WITHDRAWN

ENERGY IN A
CHANGING CLIMATE

Wind turbines

ENERGY IN A CHANGING CLIMATE

Martin Nicholson

ROSENBERG

First published in Australia in 2009
by Rosenberg Publishing Pty Ltd
PO Box 6125, Dural Delivery Centre NSW 2158
Phone: 61 2 9654 1502 Fax: 61 2 9654 1338
Email: rosenbergpub@smartchat.net.au
Web: www.rosenbergpub.com.au

National Library of Australia Cataloguing-in-Publication data

Nicholson, Martin.

Energy in a changing climate / Martin Nicholson.

1st ed.

ISBN 9781877058813 (pbk.)

Includes index.
Bibliography.

Renewable energy sources
Energy consumption—Forecasting
Power resources—Environmental aspects
Pollution prevention

333.794

Front cover: Solar PV panels (*Courtesy DOE/NREL and Aspen Skiing Co.*)

Set in 12 on 14 point Adobe Jenson Pro

Printed in Singapore by South Wind Production

Contents

Abbreviations 8
Acknowledgments 10
Preface 11
Part One — Overview of Energy 17
  1   What is a Watt? 19
  2   Cooking with Gas 32
  3   The 'Good Oil' on Oil 36
  4   Coal — Smoke Signals on Solid Fuels 42
  5   Going Nuclear 46
  6–11 A Renewed Look at Renewables 52
  6   The Sun Shines on Solar Power 54
  7   The Answer is (Well Maybe) Blowing in the Wind 59
  8   Hydropower — an Old Solution to a New Problem? 63
  9   Geothermal — Hot Rocks Can Get You Steamed Up! 67
  10 Biomass — Plant Power! 71
  11 Hydrogen — the Great Hope or Fool's Gold? 75
Part Two — The Changing Climate 79
  12 A Peek at Peak Oil 80
  13 Feel the Heat! 89
  14 Technology to the Rescue? 97
  15 We Can't Escape the Politics 116
  16 Trading, Taxing, Offsets and Other Inducements 132
  17 The Price We Have to Pay 146

Part Three — The Future of Energy   154
  18   What's Needed to Save the Planet?   156
  19   Getting More From Less   165
  20   Energy Without Carbon   169
  21   What Next for the Watt?   172
  22   Where to for Transport?   185
  23   Building Better Buildings   202
  24   The Nuclear Explosion   206
  25   The Sun Will Always Shine and the Wind Will Always Blow
       (at Least Some of the Time)   211
  26   Is There Still Hope?   217
References   223
Bibliography   227
Index   230

Boxes

Box 1   *How an Electricity Generator Works*   21
Box 2   *How We Transport Electricity*   24
Box 3   *How Nuclear Reactors Work*   47
Box 4   *How Wind Turbines Work*   60
Box 5   *How Hydro-Electric Power Stations and Pumped Storage Work*   65
Box 6   *How Hot Dry Rocks Work*   68
Box 7   *How a Hydrogen Fuel Cell Works*   77
Box 8   *Estimating the Size of an Oil Reserve*   81
Box 9   *Sources of Unconventional Oil*   87
Box 10 *Carbon Capture and Storage*   99
Box 11 *Next Generation Nuclear Reactors*   101
Box 12 *Some Issues Raised by Climate Change Sceptics*   120
Box 13 *Worked Example of a Cap and Trade Emissions Scheme*   135
Box 14 *Sources of Energy Emissions Reductions*   158
Box 15 *Worked Example of Energy Emissions Reduction Savings*   166
Box 16 *Worked Example of the Cost of Reducing Emissions by Decarbonising* 170

Tables

Table 1   *Typical Power Usage of Household Appliances*   26
Table 2   *Lifetime Generation Costs for Different Technologies*   27
Table 3   *Emissions Intensity for Different Technologies*   30
Table 4   *Transport Emissions*   41
Table 5   *Comparisons of Expert Assessments of Reserves and Peak Years* 83

Table 6   Source of Greenhouse Gases in 2000   95
Table 7   Summary of Potential New Technologies   115
Table 8   Impact of Emissions Price on Energy Costs   153
Table 9   Energy emissions Reduction Potential by Sector   160
Table 10 Opportunities to Reduce Emissions With Potential Savings   167
Table 11 Opportunities to Reduce Emissions From Decarbonising Energy   170
Table 12 Electricity generation Primary Energy Mix to 2030   173
Table 13 Electricity Generation 2004 to 2030   174
Table 14 Electricity Generation Costs 2005 to 2030   182
Table 15 Vehicle Stock by 2030   187
Table 16 Transport emissions Reduction Potential by Sector   195
Table 17 Building Emissions Reduction Potential by Sector   204

Figures

Figure 1   Electricity Load Curve   28
Figure 2   A Peak Oil Scenario   82
Figure 3   Global Annual Mean Surface Air Temperature Change   91
Figure 4   Possible Emissions Path to Stabilise Greenhouse Gases at 550ppm CO_2-e   93
Figure 5   Well-to-Wheel Transport Emissions by 2030   192

Abbreviations

ABWR	Advanced boiling-water reactor
AC	Alternating current
ASPO	Association for the Study of Peak Oil and Gas
BAU	Business-as-usual
BEV	Battery electric vehicle
BP	British Petroleum
BTU	British thermal unit
BWR	Boiling water reactor
CAES	Compressed air energy storage
CCGT	Combine cycle gas turbine
CCS	Carbon capture and storage
CCX	Chicago Climate Exchange
CDM	Clean development mechanism
CERA	Cambridge Energy Research Associates
CFC	Chlorofluorocarbons
CFL	Compact fluorescent lamp
CHP	Combined heat and power
CNG	Compressed natural gas
CO_2	Carbon dioxide
CO_2-e	Carbon dioxide equivalent
CSP	Concentrated solar power
CTL	Coal to liquids
DC	Direct current
DG	Distributed or decentralised generation
DI	Direct injection
DOE	US Department of Energy
EGS	Enhanced or engineered geothermal system
EOR	Enhanced oil and gas recovery
EPR	European Pressurised Reactor
ETS	Emissions trading scheme or system
EU	European Union
EWG	Energy Watch Group
FCV	Fuel cell vehicle
FT	Fischer-Tropsch
GDP	Gross domestic product
GTL	Gas to liquids
HEV	Hybrid-electric vehicle

HFC	Hydrofluorocarbons
HTGR	High temperature gas cooled reactors
HVDC	High voltage direct current
IAEA	International Atomic Energy Agency
ICE	Internal combustion engine
IEA	International Energy Agency
IGCC	Integrated gasification combined cycle
IPCC	Intergovernmental Panel on Climate Change
ITER	International Thermonuclear Experimental Reactor
JI	Joint Implementation
kV	Kilovolt
kW	Kilowatt (one thousand watts)
kWh	Kilowatt hour
LDV	Light-duty vehicle
LED	Light-emitting diode
LNG	Liquefied natural gas
LPG	Liquefied petroleum gas
LWR	Light water reactor
Mb	Million barrels of oil
Mboe	Million barrels oil equivalent
MJ	Megajoule
MW	Megawatt (one million watts)
MWe	Megawatt electrical
MWh	Megawatt hour
NASA	The US National Aeronautics and Space Administration
OECD	Organisation for Economic Co-operation and Development
OPEC	Organisation of the Petroleum Exporting Countries
PBMR	Pebble bed modular reactor
PEM	Proton Exchange Membrane (or Polymer Electrolyte Membrane)
PFC	Perfluorocarbon
ppm	Parts per million
PV	Photovoltaic
PWR	Pressurised water reactor
RME	Rapeseed methyl ester
SCC	Social cost of carbon
TOE	Tonnes of oil equivalent
UAE	United Arab Emirates
UN	United Nations
UNFCCC	UN Framework Convention on Climate Change
VCS	Voluntary Carbon Standard
WBCSD	World Business Council for Sustainable Development
WRI	World Resource Institute

Acknowledgments

The world issues of peak oil and climate change have intrigued me for some time. As I discussed them with friends and colleagues and read political commentary, I began to realise how little was generally understood about the energy we use and where it comes from. There seemed to be a general understanding about our dependence on oil and that carbon dioxide emissions were the culprit in global warming, but little understanding of the technical difficulties in reducing our dependence on either of them. This led me to write this book and to write it in a way that was accessible to the energy novice with limited scientific training.

I was fortunate to have the interest of a good friend, Dr Tom Biegler, a Fellow of the Australian Academy of Technological and Engineering Sciences with many years experience in the field of energy. Tom has provided very valuable assistance in making sure that the technical content was sound. I am also fortunate to have a daughter Kara who works in the publishing industry and has provided invaluable assistance with the book layout and how to find a publisher. I am grateful to my son Dylan and my other daughter Zoe and several of my close friends for their support and for providing valued comments on the various drafts. Above all I want to thank my long-suffering wife, Eva, who has lived as a 'book widow' during the gestation and birth of the manuscript.

Preface

Any meaningful solution to climate change is going to mean significant changes in our energy generation and usage. It is very important that we understand what these changes could mean for our economy and lifestyle before we rush in to solving the problem. I decided to write this book to help the interested lay reader gain some of that understanding.

Although my university eduction was in electrical science and engineering, I have spent much of my life running businesses. A couple of years ago, I left the big city where I had lived and worked for 30 years to move to the rural/coastal area of far north New South Wales. I share my new neighbourhood with hard-working small commercial farmers and others seeking an alternative lifestyle; drawn to being self-sufficient and eco-friendly. Both groups are very aware of the threat of global warming but continue to rely on their motor vehicles and on electricity to power their homes and farms with little apparent regard for the relationship between the two. The conservationists see the problem of global warming as urgent and solved by renewable energy, the farmers are concerned but just want to keep on farming, and both groups want to hang on to their personal transport as they consider it a necessity in the bush.

Meeting some of these new neighbours with their roof solar panels and batteries and no grid electricity started me thinking about other ways of living. Maybe we didn't need baseload electricity after all. As we will see later, low cost, reliable, baseload power is a challenge for solar and wind renewable energy (although this is sometimes refuted by advocates of solar and wind power). Anyway, I quickly stopped dreaming and realised these people wouldn't have their solar panels, batteries and motor vehicles or their refrigerators, gas cookers or computers without cheap mass production. Cheap mass production needs plenty of low-cost 24 by 7 electricity and, today, low-cost 24 by 7 electricity means 24 by 7 power stations using, in most places, non-renewable, often fossil-fuel, energy sources. Fossil-fuel energy means greenhouse gas emissions and greenhouse gases mean global warming.

In a little over 150 years, burning fossil fuels has given us cheap, readily available electricity and mechanisation. These have both delivered human welfare advancements in the developed world including improved life expectancy, better health care, personal mobility, intellectual opportunity, universal access to information and egalitarianism. Without the high energy density of coal and oil many of these advances would not have been possible.

Global warming has been one of the most talked about subjects in recent years. You can't open a newspaper without finding some story on climate change and how it needs to be solved and when. Most stories seem to understand that energy use is a key part of both the problem and the solution but there seems to be little understanding about the limitations of some energy sources, the maturity of new energy technology, and the economic consequences of some of the solutions. Over the next few years politicians are going to be making critical decisions about climate change that could have substantial impact on both our economy and the future of our planet.

The Intergovernmental Panel on Climate Change (IPCC) has had a big influence on the climate change debate. The press has widely reported what the IPCC has had to say about global warming and the possible impact on the Earth's environment at various stabilisation levels of greenhouse gases. Less familiar seems to be the extensive IPCC work on how to go about reducing greenhouse gas emissions. The IPCC is the best consensus of the scientific evidence about climate change. It has done a detailed critique of the short- and long-term mitigation potential for various energy related sectors using the same scientific rigour applied to the critique of the environmental impact of climate change. I rely on much of this work in this book when discussing technology and the future of energy.

Just a few centuries ago, energy use was simple. Populations were much smaller and people burned wood and peat for heating and cooking and there was no mass production. All energy was renewable and largely sustainable. In the last 300 years or so we have added coal, oil and gas to the fuels we burn for heating, lighting, cooking and to run factories and motor vehicles. The trouble is, burning fuel creates greenhouse gases that scientists tell us are changing our climate. On top of that, the new fuels we are burning are non-renewable and won't last forever.

There is a very close relationship between energy use and production. Over the last 40 years, energy use in the developed world has doubled. Over the same period energy use in the developing world has quadrupled. Despite this quadrupling in the developing world (with a corresponding growth in production), world poverty persists. Demand for more and more energy will continue throughout the world, particularly in the developing countries like China and India which strive to match the level of production and standard of living in the developed world. Without plenty of low cost energy the world economy is threatened.

Forty years ago very few individuals seriously worried about climate change. Even fewer individuals worried about running out of oil or any other fuel. Now the development of future energy will be driven by two key events: peak oil and human induced climate change. Although technically unrelated (neither caused the other) these events have much in common. They became common knowledge about the same time (in the first decade of the 21st century); they have the potential to have a big impact on energy use and cost and there is scientific uncertainty about the extent of their impact. We only have limited supplies of oil, coal, natural gas and uranium. There are many arguments about how long the supplies will last but they will all run out eventually. For coal and uranium it might be well into the 22nd century, or even longer, before they run out. For oil and natural gas it may well be in this century. Judging by the sharp oil price increase over the last couple of years, oil production may already be struggling to meet the growth in demand.

To reduce greenhouse gas emissions over the long term, significant changes to energy will be necessary in most countries. This may require fundamental changes in behaviour for both consumers and industry. We can make some reductions in energy use in the short term at low cost by finding ways to reduce our energy consumption without reducing production. As consumers we can be choosey about what we buy and how much energy it uses. We can buy more efficient cars; we can buy low-energy appliances. We can turn things off when we don't need them and we can drive our cars less often. Large-scale emissions reduction on the other hand will require a major rethink about the energy sources we use and how we convert them into the common forms we are all used to: electricity, piped or bottled gas, heating oil, petrol (gasoline), diesel and other transport fuels.

Because of the growing demand for energy, particularly from the developing world, using less energy is not going to be a complete solution to climate change or peak oil unless we think that the developing world doesn't need or deserve the standard of living that we in the developed world enjoy. We need to find ways to produce energy differently and to make better use of it — to improve the amount of value we get from the energy we use. We need new technology breakthroughs. Some conservationists believe we have all the technology we need now. I disagree. Much of the change will need to come from government-led reforms that target low carbon energy and energy efficiency. We have plenty of technology ideas to help like energy storage (which is an important component for solar and wind power) but we still require significant financial investment to change some of these ideas into cost competitive commercial realities. We need our governments to actively encourage the development of new clean energy technologies because private industry won't do it on its own in the time required.

There are widely differing views about solutions to energy and climate change. Some conservationists see the problem as relatively straightforward requiring deep cuts in emissions now by improving energy efficiency, energy conservation and using only renewable resources. Many energy industry engineers and scientists see the problem as being much more involved. In this book I look at what still needs to be done before we can return to an all-renewable energy economy, as we will eventually, and why using renewable energy sources is not quite as simple as it seems. I also look at the impact of aggressive emissions reduction targets that demand emissions reductions before we have the technology in place. I consider and reference recent works published on energy use and climate change by the International Energy Agency (IEA), Greenpeace, consultants McKinsey and the World Business Council for Sustainable Development (WBCSD). If we, either privately or publicly, are to advocate very aggressive targets it would be valuable to understand what the world impact of that might be for both the environment and the economy.

The book is structured in three parts:
• Part One gives a straight forward overview of our primary energy sources and how we utilise them.
• Part Two discusses the changing climate. This is not just the weather climate but the changing political, economic and engineering climate that surrounds energy. I discuss peak oil and its impact on the supply of our principal source of energy. I also discuss technologies that may help us move to an all-renewable energy future.
• Part Three looks at the future of energy and suggests a roadmap for surviving with much less oil and progressively weaning ourselves off non-renewable coal and gas and at the same time saving the planet from global warming.

I explore terms used liberally in the press, on radio and on TV such as 'renewable energy', 'baseload power', 'peak oil', 'biofuels', 'global warming', 'greenhouse gas emissions', 'energy security', 'emissions trading', 'carbon taxes' and 'carbon offsets'. I look at ways we can all save energy in our homes, workplaces and on the road. I also explore the thorny issue of nuclear energy. You can dip in and out of this book. You don't have to read it from cover to cover. For those who want to use the book as a reference source, I have included a comprehensive index.

Australia has been an interesting place to write this book. It is one of the world's major uranium suppliers and yet does not use nuclear power. It is also one of the sunniest places in the world but gets less than 1% of its electricity from solar power. It has the highest emissions of greenhouse gases per person of all the OECD countries; partly because 80% of its electricity is generated by coal; partly because it is a major mineral exporter and mining uses vast amounts of energy; and partly because Australia is almost as big as the US but with less than 10% of its population.

I believe we should embark on a path to reducing greenhouse gas emissions that does not require us all to make drastic changes to our lifestyle as some have advocated. Such drastic changes would not be politically acceptable in most countries and would probably never be implemented. I have aimed to provide a balanced and realistic review of all aspects of energy, including its impact on climate change. I have no association with any vested interest in the energy or climate change debate so any biases are my own. As you go through the book, you will see that there are no simple solutions to changing the way we use energy, as some would have us believe, and there is no one solution to the problem but with a realistic balance between risk to the environment and the risk to our social structure there is still hope for the future.

Martin Nicholson,
October 2008

A Quick Note on Notes
Numbered footnotes are placed at the bottom of the page to further explain the text, particularly any terms that might be unfamiliar to some readers.

Numbered endnotes are placed in square bracket (e.g. [26]) and provide source references for the material. These can be found in the References section at the back of the book.

Table footnotes use lowercase letters and are placed immediately below the table.

Part One — Overview of Energy

Energy is something we all use. Much of it comes to us in the form of electricity and gas, which we use in our homes or workplaces, and petrol (gasoline)[1] and diesel which we use in our motor vehicles. Today, most of this energy is sourced from 'non-renewable' resources. These resources — coal, oil, natural gas and uranium — will eventually run out as the Earth cannot renew them at the rate we consume them. A much smaller amount of our energy comes from renewable resources such as the sun, wind, wood or moving water (hydro power). All these energy resources are known as primary energy, or energy in its raw form.

For those who like numbers, in 2004, according to the International Energy Agency (IEA), 34% of the world total primary energy supply came from oil, 25% came from coal, 21% from natural gas, 13% from renewable resources and 7% nuclear (largely uranium). Of the renewable resources, 80% was from combustible renewables such as wood and waste called biomass, 16% from hydro, 3% from geothermal and less than 1% from solar and wind.[1]

The changing weather climate (often referred to as climate change) involves greenhouse gases that occur naturally in the atmosphere but are also produced by much of our energy. To assist our later discussion of this subject, we will briefly discuss how much greenhouse gas

---

[1] In the US petrol is referred to as gasoline. From now on we will use the term petrol.

17

is produced from each source of energy. Greenhouse gases in the atmosphere mainly consist of carbon dioxide plus a few other gases. We will discuss why they are called greenhouse gases in Chapter 13 in Part Two. At this stage we will just discuss them in terms of tonnes of greenhouse gases produced, or more accurately the amount of carbon dioxide equivalent produced. In 2000, using energy generated 63% of the total greenhouse gas emissions.[2]

In this first part of the book we will discuss each of these energy forms: what they are, where they come from, how we use them, what they cost and how we might use them more efficiently. In the first chapter we will look at the most commonly used form of energy, electricity. Electricity is strictly an energy carrier rather than an energy resource but we start with it because it really is critical to our modern society and plays a key part in the energy debate.

For comparison purposes we will use standard units of quantity and currency throughout the book, so all costs are quoted in US dollars and all units of volume or length are in metric unless specified otherwise.

1 — What is a Watt?

Or Everything About Electricity That You Wanted to Know but Didn't Dare Ask

A watt is a unit of power.[2] If you like, it's a way of measuring the rate of energy production or usage. A typical electric light lamp uses 40–100 watts of power. An electric swimming pool pump uses a thousand watts — also called a kilowatt (kW). The amount of energy we use depends on how long we use the light or the pump. Running a 1kW pump for one hour uses what is called a kilowatt hour (kWh) of energy, so a kWh is a unit of energy and a watt is a unit of power. The term watt isn't limited to electrical power. In fact the name came from the Scottish inventor James Watt, who did pioneering work on steam engines back in the 18th century. But this chapter is about electricity, what it is, where it comes from and how we use it.

What is Electrical Energy?
Electricity is the most widely available energy source and the only one able to run the full range of household appliances. It can be used to power everything from the lights to the refrigerator. Without getting too scientific, electricity is the flow of an electric charge along a conductor — typically a copper wire. Electrons move from one atom to another along the wire. These moving electrons are what we call an electric current or just electricity. Electricity needs a closed loop or cir

---

[2] A watt is one unit of energy (called a joule) expended in one second.

cuit to flow. When we turn on a light switch we close that circuit and allow the electrons to flow through the wires and through the light. For an incandescent lamp (the ones with a glowing element) the electrons flowing through the element in the lamp cause it to glow brightly, giving us light. Turning the switch off breaks the circuit and the electrons stop flowing so the element stops glowing.

Where Does the Electricity Come From?

The electricity we use in our homes and workplaces is produced from a primary energy source which could be coal, oil, gas, biomass, wind, hydro, geothermal, solar or nuclear. The electricity is typically produced by electricity generators owned by a power company. The principles of an electricity generator are the same for all primary energy sources (see Box 1).

The electric current is transmitted from the power company to our homes and workplaces along the big transmission lines (high voltage) and distribution lines (low voltage) we see crossing the countryside and the cities. We will discuss electricity transmission in the next section.

The shaft of the electricity generator is driven by a turbine or engine of some kind. Turbines typically use steam, gas combustion, water or wind to drive them. Today, most of the electricity is produced using steam turbines. Steam turbines have a series of blades mounted on a shaft. Steam is forced against the blade rotating the shaft connected to the generator. In a coal, oil, gas or biomass steam turbine, the fuel is burned in a furnace to heat water in a boiler to produce the steam. In a nuclear power plant steam is produced by heating water through a process called nuclear fission (see Chapter 5). Geothermal steam power comes from heat energy buried beneath the surface of the Earth (Chapter 9). Solar-thermal electric generators use the radiant energy from the sun to heat water and produce steam (Chapter 6).

In some countries as much as 90% of electricity is produced in steam-powered generators. Unfortunately, steam generator plants are only about 35% efficient. That means that for every 100 units of energy that go into a plant only 35 units are converted to usable electrical energy. As much as two-thirds of the primary energy used in conventional thermal plants is lost in the form of heat. Some plants capture the excess heat for use in buildings or industrial processes. These are referred to as cogeneration plants or combined heat and power plants (CHP). These plants can increase the overall conversion efficiency to over 80%, which lowers costs and reduces greenhouse gas emissions as we will see later.

As well as using steam to drive the turbine, gas can be burned to produce hot combustion gases that pass directly through a turbine,

Box I

How an Electricity Generator Works

A generator converts rotating mechanical energy into electrical energy. An electricity generator uses what is called electromagnetic induction. When an electric conductor, such as a piece of copper wire, is moved through a magnetic field an electric current is induced in the conductor. So if a loop of copper wire is rotated between two magnets, as shown in the illustration, an electric current will flow round the loop. The rotating part of a generator is called the rotor and the stationary part is called the stator.

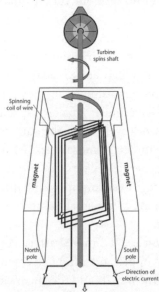

A generator at a power station uses an electromagnet,[a] not a traditional magnet as show in the illustration. The electromagnet can be in the stator or the rotor. A typical power generator has a series of insulated coils of wire that form a stationary cylinder around a rotating electromagnetic shaft (opposite to the diagram above). When the electromagnetic shaft rotates, it induces an electric current in each section of the stationary wire coil. The small currents in each section together form one larger current that is transmitted from the generator. The shaft can be rotated by a turbine, engine, windmill or waterwheel.

The electric current produced by power generators is normally alternating current (AC), which means the current constantly changes direction, usually 100 or 120 times a second (50 or 60 cycles per second) depending on the country we live in. This is the form of electricity we normally use in our homes and workplaces. The big advantage of AC is that the voltage can be readily changed using a transformer.

[a] A magnet produced by electricity.

Image Source: Energy Information Administration

spinning its blades. Gas turbines can be used stand-alone or with steam turbines called combined cycle gas turbines (CCGT) where the waste heat from the gas turbine is used to make steam to generate additional electricity in a steam turbine.

With hydro-electricity, flowing water from a reservoir is used to spin the turbine much like with a waterwheel (Chapter 8). With a wind turbine large blades are aligned to rotate in the wind like a giant windmill (Chapter 7). Internal combustion engines using either petrol or diesel can also be used to drive generators.

So there are many ways to power electricity generators. As we progress through the book we will discuss some of the advantages and disadvantages of each of these energy sources. In the US about half the electricity comes from coal. In France only about 5% comes from coal because France is the second-largest producer of nuclear power in the world.[3] Worldwide, electricity uses about 40% of our total primary energy.

A very different sort of electricity generation can be achieved using the sun. Photovoltaic (PV) conversion generates electric power directly from the light of the sun in a PV or solar cell (Chapter 6). Today, this is a much more expensive source of electricity than using steam-powered generators. PV power stations generally have much smaller capacity than generator power stations and don't work well when the sun isn't shining. Typical PV power plants produce under 50 megawatts (MW) (50 million watts) of electricity whereas generator plants can produce over 1,000 MW. PV cells have a big advantage over rotating generators. They are silent (no moving parts) and can have a very small footprint so they can be installed on a suburban house.

Electricity can also be produced in batteries. A simple battery consists of two different metals (for example, copper and zinc) in a chemical solution. A chemical reaction between the metals and the chemicals frees more electrons in one metal than in the other. Each terminal of the battery is attached to each of the metals. The terminal end that frees more electrons develops a positive charge and the other end develops a negative charge. If a closed wire loop or circuit is formed by attaching each end of the wire to each battery terminal, electrons flow directly through the circuit to balance the electrical charge in the battery so batteries produce direct current (DC) electricity. PV cells also produce DC electricity.

A fuel cell is a device that produces electricity from an external fuel source such as hydrogen. This means that the fuel cell must be continually replenished with fuel. This is different from a battery, which generates the electricity in a closed system and does not need a continuous external source of chemicals — but the battery will eventually need to be recharged or replaced as the chemicals are consumed. The fuel cell converts chemical energy into electrical energy (see Box 7 in Chapter 11). Fuel cells are still relatively experimental and not yet widely used in commercial systems.

How Is Electricity Transmitted and Distributed?

Electricity provides a way of moving energy from the primary energy source which might be coal, gas, wind or water to where it is needed, which could be our home or our place of work. What has made it possible to have the electricity generator some distance from where we use the electricity is a large network of transmission infrastructure that can transmit the electricity long distances — what we refer to as the 'grid'. (see Box 2).

The transmission lines from power stations are usually interconnected in a network. This allows the electricity we use to come from many different power stations so we are not dependent on one station. It means the electricity utilities can monitor the supply and demand around a country or region and maximise the availability for users. This makes the electricity grid very reliable in most countries. It also means that we never know where our electricity has come from (unless we generate our own), so we should remember that when our utility signs us up for green power. We probably still get our electricity from multiple sources both green and non-green.

How Much Electricity Do We Use and What Do We Use it For?

Worldwide, we generate over 16 trillion kilowatt hours of electricity per year with about half used in North America and Europe. [4]

Depending on where we live and our pattern of usage, a typical four-bedroom home in the developed world might use 6,000–10,000 kWh

Box 2

How We Transport Electricity

When electricity is transmitted along a wire some of the energy is lost as heat because of what is called 'resistance' in the wire. The longer the wire the greater the resistance and the greater the loss. Using thicker wires reduces the resistance and the loss but there is a limit to how thick you can run a cable economically. Another way to address this problem is to transmit the electricity at very high voltage and this is what happens in the big electricity transmission lines mounted on very high towers that run from the power stations to population centres. The voltage used on these transmission lines is usually greater than 200,000 volts (200 kilovolts or kV). The voltage from the generator might be only 15–25 kV so this has to be increased using a step-up transformer before it is sent over the transmission lines. Closer to our home or workplace the voltage is lowered again using step-down transformers to a final voltage around 100–400 volts that we use for our appliances. In practice several transformers progressively lower the voltage as the line gets closer to the final place of use. Electricity travels at close to the speed of light, so even if we live a long way away from the power station the electricity we use in our home is generated almost at the same time as we use it.

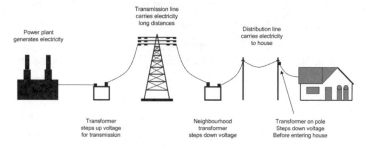

Even using very high voltages still creates transmission and distribution energy losses in the grid. These losses can be of the order of 5–10% for some grids. The losses can be reduced by transmitting the very high voltage as direct current (DC) rather than alternating current (AC), particularly where the cables run under the sea.[b] This is often referred to as high voltage DC (HVDC). There are some losses and costs in converting the generated AC to DC and then back to AC, so HVDC is only used where there are sufficient advantages. HVDC typically begins to pay off when above ground lines are longer than 600 km and undersea cables reach 60 km.

[a] The power loss on a transmission line is given by the formula $Loss = P^2R/V^2$ where P is the power demand on the network, R is the resistance of the line and V is the voltage. So the higher the voltage the lower the loss but the higher the power demand the greater the loss. The longer the line, the greater the resistance R so the greater the loss.

[b] Underground and undersea cables have high capacitance which cause greater losses with AC than DC.

of electricity each year. As we might expect, household appliance use different amounts of electricity. As a rule of thumb, appliances that have electric motors (refrigerators, air-conditioners, washing machines, pumps) or heating elements (ovens, space heaters, hot water heaters, kettles, toasters) use much more electricity than lights or electronic devices (radios, stereos, computers). Table 1 shows the typical rate of electricity usage by some common household appliances.

Of course the rate of electricity usage of an appliance while it is working is only half the issue. Equally important is how long we use the appliance for, and this is where the kilowatt hour (kWh) comes in. Our electricity supply company charges us for kilowatt hours used. Running our 3,000 watt air-conditioner for 10 hour uses 30 kWh of electricity and costs the same as leaving a 100 watt light on for 300 hours. According to the US Department of Energy (DOE)[5] in the US the average split of electricity use in domestic households is air-conditioners (16%), refrigerators (14%), space heaters (10%), water heaters (9%), lighting (9%), clothes dryers (6%), freezers (3%), televisions (3%), all other appliance (30%).

Hidden in these numbers is a thing called 'standby' power. There is some debate about how standby power should be defined, but at a minimum, standby power is the power used while the device is performing no function. An appliance uses standby power when it is connected to the power, turned on and waiting to be used. Typical examples of standby power would be a television or stereo that is waiting to be activated by the remote control, a microwave with a built-in clock, a phone battery charger left in the wall socket or a computer printer left on when not being used. A TV/video recorder in standby mode can use 5 watts and is often left on most of the time. The amount of standby power in an average household has been estimated at between 5% and 10% of total power usage.[6]

What About the Non-Residential Use?
In the US, residential usage of electricity represents about one-third of the total. Commercial and industrial usage largely makes up the rest.[7] Commercial use in offices and shops is similar to the domestic use discussed above, with perhaps more air-conditioning and electrical equipment use such as elevators. Industrial use often involves both heat and power.

Table I — Typical Power Usage of Household Appliances

Appliance	Typical Watts
Air-conditioner — central	3000
Air-conditioner — wall	1200
CD player	100
Clothes dryer	2000
Coffee maker	1000
Computer with screen	450
Dishwasher	1200
Electric grill	1500
Fax machine	100
Freezer	700
Frying pan	1200
Garage door opener	800
Hair dryer	1200
Heater — portable	1500
Hot plate	1500
Ink jet printer	150
Iron	1200
Laser printer	350
Microwave	800
Mixer	150
Pool pump	1000
Range w/oven	10000
Refrigerator	700
Space heater	1800
Stereo	100
Television	300
Toaster	1000
Vacuum cleaner	1300
Video recorder	25
Wall clock	5
Washing machine	1200
Water heater	4000

Industry consumes large amounts of electricity using machines driven by electric motors and industrial processes that involve electricity like manufacturing aluminium. If an industry is a big user it will often generate its own electricity and sell any excess capacity back to the grid.

How Much Does Electricity Cost to Generate?

The generation cost of electricity varies depending on the technology used, the primary energy source and the geographic location. A recent (2005) study of new generator costs from around the world prepared by the OECD[3] and the International Energy Agency (IEA) considered the lifetime cost of several state-of-the-art technologies for new generators to be commissioned between 2010 and 2015 and gives some indication of the future range of costs per kWh for different technologies. These costs do not include external costs such as the impact on the environment. Adding in the cost of greenhouse gas emissions can change some of these cost significantly and we will discuss this in detail in Part Two.

Table 2 — Lifetime Generation Costs for Different Technologies

Generation Technology	US $/kWh
Coal-fired	0.035–0.060
Gas — combined cycle	0.040–0.063
Nuclear	0.030–0.050
Wind	0.045–0.140[a]
Solar	0.200–0.600[b]
Hydro	0.065–0.100

[a] Depends on wind availability. *Source*: OECD/IEA[8]
[b] Depends on sun availability and technology used (solar-thermal or PV).

How Much Does Electricity Cost Us?
The cost of electricity depends on where we live, how much we use and possibly when we use it. Most electricity suppliers offer lower rates for usage at low demand times. We will discuss why this is so shortly. There are also fixed charges that we pay every month no matter how much electricity we use to cover the cost of providing the service to our home or office. Residential prices differ around the world but vary from about $0.08/kWh to $0.24/kWh, a threefold difference.[9] The simple average international price is $0.16/kWh. In the US in February 2007 the average residential price was $0.10, the average commercial price was $0.09 and the industrial price was $0.06.[10]

So why do suppliers charge different rates at different times of the day? Unfortunately, unlike oil or gas, it is very difficult to store electricity although not impossible (see pumped storage systems in Chapter 8). Small amounts can be stored in batteries but this is very expensive storage and not practical for high demand usage. Electricity demand varies over the day, higher in the middle of the day and early evening

[3] Organisation for Economic Co-operation and Development

and lower at night. It also varies over the seasons. Because electricity cannot be economically stored, generators are required to match supply with demand. What are called 'baseload' generators run all the time to match most of the demand with 'quick-start' generators used to meet short-term peak demands. These quick-start generators are only used intermittently and are relatively expensive to operate compared to base-load generators, so the electricity produced during these peak periods is much more expensive than electricity produced at off-peak times.

How Does Demand Vary Throughout the Day and How is it Supplied?

Figure 1 show an example of what is called a load curve which shows the electricity demand on an electricity grid throughout a 24 hour period. Load curves vary by region and season. This is a curve for a summer's day in a warm climate and shows a peak demand between 10:00 (10 am) and 17:00 (5 pm) when there was a high demand for air-conditioning. A curve for a winter's day may show a high demand early in the morning and late in the afternoon when users turn on heaters rather than in the middle of the day.

Figure I

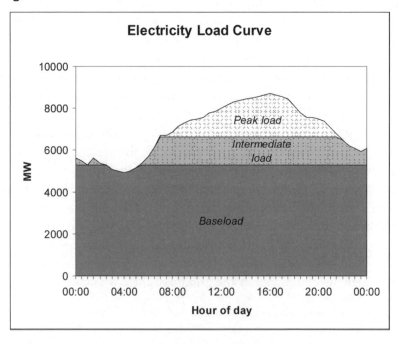

The baseload can account for a substantial proportion of the demand throughout the day, particularly if the grid is supplying a significant amount of 24 hour a day commercial and industrial demand. This baseload is normally supplied by plants that operate continuously using coal, gas, nuclear or geothermal resources. Baseload plants are often slow to start but relatively cheap to run.

As we can see from the load curve, the peak demand could be half as much again above the baseload and needs to be supplied by generators that can be started reasonably quickly as demand requires — the quick-start generators we discussed earlier. These are often referred to as intermediate (or cycling) load and peak-load generators that might be gas turbine or hydro plants that are quick to start. Peak-load plants are usually much smaller and cheaper to build than baseload plants but more expensive to run so they are only used when needed. Intermediate-load plants occupy a middle ground between baseload and peak-load plants. They are typically cheaper to build than baseload but cheaper to run than peak-load plants.

Understanding the load curve and the need for reliable baseload supply will become important when we talk about the future of energy in Part Three.

How Much Greenhouse Gas Does Electricity Generation Produce?

Just over a quarter of all man-made greenhouse gas emissions come from generating electricity. On average worldwide, about 0.6 kilograms of emissions are produced per kWh of electricity generated. This is known as the emissions intensity. Worldwide, man-made greenhouse gas emissions totalled 44 billion tonnes in 2000.[2] The proportion from electricity generation in each country will depend on the average emissions intensity and this depends on the energy sources and technology used to generate the electricity, as can be seen from Table 3. A country with a high use of nuclear, wind or hydro power will have a much lower emissions intensity than a country relying on coal or gas-fired power stations.

How Can We Reduce Our Electricity Usage?

For reasons we will discuss in Part Two, we can expect the cost of

Table 3 — Emissions Intensity for Different Technologies

Electricity Generation Technology	Emissions Intensity kg CO_2-e/kWh[a]	
	Current	Future[b]
Coal-fired	1.0–1.3	0.8
Oil-fired	0.8–0.9	0.5
Natural gas — combined cycle	0.4–0.7	0.4
Nuclear	< 0.1	
Wind	< 0.1	
Solar	0.1–0.3	< 0.1
Hydro	< 0.2	

[a] The figures from the source document are for the full energy chain (not just generation) and have been converted from carbon to carbon dioxide equivalent for consistency in this book by multiplying by 44/12.
[b] Current figures related to power stations built in the 1990s. Future figures are newer stations being built using more advanced technologies.

Source: IAEA[11]

electricity to rise significantly over the next few years so there will be growing financial incentive to reduce our electricity consumption. The most effective way of reducing electricity consumption is to restrict the use of the energy hogs like the air-conditioners, space heaters or that second refrigerator. Each of these may have some impact on our quality of life, unless we can compensate with better home insulation, so what else can we do that won't mean compromising our lifestyle too much?

We can be more careful next time we buy a new appliance and make sure we buy the most energy-efficient model. We can also replace appliances with ones that use a different energy source. Solar hot water heaters will save electricity on bright days (see Chapter 6). Gas appliances are generally less costly to run than those using electricity (see Chapter 2). We can save electricity by replacing electric space heating with electric heat pumps or reverse-cycle air-conditioners. We can reduce the need for heating and cooling by improving the insulation in our homes. We can replace incandescent lamps with compact fluorescent lamps that use only about a quarter of the electricity for the same light output. We should avoid using low voltage spotlights and down-lights as they use more power than equivalent brightness mains voltage lights. Just because they are low voltage it doesn't mean they are low power users.

Some of these ideas come with a cost of replacement of an existing device, so make sure they are cost effective. For example, a 25W compact fluorescent lamp might cost $5 more than a comparable 100W incandescent lamp. If electricity is costing us 16 cents a kWh we will need to use the lamp for over 400 hours before we recover the additional cost, so replacing a lamp that we don't use very often may not be economical although it will reduce our electricity usage.

One thing we can do to save electricity that won't cost money is to turn off devices that we are not using to reduce the standby power. There are some devices we wouldn't want to turn off because it would mean some reprogramming each time we used it (like resetting the time on a clock) but we should be able to save part of that 5-10% of total power that goes to providing standby power. The most effective way of reducing standby power long term is to urge the manufacturers to use better standby design for future models to reduce the standby power. Some industry associations and governments are already encouraging manufacturers to do this but we can also help by only buying devices with low standby power usage, so check it when next buying an appliance (most manufacturers now tell us what standby power the appliance requires).

Most electricity suppliers allow households to buy off-peak electricity at a much lower tariff than peak electricity. With normal electricity meters this requires appliances to draw power through a separate off-peak meter to take advantage of using cheaper off-peak electricity. This means that the appliance can only be used during the off-peak period. This works fine for appliances like hot water heaters but is usually impractical for appliances like air-conditioners. It may be worth considering using a smart meter (sometimes called an interval meter) if our electricity supplier supports them. A smart meter is an advanced electrical meter that monitors usage over the day and communicates that information over a network to the supplier for billing purposes. This allows the supplier to vary the tariff for all our electricity use depending on the time of day and season. Even just the introduction of simple 'shoulder periods' (typically 7am–2pm and 8pm–10pm) with a tariff midway between the peak and off-peak tariff can reduce the total cost significantly. Some of these meters provide an in-house display so we can see just how much electricity we are using at any one time and how much it is costing us. There may be a charge for the meter, so make sure your savings offset the additional costs.

2 — Cooking With Gas

Or Everything About Gas That You Wanted to Know but Didn't Dare Ask

What Types of Gas Energy Are There?
Basically today there are two types of gas energy, natural gas and petroleum gas.

Natural gas is a fossil fuel. That means it was formed millions of years ago from the remains of animals and plants. It occurs naturally, trapped between layers of rock in the ground. It is converted from its raw natural state in a gas processing plant before being piped to our homes, factories and electricity power stations. Natural gas can be piped economically but it is expensive to transport or store because of its low density. To make it economic to store and transport it is sometimes converted to a liquid called LNG (liquefied natural gas) by cooling it and storing it in special cryogenic[4] tanks. Natural gas can also be compressed into CNG (compressed natural gas). CNG requires very high pressures and requires more volume to store the same amount of natural gas as LNG but has a lower cost of production and storage.

LPG or liquefied petroleum gas occurs naturally in crude oil and natural gas production fields and it can also be produced in the oil refining process. The raw LPG is put through a process called fractionation.[5]

---

[4] Cryogenic means producing, or related to, low temperatures.
[5] Fractionation separates the LPG into different gases for different uses.

It is then turned to a liquid by cooling and applying pressure for more efficient storage and transportation. LPG can be piped to manufacturing plants, sent by trucks to road fuel outlets or supplied in pressurised steel bottles to households.

Town gas or manufactured gas was used in homes and industry before the long-distance transmission of natural gas became widely available. Town gas was manufactured by heating coal in the absence of air to produces coke and crude coal gas. This coal gas was purified to produce town gas. Town gas was largely replaced by natural gas during the second half of the last century.

What Is Gas Used For?
In households, piped natural gas is used for cooking, space heating, water heating and clothes drying where it is usually cheaper than electricity (see below). Where piped gas is not available, bottled LPG can be used for the same purposes. LPG is usually twice as expensive as piped natural gas.

For commercial use, natural gas is used for cooking, water heating, steam raising and space heating. Industry uses natural gas in a variety of ways. It is used in direct heating in a number of production processes, for steam raising in the food, chemical and paper industries, and as a feedstock in the manufacture of certain products. It is also used in power stations to generate electricity as we discussed in Chapter 1. This is likely to increase as we try to control greenhouse gas emissions because gas-fired power stations produce less than half the emissions of coal-fired power stations (see Table 3 in Chapter 1).

Today, a relatively small amount of gas is also used in vehicles as a replacement for petrol or diesel. CNG, LNG and LPG can all be used for this purpose. CNG is typically used in buses and light to medium trucks that do not travel long distances away from their refuelling home base as CNG needs more regular refuelling than liquid fuels and there is limited public refuelling infrastructure for CNG. LPG is often called autogas or propane in some countries when used in vehicles. LPG already has extensive public refuelling infrastructure in many countries so it can be used in light vehicles like cars and taxis that require refuelling away from their home base.

LNG has an advantage as a transport fuel because it requires much less storage space than CNG. To become widely used, both CNG and LNG would require infrastructure to handle public vehicle refuelling.

How Much Does Gas Cost?

Unlike electricity, which is always priced in kWh, different parts of the world price gas in different ways. It can be priced by megajoule (1 million joules[6] — MJ) by BTU[7] or therm[8] or by volume (cubic feet or cubic metres). Household natural gas prices vary widely throughout the world depending on availability, cost of transport and government subsidies. In 2006 the variation ranged from $7 per million BTU in Hungary to $32 in Denmark[12] — a more than fourfold difference. If we take the simple average of $19 per million BTU and convert it to the kWh equivalent, the average price of natural gas is $0.07/kWh. This compares with the average price of electricity of $0.16/kWh we calculated in Chapter 1 so, on average, electricity is over twice the price of natural gas for equivalent units of energy.

How Much Greenhouse Gas Does Natural Gas and LPG Produce?

Natural gas used for electricity generation produces between 0.4 and 0.7 kg/kWh of emissions with the future trend toward 0.4 kg/kWh (see Table 3 in Chapter 1). This is less than half the emissions from coal-fired power stations but over four times the emissions from nuclear power or most renewable sources.

Natural gas used in households and commercial premises for cooking and heating produces about 0.19 kg/kWh or 0.05 kg/MJ of emissions. LPG produces a little more at 0.25 kg/kWh. LPG used in motor vehicles produces about 1.53 kg/litre (see Table 4 in Chapter 3).

How Can We Reduce Our Gas Usage?

There is only a limited quantity of gas and oil in the ground. As gas and oil get used up and more difficult to extract we can expect the price to

---

[6] A joule is a unit of energy.
[7] British Thermal Unit is a unit of energy used in the power, steam generation and heating and air-conditioning industries.
[8] A therm is 100,000 BTUs or about 106 million joules or about 29 kWh.

rise so we have an incentive to reduce our gas usage.

As with electricity, some gas appliances are more efficient than others. So when we are replacing an appliance such as a hot water heater we need to look for the most energy-efficient model to reduce gas usage. We should consider using a solar hot water heater rather than gas but we should make sure that the electric booster needed on the solar hot water heater doesn't finish up costing us more to run than a gas water heater. This might be the case if the solar panel is not facing the sun, blocked by trees or doesn't get enough sunny days particularly in winter.

We should consider turning down the thermostat on the hot water heater or space heater and make sure that hot water pipes are well insulated to prevent heat loss. Showers are big hot water users so we should install water-saving shower heads. Even remembering to turn off the hot water heater when we are on vacation can make a difference.

3 — The 'Good Oil' on Oil

All About Oil and its Derivatives, Petrol, Diesel and Liquefied Petroleum Gas (LPG)

What Is Oil?

Like natural gas, oil, or more specifically crude oil (or petroleum) is a fossil fuel. It was made naturally from decaying plants and animals by compression and heating over millions of years. It is found in porous rock formations in the ground or in oil sands. Crude oil contains hydrocarbons[9] and can vary in colour from clear to black, and in viscosity (thickness) from water to almost solid.

Oil is the world's principal energy source. In 2004, 34% of all energy came from crude oil.

Where Does Oil Come From?

Crude oil is extracted from the ground using an oil well drilled into the earth. Oil wells are drilled all over the world and an estimate from the US DOE[13] suggests that about one-third of crude oil comes from the Middle East, 20% from Europe (including Russia), 14% from North America, and the rest from South America, Africa, China and other parts of Asia.

Crude oil contains hundreds of different types of hydrocarbons all mixed together. These have to be separated before they can be used as fuel sources. This is done in a process called oil refining in which the

[9] Hydrocarbons are molecules that contain hydrogen and carbon atoms.

crude oil is heated and the different hydrocarbon chains are released at different vaporisation temperatures. Each different chain has a different property that makes it useful in a different way. The key energy products derived from crude oil are petrol, diesel distillate, jet fuel and other fuel oil as well as petroleum gas (discussed in Chapter 2).

How Do We Use Oil?

There are three major categories of petroleum products: transport and heating fuels, non-fuel products such as solvents and lubricating oils, and feedstocks for the petrochemical industry.

Worldwide in 2004, 27% of crude oil was converted to petrol, 28% to diesel, 14% to other fuel oil for ships, electric power generators and space heating, 6% to jet fuel, 5% to LPG with the rest for various industrial processes.[14] In 2004 transportation used about half of the refined crude oil, industry used about a third, electricity generation used about 7% and domestic/commercial use for heating and cooking used about 8%.[13]

Industry uses oil for steam raising and water heating but also as solvents and lubricants, asphalt for roads and to provide the petroleum-based components of plastics, synthetic fibres, medicines, food items, and several other products.

In Part Two we will discuss a thing called peak oil. Once you have read that chapter you will understand that products produced from crude oil are likely to get more difficult to obtain and be much more expensive over the next few decades. This means we have a good reason to consider how we could manage with less of these oil products. Given that about half of crude oil is used to make fuel for motor vehicles, that seems like a good place to start.

How Much Does Oil Cost and How Much Do We Use?

Crude oil used in the refineries is priced per barrel and is most commonly quoted in US dollars. A barrel of oil contains 159 litres or 42 US gallons or 35 imperial gallons. A barrel of oil will typically make 74 litres of petrol (19.5 US gallons of gasoline). Worldwide we consume about 30 billion barrels of oil a year.

The actual price of a barrel of oil is of little interest to petroleum product users, but any change in the price of crude oil will generally get reflected in the price of petrol at the retail pump. Worldwide the price of crude oil has almost tripled over the last 10 years, even allowing for inflation, so we should not be surprised at the high increase in motor vehicle fuel prices over recent years.

The price of motor vehicle fuel varies substantially around the world, with most of the variation coming from local taxes. In September 2008 petrol[10] in the US cost $0.98 per litre. In Japan the same litre cost $1.63, in Germany $2.08 and in the UK $2.01. Petrol in Europe typically costs significantly more than the price charged in the US even though the ex-tax price is very similar.[15] The variation in diesel prices is less, mainly because of lower local taxation on diesel.

The substantially higher price of petrol in Europe over the US has created a greater demand there for fuel-efficient motor vehicles, which brings us to the next section.

How Could We Reduce Our Oil Usage for Transportation?

Prior to the 1973 oil crisis (see Chapter 15), motor vehicle fuel consumption was not a high priority for most vehicle manufacturers. However, the subsequent shortages in oil supply encouraged the production of more fuel-efficient cars so new vehicles today are generally cleaner and more efficient than vehicles produced 30 years ago. But there are things we can all do to reduce our motor vehicle fuel consumption further. Driving more efficiently by accelerating more slowly, not speeding and avoiding unnecessary braking can reduce our fuel consumption by 5–33%.[16] Keeping our cars and trucks well maintained with the engine tuned properly and air filters clean can also help. We can plan our trips better by avoiding peak periods and sharing trips with others. Alternatively we can chose a more efficient vehicle that uses less fuel or choose a different fuel, such as switching from petrol to diesel. As fuel prices rise further we will all be considering these alternatives so we will discuss a few of the different fuels here.

Today transportation relies on crude oil. Ninety-five percent of the total transport energy used comes from crude oil but alternative fuels can be derived from other resources. These alternatives often produce less

---

[10] Unleaded premium petrol.

pollution than petrol or diesel. We have already discussed CNG, LNG and LPG in Chapter 2 all of which can be used as substitutes for petrol or diesel. Unfortunately they are still derived from fossil fuels and will eventually run out like the crude oil products. There are other petrol/diesel replacement fuels that can be derived from renewable resources. Ethanol, a replacement for petrol, is derived by fermenting and distilling starch crops (such as corn or wheat) or sugarcane. Biodiesel, a direct replacement for petroleum-derived diesel, is made from vegetable oil or animal fat. We will discuss biofuels in more depth in Chapter 10.

Hybrid-electric vehicles (HEVs) combine the benefits of petrol or diesel engines and electric motors. With a 'series' HEV, the electric motor running off batteries drives the wheels and the petrol or diesel engine drives a generator that charges the batteries. In a 'parallel' HEV both the electric motor and the engine can drive the wheels. Typically the electric motor provides additional power to assist the engine in accelerating, passing, or hill climbing. HEVs can use a smaller, more fuel-efficient engine than conventional vehicles. The battery packs generally need to be larger in series HEVs than in parallel HEVs. In some parallel HEVs, the electric motor alone provides power for low-speed driving conditions where engines are least efficient. The engine can be shut off automatically when the vehicle slows down and restarted when needed. This prevents wasted energy from idling and the electric motor will even recharge the batteries during deceleration and braking. A Toyota Prius is a parallel HEV that travels over 50% further on the same amount of fuel than the slightly smaller, non-hybrid Toyota Corolla.[17] The General Motors Volt is an example of a series HEV.

All-electric cars are also attracting interest. These vehicle have batteries that are charged from grid electricity at home or at work using the normal electricity supply. They are often referred to as 'plug-ins' and generally have a fairly short driving range before they need recharging and can take about five hours to recharge. Plug-in hybrids combine grid charging with a small petrol or diesel engine to extend driving distance between battery charging.

Another way to reduce oil usage is to use a different mode of transport. For example, moving road freight to rail or coastal shipping may reduce fuel use per tonne carried. We could use public transport more or car pooling which would both reduce our emissions per person per km (see Table 4).

The big challenge for transportation oil replacement will be jet aircraft. As discussed earlier, 6% of crude oil goes to making jet fuel. Some success has been made in producing synthetic jet fuel from coal and natural gas but it is not yet commercially viable. Ethanol, methanol and liquid hydrogen could also be used as a jet fuel but they each have significant challenges to meet the testing environment of high-altitude commercial flying as well as substantial cost disadvantages. Work continues on making jet aircraft more fuel efficient, as is demonstrated by a recent announcement from Boeing about the 787 jetliner claiming a 20% reduction in fuel usage.[18]

How Could We Reduce Our Oil Usage for Electricity Generation?
In Chapter 1, we discussed electricity and where it came from. The use of oil in electricity generation has been reducing since the 1970s. Worldwide, 5% of electricity is still generated from crude oil products but only 3% is generated from crude oil in the US.

How Much Greenhouse Gas Does Oil Produce?
Table 4 shows the amount of emissions produced per litre for transport fuels. It also shows the emissions per passenger kilometre for typical passenger loads in various vehicles. The last column shows an estimate of the annual emissions for each vehicle based on driving 15,000 km per year for a medium sized car, 5,000 km for a scooter, and 30,000 km for a bus. The table shows that public transport is significantly more energy efficient per passenger than private transport.

With jet aircraft the actual climate impact has been estimated to be double the effect of the carbon dioxide emissions alone. We will discuss this in Chapter 22 in Part Three.

Oil used for electricity generation produces between 0.8 and 0.9 kg/kWh of emissions, with the future trend toward 0.5 kg/kWh (see Table 3 in Chapter 1). This is better than coal but not as low as natural gas.

Table 4 — Transport Emissions[19]

Vehicle	Emissions kg CO_2-e/ litre[a]	Passengers	CO_2 Emissions kg CO_2-e per passenger/ km	Annual CO_2 Emissions (tonnes)
Car (petrol/gasoline)	2.35	2	0.12	3.5[b]
Car (diesel)	2.68	2	0.12	3.6[c]
Car (LPG)	1.53	2	0.11	3.0[d]
Scooter (petrol)	2.35	1	0.09	0.5[e]
Minibus (diesel)	2.68	12	0.04	16.1[f]
Bus (diesel)	2.68	40	0.03	32.2[g]
Mid-sized jet (jet fuel)	2.53	100	0.09[h]	

[a] Fuel emissions coefficients from US DOE EIA converted from pounds per gallon to kg per litre.
[b] Based on driving 15,000 km using 10 litres of petrol per 100 km.
[c] Based on driving 15,000 km using 8 litres of diesel per 100 km.
[d] Based on driving 15,000 km using 13 litres of LPG per 100 km.
[e] Based on driving 5,000 km using 4 litres of petrol per 100 km.
[f] Based on driving 30,000 km using 20 litres of diesel per 100 km.
[g] Based on driving 30,000 km using 40 litres of diesel per 100 km.
[h] Based on using 360 litres of jet fuel per 100 km with no allowance for upper atmosphere emissions.

4 — Coal — Smoke Signals on Solid Fuels

Solid fuels include coal, wood, charcoal[11] and peat.[12] Over many centuries these fuels have been used for domestic heating by burning them in an open fire or a stove. Today they are restricted or banned in some urban areas because of the generated smoke which causes pollution and health risks. They are still used in 'smokeless' forms or burned in special solid fuel stoves that minimise the smoke.

Of the solid fuels, coal is the major fuel source worldwide although wood is widely used in developing countries. As we discussed above, more than a quarter of all energy used comes from coal.

What Is Coal?

Coal is a combustible black or dark brown rock composed mostly of carbon and hydrocarbons. Like oil and gas it is a non-renewable fossil fuel that took millions of years to create. Coal is formed from partially decayed vegetable matter (peat) that is transformed by bacterial decay, pressure and heat in a process called coalification. The 'youngest' form of coal is lignite or brown coal. As more heat and pressure is applied over time the lignite matures into bituminous coal which becomes more black and finally into anthracite which is a glossy black coal.

[11] Charcoal is produced from wood burned in the absence of oxygen.
[12] Peat is partially decayed vegetable matter that is found in marshy (waterlogged) areas.

Where Does Coal Come From?

Coal is mined using two main methods — underground mining and surface or open-pit mining. Typically the depth of the coal in the ground will determine whether it is mined underground or open-pit. Underground mining involves tunnelling into the coal seam whereas open-pit mining involves excavating the coal from the surface. Worldwide, about two-thirds of all coal is mined underground.

How Do We Use Coal?

Today most coal is used to generate electricity; the rest is largely used in industry to produce products like steel, cement or paper. In the US over 90% of coal is used for electric power generation. The coal is burned in electricity power plants to produce steam which turns turbines and generators as discussed in Chapter 1. Coal is also used to manufacture steel by burning it in hot coking ovens to make coke and then mixing the coke with iron ore and limestone in a blast furnace to make steel. Coal is used to fuel high temperature kilns to manufacture cement. It can also be liquefied to produce petroleum replacement products like petrol, diesel and fuel oil. It can be gasified to produce syngas — a combination of hydrogen and carbon monoxide which can be used for industrial heating, power generation or the production of hydrogen, synthetic fuels or other chemicals.

How Much Does Coal Cost and How Much Do We Use?

Steam coal prices for electricity generation vary significantly around the world. Measured in US dollars per tonne (metric ton) the 2005 average end-user price in the US was $35.30, in the UK $65.60, and in Germany $79.70, whereas in India it was $21.40.[20] As with oil, local taxes explain some of the differences, as do variations in mining and transport costs. Coking coal, used in making steel, is generally much more expensive. For example, in 2005 the US coking coal price was $92.40 per tonne.

The average thermal energy content of coal is about 6,800 kWh per tonne. Electricity generation from coal is only about 35% efficient using thermal generation, so the electricity generated from a tonne of coal today is about 2,400 kWh. Based on a coal price of $60 per tonne, the coal fuel cost for electricity is about $0.025/kWh.

Worldwide we use about 6,000 million tonnes of coal a year. A home using, say, 10,000 kWh of electricity per year would use around four tonnes of coal to make that electricity if all the electricity came from coal-fired power stations. New technologies are expected to improve the generating efficiency of coal to over 50% which would reduce the usage to around three tonnes per year. The same home would use only 250 grams of natural uranium if all the electricity came from nuclear power.

How Much Greenhouse Gas Does Coal Produce?

Coal is the worst producer of greenhouse gases. As we saw in Table 3, Chapter 1, coal used for thermal electricity generation produces an average of over one kilogram of emissions for each kWh generated. So our home using 10,000 kWh of electricity per year could generate over 10 tonnes of greenhouse gas emissions over that period if all the electricity came from coal-fired power stations. Even at the world average emissions intensity of 0.6 kg/kWh, the home will generate six tonnes of emissions a year just from electricity use. Future technologies that could substantially reduce the carbon dioxide released into the atmosphere from coal-fired power stations can significantly reduce these greenhouse gases (see Part Two, Chapter 14).

Coal used in steel-making produces between 1.5 and 2 tonnes of greenhouse gas emissions for each tonne of steel produced, depending on the steel-making technology used.[21] Some 60% of steel production worldwide comes from iron made in blast furnaces which use coal and world crude steel production was 1.2 billion tonnes in 2006.[22] That means that 1.1–1.4 billion tonnes of greenhouse gas was produced from making steel alone.

How Do We Reduce Our Usage of Coal?

Like oil and gas, there is only a limited amount of coal in the ground. The world coal proven reserves, estimated at 147 years,[23] are believed to be significantly higher than our reserves of oil and gas and more widely distributed throughout the world. So although oil and gas can be used as alternatives to coal in electricity generation, they are generally more expensive and less plentiful. In Chapter 1 we have discussed several alternative energy sources for electricity generation. In Chapters 6–11 we will discuss other, renewable energy sources in more detail but as you will see, most of these are not well suited to baseload generation, which is where coal is generally used. Today the most effective replacements for coal in electricity generation are natural gas or nuclear power. Nuclear power is used extensively throughout the world to generate about 16% of all electricity. It is well suited to baseload[13] generation, generates much less greenhouse gas emissions than coal but does create a nuclear waste disposal issue. We will consider the nuclear option in the next chapter.

[13] Baseload generators run all the time to meet most of the electricity demand (see Chapter 1).

5 — Going Nuclear

Or Everything About Nuclear Energy That You Probably Didn't Want to Know

What Is Nuclear Power?

Nuclear energy is energy released from the nucleus or core of an atom. The bonds that hold atoms together contain enormous amounts of energy. Nuclear power is generated when this energy is released. The energy can be released in two ways: nuclear fission and nuclear fusion. With nuclear fission the energy is released by splitting apart the atom to form smaller atoms. This is the process used in nuclear power plants for generating electricity. With nuclear fusion the energy is released when atoms are combined or fused together to form a larger atom. This is the process that takes place in the sun.

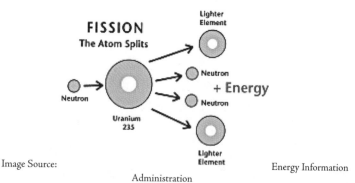

Image Source: Energy Information Administration

Where Does Nuclear Fuel Come From?

The most commonly used fuel in nuclear power plants is uranium. Uranium is a naturally occurring metallic substance found in rocks and is common and widely distributed throughout the world although the major supplies are from Canada and Australia. It occurs in low concentration and must be mined and extracted from the soil and rocks in a process called milling. It is also possible to extract uranium from the oceans.

The milled uranium oxide concentrate (sometimes called yellowcake) contains about 80% uranium. Naturally occurring uranium is 99% uranium-238 with a small amount (0.7%) of uranium-235.[14] Nuclear power plants use the uranium-235 as a fuel because its atoms can be readily split apart to release nuclear energy. This means the uranium oxide has to be enriched to increase the concentration of uranium-235 to above 3% by removing much of the uranium-238.

Uranium is a very energy rich source of power. One tonne of uranium fuel produces more energy than 100,000 tonnes of coal. If our home uses four tonnes of coal a year to produce its electricity (see Chapter 4) then the same home would use only 40 grams of enriched uranium fuel per year!

To release the energy from the enriched uranium a neutron hits the uranium atom, causing it to split and release a great amount of heat and radiation as well as more neutrons (see diagram above). These neutrons go on to hit other uranium atoms to release even more energy and the process continues in a chain reaction.

Box 3

How Nuclear Reactors Work

The nuclear fission process to release nuclear energy takes place in a nuclear reactor. The uranium fuel is formed into small ceramic pellets that are stacked into long fuel rods. These rods are collected into bundles or assemblies that are submersed in water in a pressure vessel. To control the rate of nuclear reaction in the fission process, control rods are inserted into the fuel rod bundles. These control rods absorb neutrons and slow the reaction. To increase the reaction and the amount of heat generated, the control rods are raised out of the fuel rod bundles. If the control rods are fully inserted into the bundles the reaction stops and allows the reactor to be shut down. A reactor can contain several hundred fuel rod assemblies.

---

[14] Uranium-235 and uranium-238 are called isotopes of uranium. Isotopes are just a different form of the same element — in this case the element uranium (U).

There are two main types of reactors currently in use. In boiling-water reactors (BWR), the water heated by the fuel rods turns to steam in the reactor vessel and is used to directly power the turbine and electricity generator. In a pressurised-water reactor (PWR), the water is kept liquid under pressure and converted to steam in a separate steam generator that uses a clean water source (not from the reactor vessel). The advantage of pressurised-water reactors is that the radioactive water/steam is redirected back into the reactor and does not enter the turbine. BWR and PWR reactors are also known as light-water reactors (LWR) and are considered to be second generation (Generation II) reactors. Generation III reactors include a new PWR design called the European Pressurised Reactor (EPR) and an advanced boiling-water reactor (ABWR) with improved economics, safety features, fuel utilisation and reduced waste. Several Generation III reactors are currently being built or commissioned. We will discuss the next generation of reactors (III+ and IV) in Chapter 14.

How Much Nuclear Power Do We Use?

There are almost 440 nuclear power stations throughout the world generating some 2,700 billion kWh/year of electricity or about 16% of the total. Of the larger electricity users, France is the biggest generator of nuclear power by percentage with 79% of its electricity coming from nuclear energy. Of the other major generators of nuclear power next are Ukraine (47%), Sweden (45%), South Korea (38%), Germany (27%), Japan (27%), UK (20%), Spain (20%), US (19%), Russia (16%) and Canada (14%). Brazil, China and India get less than 3% of their electricity from nuclear power plants.[24]

A 1000MW reactor uses about 75 tonnes of nuclear fuel at any one time with about 25–30 tonnes replaced each year. The spent fuel rods from the reactor — replaced with new ones every 12–18 months — are highly radioactive and give off a lot of heat. They are initially stored in ponds like large swimming pools close to the reactor where the water cools the rods and provides a shield against the radioactivity. They can be left in the ponds for some time while the radioactivity decreases before they are either reprocessed or sent for final disposal. Reprocessing involves recovering the unused uranium in the rods and reprocessing and re-enriching it for future use in a reactor. The waste from the reprocessing is stored in stainless steel containers. A 1000MW reactor produces about five tonnes of reprocessing waste each year which can be stored or transported with suitable radioactive shielding.

How Much Does Nuclear Power Cost?

The construction cost of a new nuclear power plant varies from $1000–2000 per kW. So a 1000MW plant costs $1–2 billion to build. Once built, the plant needs to be operated and maintained and there is a fuel cost for the uranium. If we than add the costs of decommissioning at the end of the reactor's life the cost of nuclear generated electricity varies from $0.03-0.05/kWh (see Table 2 in Chapter 1). This makes the lifetime cost of nuclear power comparable with any other fuel source.

How Much Greenhouse Gas Does Nuclear Power Produce?

As we saw in Table 3 in Chapter 1, nuclear power is one of the lowest greenhouse gas producers of all the electricity generating technologies, producing less than 0.1 kg/kWh over the full life cycle including processing the uranium used.

The Downside and Upside of Nuclear Power

In Part Two of the book we will discuss the worldwide concern about the amount of greenhouse gas we are putting into the atmosphere. Coal burning is one of the biggest culprits. Most coal is used to generate electricity and coal is the most frequently used fuel in electricity generation. Nuclear power generation on the other hand generates very little greenhouse gas and delivers large amounts of baseload power, while the generation cost of electricity from nuclear power stations is comparable with coal-fired stations in many parts of the world. So if coal is so bad, why not switch to nuclear?

Firstly, uranium is a non-renewable energy source. At the current rate of usage, we have about 100–300 years supply, which is better than coal or petroleum. Secondly, final (very long-term) disposal of the radioactive waste and spent fuel rods from reactors is a problem yet to be addressed. The volume of waste is relatively small where reprocessing is done — less than 30 cubic metres (about the size of a small room in a house) of disposable volume per year for a 1000MW reactor. The longer it is stored the less radioactive it becomes. After about 40–50 years the radioactivity is down to 1/1000 of the level at removal and this makes transportation and final disposal easier. So the waste is often 'temporarily' stored close to the reactor or in a central location awaiting a final disposal site. As well as waste from fuel rods, there is also the issue of decontaminating and safely disposing of decommissioned nuclear plants. Uranium enrichment and the processing of spent fuel are critical steps for nuclear weapons proliferation, which naturally causes safety and security concerns.

The likely final disposal solution for nuclear waste is to bury it in stable rock structures deep underground and several countries are already selecting suitable sites for their own waste. It will still take a further thousand years before the radioactivity returns to that of the naturally occurring uranium ore from which the fuel originated (although it will be more concentrated). Needless to say, radioactive contamination issues are very political and an environmental and public safety concern. Governments require nuclear utilities to set aside a small levy (0.1 cents per kWh in the US) for future management and disposal of this waste but the first facility is yet to be built and not expected before 2010. International repositories have also been proposed with the US, Russia and Australia as possible locations. Because the waste is stored on the surface for 40–50 years (about the age of the nuclear power industry) there has not been a pressing need for final disposal.

Thirdly, there is a community concern about the safety of nuclear reactors themselves, which are often installed close to populations that need the electricity. Reactors also need easy access to water and the electricity grid. There have been only two significant accidents in the 50-year history of commercial nuclear power generation, although there have been several 'minor' accidents. The first significant accident, and the worst in the US, was at Three Mile Island in 1979 where the reactor was severely damaged but radiation was contained and the consensus seems to be that there were no adverse health or environmental consequences. This has been disputed by fellow Australian, Dr Helen Caldicott, a passionate advocate against nuclear power, who claims that a long-lived radioactive isotope (Strontium-90) escaped from the reactor site. This has been refuted in an article by Thomas Gerusky, Director of the State Bureau of Radiation Protection, published in the

Annals of the New York Academy of Sciences.[15] The second accident was at Chernobyl in the Ukraine in 1986, where the destruction of the reactor by steam explosion and fire killed over 50 people and had significant health and environmental consequences resulting in permanent evacuation of the city. Reactor technology has developed significantly over the last 30 years and a reactor like Chernobyl would not be built or operated today.

Another community concern is that rogue nations or terrorists will create nuclear weapons from the reactor fuel. This is often referred to as nuclear proliferation. We discuss nuclear weapons proliferation in Chapter 15 but it is considered to be a low risk.

Of course, no industrial process is completely safe and energy generation is no exception. Even the most common source of renewable electricity, hydro-electricity, has killed thousands more people through dam failures than have been killed in nuclear reactor accidents and coalmining has killed and injured thousands more. Despite this, public concern about nuclear reactors persists and the development of new reactors has slowed substantially over the 20–30 years since the Three Mile Island and Chernobyl accidents. This is starting to change with rising concerns about greenhouse gas emissions. In April 2008 there were 35 power plant reactors under construction, mainly in developing countries, and a further 91 on the drawing boards.[25]

---

[15] 'Three Mile Island: Assessment of Radiation Exposures and Environmental Contamination', *Annals of the New York Academy of Sciences*, Vol. 365, Issue 1, April 1981, p. 54.

Chapters 6–11 — A Renewed Look at Renewables

In the next few chapters we are going to look at the renewable energy resources—solar, wind, hydro, geothermal and biomass. We also cover a developing source of renewable energy storage in hydrogen. About 13% of primary energy comes from renewables today, mainly biomass and hydro for electricity.

Sources of renewable energy are either continuously replaced (such as from the sun or wind) or can be replenished in a relatively short period of time of months or a few years. Renewable resources include solar (from the sun), wind, hydro (water), geothermal (heat from the Earth), biomass (plant and animal matter) and hydrogen. In the early history of man, all fuel sources were renewable — mainly wood, peat and animal dung for fires. The first non-renewable energy resource used was coal that had taken millions of years to create, so it is clearly a non-renewable resource.

Non-renewable energy resources will all run out eventually or get so expensive to recover that they are no longer attractive. This is probably going to happen to oil within a few decades (some would say much sooner). Coal will last a bit longer (about 150 years) but will get more expensive to mine. So renewable energy resources will become increasingly more important as the non-renewable resources become more scarce and expensive. Several large international companies such as

General Electric, Siemens, Shell and BP have invested in renewable energy products.

The World Business Council for Sustainable Development[26] reports that renewable energy resources have been estimated as adequate to meet the energy needs of 10 billion people. This is fortunate because the world population is likely to reach that figure before the end of the 21st century.

For each of the renewable resources we will discuss where the energy comes from and how we use it. We will also discuss the upsides and downsides of each energy source. Greenhouse gas emissions from renewable energy sources are generally small so we will not discuss the emissions from these sources in greater detail than was covered in Table 3 in Chapter 1.

6 — The Sun Shines on Solar Power

In Chapter 5 we discussed nuclear power initiated by man using nuclear fission. In this chapter we will look at natural nuclear power that comes from the sun. The sun is a giant nuclear reactor that produces energy through nuclear fusion, where atoms are combined or fused together to form larger atoms. Solar energy is the solar radiation that reaches the Earth. The total solar radiation hitting the Earth is about 7,000 times the total current global energy consumption so we are unlikely to run short of energy. The difficulty is in converting it to a usable form.

Where Does Solar Energy Come From?
Nuclear fusion happens deep in the core of the sun where the pressure is so great that hydrogen atoms can be fused together to create helium and energy. The energy is emitted from the sun in several forms including ultraviolet light, X-rays, visible light, infrared light, microwaves and radio waves. This energy warms the Earth, drives our weather and provides energy for life.

On a bright sunny day around noon, about 1,000 watts of solar energy shines on a square metre of the Earth's surface at the equator. The sun has been emitting this energy for billions of years and it can be truly said to be renewable — while ever man lives on the Earth, there will be solar energy irrespective of how much we use.

Where Can We Use Solar Energy?

We can basically use solar energy either as a heat source or to make electricity. These two forms are often referred to as solar-thermal and solar-photovoltaic or PV.

Solar-thermal energy is where the sun's radiation is used as a heat source to heat, for example, water or air for buildings. There are two types of solar-thermal collectors, concentrating and non-concentrating. With non-concentrating or flat-plate collectors the area that is exposed to the sun (collector area) is the same as the area that absorbs the radiation (absorber area). With concentrating collectors the collector area is greater (often much greater) than the absorber area which means that the sun's radiation is very concentrated at the absorber. Where temperatures up to 95°C are adequate (such as with swimming pools, domestic hot water or space heating) then non-concentrating flat-plate collectors are adequate. Above that temperature we need to use concentrating collectors.

Flat-plate collectors typically consist of a blackened metal flat absorber plate within a glazed metal box. The absorber absorbs the solar energy that passes through the glass and uses a heat-transport fluid (usually water or air) that flows through tubes attached to the absorber plate to remove the heat from the absorber. With a concentrating collector a parabolic reflector focuses the solar energy from the collector onto a much smaller absorber. This concentrates the energy and heats the absorber to a much higher temperature than is possible with a flat-plate collector. Solar-thermal electricity power generators use concentrating collectors to heat a fluid (such as oil) that creates steam in a steam generator using a heat exchanger. The steam drives a turbine and generator to produce electricity (see Chapter 1). We will discuss some developing technologies in solar-thermal large-scale grid power in more depth in Part Two, Chapter 14.

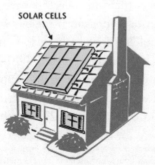

SOLAR CELLS

Image Source: Energy Information Administration

Photovoltaic energy is the conversion of sunlight into electricity through a PV cell, commonly called a solar cell. PV cells are made of a semiconductor[16] material (typically silicon). When light strikes the cell some of it is absorbed in the semiconductor material, releasing free electrons and creating an electric current. Individual PV cells vary in size from 1 to 10 cm across and generate about 1 or 2 watts of power. They are typically connected together in PV modules to produce greater power. PV cells only convert about 25% of the solar energy into electrical energy under ideal conditions. The amount of electricity produced depends on the amount of solar energy hitting the PV cells, so it depends on the weather and the time of day. When it is cloudy the PV cells might produce very little electricity. To make electricity available at any time of day, it can be stored in batteries (see Chapter 1). PV cells produce a direct current (DC) whereas most households and appliances require an alternating current (AC). Converting DC to AC is done using an inverter.

PV cells are used for many applications, from powering small calculators to generating power for the electricity grid. They are often used for powering devices in remote areas away from mains power sources such as road signs, lighting or communications equipment. They are also becoming integrated into building products such as roof tiles, shingles and standard metal roofing. These are commonly referred to as PV roofing.

How Much Does Solar Power Cost?

It might be tempting to think that solar power is free. Unfortunately, to capture and convert it requires investment in collectors or PV cells, batteries and inverters. Solar PV installations are usually priced in dollars per watt. For domestic or building installations, PV modules cost between $4 and $5 per watt.[17] The module represents 40–50% of the total installation cost depending on the nature of the application, for example, whether it has batteries or is connected to the grid. So an installation can cost between $8 and $10 per watt.[27] If the installation

---

[16] A semiconductor has an electrical conductivity between a conductor and an insulator.
[17] Technically a peak watt. A peak watt is the DC watt output of a solar module as measured under an industry standardised light test.

is 2,000 watts of solar power, which is typical for an average home, the cost will be between $16,000 and $20,000.

Remember solar power only works when the sun is up. So in a sunny place like southern California or Australia we might get around 4,000 kWh per year from a 2,000 watt system. If we are in northern Europe we will get much less — maybe half. If our home uses 10,000 kWh per year and we live in a sunny part of the world then this solar system is supplying about 40% of our electricity needs. To install a solar system to provide all our electricity needs including connection to the grid and battery back-up storage might cost us $50,000. In some regions, if we can generate more electricity than we can use at any time, we can sell it back to the electricity utility and this will help reduce the overall cost.

According to Solarbuzz LLC[28] in August 2008 the average international solar energy cost for residential use was $0.38/kWh, spreading the capital cost over 20 years. Based on the international average price of $0.16/kWh for grid electricity quoted in Chapter 1, domestic solar electricity is 2.4 times more expensive than the average grid electricity price. Another way to look at it is, if we invest $20,000 to install a 2,000 watt solar PV system and it produces 4,000 kWh then it would save us $640 a year in electricity (4000 x 0.16) which is a small 3.2% annual return on our investment.

A domestic solar-thermal hot water heater system without a pump will cost us $1,000–2,000. We will save electricity or gas, although all solar-thermal water heaters need an electric or gas booster to provide hot water on cloudy days. Some utilities claim we can save up to 75% of our hot water electricity costs depending on the location and climate. In some countries a third of the domestic electricity usage can be for hot water. Even if most of this is at off-peak rates of say $0.08/kWh and we use 3,000 kWh per year for electric hot water, then we could save around $150 per year with solar water heating which would give us an attractive 8–15% annual return on investment.

For commercial PV solar power plants for the grid, typical construction costs are about $4,000 per kW. The cost per kWh varies significantly around the world depending on the availability of sunlight and can range from $0.20/kWh to $0.60/kWh (see Table 2 in Chapter 1). This makes it the most costly generating technology available. For commercial solar-thermal power plants (sometimes referred to as concentrating solar power or CSP) construction costs are a little less at about $3,000 per kW but still twice the price of a modern coal-fired power station and three times the price of a gas-fired station. As with PV, generation costs per kWh will vary with location but a recent plant in the US cost around $0.20/kWh. These costs are likely to reduce over time with more research and development.

The Downside and Upside of Solar Power

The downsides of solar energy are that it is not available at night and its power is significantly reduced in cloudy conditions or when the sun is not directly over the collector. We also need to make a significant capital investment (probably $10,000–30,000) to use solar energy domestically for electricity and we will have some maintenance costs — particularly batteries which have a life of around 8 to 15 years if used properly and can account for 15% of the total system cost. Today the cost of domestic solar electricity cannot compete with grid electricity.

Where I live in Australia, about the same latitude as Orlando in Florida but in the Southern Hemisphere, we have plenty of sunshine but, being near the Pacific coast, we also have lengthy periods of cloudy and warm but very wet weather. There are people in my area using solar panels who have elected not to be connected to the grid (and can snub their noses at the electricity companies) but they all have to own petrol or diesel generators to recharge their batteries after about five or six days without sunshine. Apart from the noise, these generators are not very greenhouse gas friendly or cost effective.

The obvious upsides with solar energy are that there is a lot of it, it is renewable and it doesn't generate any waste or pollution while generating electricity or heat. By using solar power, we can reduce our dependence on non-renewable fuels which will get more expensive as supplies dwindle (unless we have to buy a generator). Once we have paid for the installation of the equipment, the fuel cost is zero and it can be used in remote locations away from the electricity grid. Over the life of the system (including manufacturing the collectors) it will generate far fewer greenhouse gas emissions than fossil fuels.

We will discuss more upsides and downsides of using solar energy to produce electricity for the grid in Part Two, Chapter 14.

7 — The Answer Is (Well Maybe) Blowing in the Wind

Wind is probably the most promising resource for renewable energy in terms of cost. However, as with most of the renewables, wind has its downsides.

Where Does Wind Energy Come From?

Wind is moving air. The sun heats the Earth's surface unevenly because different types of land and water absorb the sun's heat at different rates. During the day, the air above the land heats up more quickly than the air over water. The warmer air over the land expands and rises, and the heavier cooler air rushes in to take its place, creating winds. So technically wind is another form of solar energy.

Wind turbines use blades to collect the wind's kinetic[18] energy and rotate the blades to convert it into mechanical energy. The wind flows over the aerofoil (airfoil) shaped blades causing the blades to lift and turn on a shaft (see Box 4). The shaft can be used to drive a mill wheel, pump or electricity generator.

How Do We Use Wind Energy?

Man has harnessed wind energy for thousands of years using sail boats and windmills. Early windmills were used for grinding grains such as wheat into flour. Later they were also used for pumping water and driving wood saws in sawmills. Today windmills or wind turbines are largely used for generating electricity.

[18] The kinetic energy of a body is the energy it possesses because of its motion.

Most wind turbines use a horizontal shaft on a high tower and are located on land or offshore (see Box 4). Commercial wind turbines are usually installed in clusters called wind farms to provide power to the grid. The largest wind farm in the world is in Texas and has over 400 wind turbines with a peak capacity of over 700MW. Most wind farms are much smaller than this, ranging from 1MW to 500MW.

Let's look at the example of building new wind farms to replace a 1000MW coal-fired power station. If we assume that the coal-fired station has a capacity factor of 75% — that means that on average over the course of a year it generates 750MW because it is sometimes shut for maintenance or not required at full capacity — then the station will generate 6.6 million MWh of electricity over the year. A typical capacity factor for a wind farm is around 30%, so to generate 6.6 million MWh[19] of electricity we will need to build wind farms to a total peak capacity of 2,500MW. This will probably require several wind farms in different locations using 1,250 wind turbines.

Box 4

How Wind Turbines Work

Large commercial wind turbines typically use three giant blades about 30 metres in length to rotate a horizontal shaft at the top of a 100 metre tower. Attached to the shaft at the top of the tower is an electricity generator. A typically 2MW turbine might generate 6 million kWh per year in good wind conditions (about 34% capacity factor[a])[29]. Some turbines are approaching a peak capacity of 5MW.

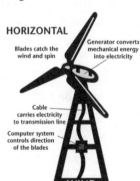

HORIZONTAL

Blades catch the wind and spin

Generator converts mechanical energy into electricity

Cable carries electricity to transmission line

Computer system controls direction of the blades

WIND MACHINE

Wind turbines can also have the shaft mounted vertically rather than horizontally. The advantage is that the generator can be located at the bottom of the shaft near the ground rather than on top of a high tower. Typically vertical-axis turbines only stand 30 metres high so a disadvantage is that they collect less wind and extract less energy than horizontal-axis turbines.

[a] Capacity factor of a wind turbine is the actual annual energy output divided by the theoretical maximum output if the machine was running at its rated (maximum) power for 24 hours a day, 365 days a year.

Image Source: Energy Information Administration

[19] 750MW x 24hr x 365days = 6.57 million MWh.

There are some grid connection issues with wind farms. As we discussed in Chapter 1, electricity utilities are required to match supply with demand because electricity cannot be readily stored. The electricity generated from a wind farm is intermittent (the wind doesn't blow all the time or at a steady rate — see the section below on wind power cost) and so cannot be delivered on demand in the same way as from a coal, gas or nuclear power plant. This presents reliability issues in some networks and requires network upgrades to handle more variable loads and smaller-scale generators. Solutions such as aggregating the supply from different wind farms and hydro-power plants to smooth variations, improved weather forecasting methods and use of pumped storage hydro system (see Chapter 8) are being evaluated but require increased network interconnections and upgrades at ultimate cost to the end user. Today, for many grids, intermittent sources such as wind and sun are limited to 15–20% of the total grid capacity.

Single small wind turbines can also be used for domestic purposes or remote off-grid applications. They work in the same way as large commercial turbines but are typically under 100kW in capacity and are used to charge batteries as an alternative to or in conjunction with solar cells.

How Much Does Wind Power Cost and How Much Do We Use?

Like solar, it might be tempting to think that wind power is free. The fuel cost is certainly free but wind farms need to be built, operated and maintained. The construction costs for a wind power plant range from $1,000 to $2,000 per kW. So a 100MW plant will cost $100–200 million to build. Add another 20–40% to the construction cost for operating and maintenance spread over 20-30 years life and the cost at best in good wind sites (high capacity factor) is in the range for coal, gas and nuclear power plants (see Table 2 in Chapter 1).

The cost of wind power has dropped significantly over the last 25 years from above $0.20/kWh in 1980 to under $0.05/kWh at good wind sites[30]. Wind power varies as the cube of the wind speed, so doubling the wind speed gives eight times the wind power. Even a small increase in wind speed can result in a large increase in electricity generated. For example, an increase in wind speed from 20 km per hour to 25 km per hour will almost double the power generated from a turbine. As the cost of generation doesn't change, the cost per kWh almost halves. So we can see that the cost per kWh of wind power can vary significantly between wind farm sites even if the farm peak capacity is identical. Farms typically generate between 25% and 40% of their peak capacity depending on wind availability with a worldwide average of around 28%. Wind turbines need a wind speed of 14–90 km/h to operate effectively.

In 2007, worldwide wind peak power capacity had reached almost 94,000MW and is forecast to reach 170,000MW in 2010.[31] At 30% capacity factor this capacity represented just over 1% of total electricity generation, rising to 2% in 2010. Wind generator capacity is the fastest growing of all electricity technologies. The largest user of wind power today is Germany, with 28% of the world capacity. Other big users are Spain (16%), the US (16%) and India (8%).

A 2MW wind turbine can power about 600 homes each using 10,000 kWh per year. A 500MW wind farm with around 250 turbines could (in theory) provide enough power for a city of 150,000 homes.

The Downside and Upside of Wind Power
On the downside, electricity generated by wind turbines is still more expensive than from non-renewables such as coal, gas or nuclear, particularly in low to moderate winds areas. The initial investment cost per kWh for wind is higher than for coal, oil or nuclear although the operation and maintenance costs are similar with no fuel cost. As discussed above, the wind is intermittent and not always available on demand. This limits its usability for grid electricity and creates some grid integration issues. Good wind sites are also often remote from the grid. There is some environmental impact as rotor blades produce noise and some people are unhappy about the visual impact on the landscape.

Like solar power, the obvious upside with wind is that it is renewable and is one of the cheapest of all the renewables at producing electricity. Also like solar, there is no greenhouse gas or other pollution generated in the electricity production process although there is some in the construction and maintenance. Wind blows everywhere some of the time so it can be widely used. The wind is free so there is no exposure to variable fuel supply costs. Wind turbines have a small footprint (base area) so the land used for wind farms can be shared with other uses like stock grazing.

8 — Hydropower — an Old Solution to a New Problem?

Hydropower, or power from moving water, is one of the oldest forms of energy. It has been used for thousands of years for irrigation and driving various machines such as grain grinding mills and potters' wheels. Today, it is the most commonly used source of renewable power (mainly electricity) with over 80% of all renewable power coming from hydropower.

Where Does Hydro Energy Come From?

In hydropower, mechanical energy is derived from moving water in a river or channel. The amount of energy depends on the flow or fall of the water. Fast flowing water or water that falls from a great height, as in a waterfall, carries a lot of energy. To harness this energy, the water is directed into a narrow channel or pipe and then pushed against blades in a turbine causing them to rotate. Early water turbines were the large wooden paddle wheels that can still be seen on some old water mills.

There are basically two types of hydropower in use today for electricity generation. In a run-of-the-river system the force of the current in the river provides the energy to drive the turbine. In a storage or dam system the water from a flowing river or lake is collected into a reservoir behind a dam wall and the height of the water above the turbine produces a fast current to turn the turbine blades (see Box 5).

Power from water can also be harnessed from the oceans where the power comes from the rise and fall of the sea level or from waves. These are often called tidal power and wave power but they are not yet widely used for electricity generation. There are only a limited number of sites around the world that are likely to be suitable for ocean power and we will discuss this in more detail in Chapter 14.

How Do We Use Hydro Energy?

As with wind, the ancient uses for water power have largely disappeared. However, it is still used extensively for generating electricity in hydro-electric power stations (see Box 5), particularly in countries that have plenty of access to running water like Canada, Brazil and Norway. In Norway, 99% of their electricity comes from hydropower.[32]

Dam system hydro-electric power stations can also be used for storing grid electricity. Pumped storage schemes (see Box 5) can improve the capacity factor of hydro-electric power stations. Hydro-electric generators make excellent quick-start generators for meeting peak demand. Pumped water storage is currently the most effective, commercially viable, large-scale grid energy storage system.

How Much Does Hydropower Cost and How Much Do We Use?

The cost of building hydro-electric power stations can vary greatly depending on the location. As with most sources of renewable energy, the construction cost typically covers 80–90% of the total lifetime cost of the power station. As we saw from Table 2 in Chapter 1, a new hydro-electric power station can have a lifetime cost of $0.065–0.100/kWh which, at the lowest cost, makes it more expensive than wind but cheaper than solar.

Worldwide, we generate 2,900 billion kWh per year from hydro-electricity or about 16–17% of the total electricity generated. China is the biggest generator at 400 billion kWh/year and next is Canada at 360 billion kWh/year.[32]

The Downside and Upside of Hydropower

The downside of hydropower is that dams are expensive to build although they are often built for other reasons such as water storage or flood control. There are only a limited number of locations to put hydropower plants so they are unsuitable for some countries. They

Box 5

How Hydro-Electric Power Stations and Pumped Storage Work

Most hydro-electric power stations use a dam system from water stored in a reservoir. The power that can be generated from a dam system is directly related to the height of the water and the rate of the water flow. So the higher the reservoir water level above the power station and the greater the volume of water flowing through the turbines the more electricity that can be generated. Water is directed from the reservoir to the power station through pipes called penstocks with gates that control the flow of water and hence the amount of electricity produced from the station. The turbine shafts are usually mounted vertically with the generator on top of the turbine. The amount of electricity that can be generated in a hydro-electric system depends on the availability of flowing water and this can vary considerably throughout the year depending on the flow in the river source. The largest hydro-electric power station is in China and is expected to have a capacity of 22,000MW when it is fully completed. This is much larger than any thermal power station. Capacity factors for hydro-electric power stations can vary considerably depending on the availability of water flow and can range from 30% to 80%. A power station with year-round flows should exceed 50%.

Pumped storage hydro plants store water in a lower reservoir rather than letting it flow down the river. In off-peak times when electrical demand is low, the excess electricity generation capacity in the grid (which could be from thermal power plants or wind farms) is used to drive pumps that move the water back into the higher reservoir. This water can then be used to generate more hydro-electric power in peak times. In some pumped storage plants the pumps used are actually the existing turbines and generators run in reverse, with the generator becoming an electric motor and the turbine a pump.

Some pumped storage systems simply use two reservoirs, one above the other, with no river flow and these are used only for electricity energy storage. These systems do not generate any net electricity; they simply use less expensive off-peak electricity to generate more valuable peak electricity on demand.

Image Source: Energy Information Administration

need a good supply of running water and/or the ability to build a dam and space for a reservoir. There can be some environmental impact on flooded land upstream from the dam and interruption to downstream flows which can affect the ecology. Rainfall or snowmelt may be variable in the catchment areas, affecting the river flow, and this problem may get more acute with climate change. Lastly, dams have been know to fail with catastrophic consequences for people living below them. As we mentioned in Chapter 5, thousands more people have died through dam failures than have been killed in nuclear reactor accidents.

Hydropower does have an advantage over wind or solar in that in some locations adequate water flow runs continuously so it doesn't suffer from intermittency. This makes hydropower a much more reliable and predictable source of electricity. Water flows can be readily controlled so a hydro turbine can be increased to full power quickly (within several seconds) unlike a steam turbine which can take several hours to reach full power. This makes hydro-electricity very good for peak-load generation. Pumped water storage is the most effective way of storing grid electricity today and a large amount of energy can be stored for a long time, even several months.

9 — Geothermal — Hot Rocks Can Get You Steamed Up!

Geothermal energy is heat generated from within the Earth. We can use the steam and hot water naturally produced inside the Earth to heat buildings or generate electricity or we can pump water down into the Earth's hot rocks to be heated. The heat inside the Earth is continuously produced so geothermal is a renewable energy source.

Where Does Geothermal Energy Come From?

The core of the Earth is extremely hot. This heat is generated by the slow decay of radioactive particles. The core consists of a solid iron inner core, about the size of the moon, surrounded by an outer core of molten rock called magma. Around the core is a layer of magma and rock called the mantle. The outermost layer of the Earth, called the crust, is roughly 2–3 km thick. In places the crust is broken, allowing the magma to get close to the surface causing volcanos and larva flows. Most of the magma remains beneath the crust where it heats the surrounding rock and underground water at depths from a few hundred metres to three km. Drilling a well into a hydrothermal reservoir can release very hot water and steam which can be used for heating or generating electricity.

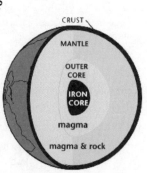

THE EARTH'S INTERIOR

There is another form of geothermal energy called enhanced or engineered geothermal system (EGS) and often referred to in Australia as hot dry rocks (see Box 6). As the name implies, it uses hot rocks deep in the earth that do not have a naturally occurring hydrothermal reservoir. The heat is extracted from these rocks by circulating water through them in a man-made reservoir or underground heat exchanger.

Box 6

How Hot Dry Rocks Work

In some places beneath the Earth's crust there are deep masses of hot dry rock (often granite) that can be over 200°C. This hot rock is heated partly by natural radioactive decay and partly by the surrounding heat of the Earth and protected from losing that heat by a blanket of insulating sedimentary rock. Hot granite masses can contain a substantial amount of heat energy. Deep bore holes (4–5 km) are drilled into the hot rock and fluid is pumped down under high pressure into the rock, where it opens existing fractures in the rock (hydraulic fracturing) creating an artificial underground reservoir and heat exchanger. In production, water is pumped down a bore hole through the fractures in this EGS reservoir where it is heated by the surrounding rock. The superheated[a] water is then returned to the surface through another bore hole,to be used as steam or in a heat exchanger to produce steam for a generator turbine. EGS largely relies on existing technologies for deep well drilling and hydraulic fracturing that were developed in the oil and gas industry.

[a] Superheating is where a liquid is heated to a temperature higher than its natural boiling point without actually boiling.

How Do We Use Geothermal Energy?

Conventional geothermal power, where an existing underground hot water or hydrothermal resource is used, has been in use for centuries for bathing, cooking and heating. It was, and still is, used for heating buildings where the hot water is piped to local homes and industries. Existing geothermal electricity power plants use hydrothermal resources at 150–350°C to drive steam turbines. The US produces the most geothermal electricity with about 50 power plants but it still amounts to less than 1% of the total electricity generated.

Geothermal heat pumps use the ground close to a building as a heat source or heat sink. Below the top 1–2 metres, the Earth holds a fairly constant temperature throughout the year even though the air temperature above can vary considerably. This means that for most places around the world the ground temperature is higher than the air temperature in winter and cooler in summer. So by transferring heat from the ground into the building in winter it can heat the building. The reverse is true in summer. Geothermal heat pumps are very efficient although expensive to install and have been in use for several decades in both residential and commercial buildings.

EGS is an emerging source of energy for producing electricity (see Box 6). Potentially it could be the most attractive source of renewable baseload power in countries that have access to suitable geothermal resources. A demonstration plant was built and tested in the US in New Mexico between 1970 and 1996. There are several commercial developments taking place in countries such as France, Japan and Australia but so far there are no commercial EGS power plants after over 30 years of development.

How Much Does Geothermal Energy Cost and How Much Do We Use?

A conventional geothermal electricity power plant costs $2,500–5,000 per kW to build. These plants have a high capacity factor of above 90% with a typical cost per kWh of around $0.05.[33] This makes it a little more expensive than coal, gas and nuclear but cheaper than wind and solar.

Geothermal energy use falls into two categories, direct use (such as heating) and electricity generation, with each category producing about the same amount of energy.

About 0.4% of worldwide total primary energy is generated by geothermal power so it makes a very small contribution to our total energy use.

The Downside and Upside of Geothermal Energy

With the exception of geothermal heat pumps, there are limited locations where geothermal energy can be used. Conventional geothermal electricity generation is not a true renewable power source because the hydrothermal resource (the hot water) can (and does) run out. EGS is the most promising geothermal energy source for producing baseload electricity but it is still unproven commercially and the hydraulic fracturing can cause seismic activity (earthquakes or earth tremors).

Here in Australia, we have a company called Geodynamics which is building an EGS plant in the Cooper Basin in South Australia. EGS exploratory drilling first started in the Basin in 1983 to a depth of almost four km. In 2003, a 'proof of concept' well was drilled with a second well drilled in 2004. This second well hit a snag and operations were suspended in 2006. A third well, which was a commercial-scale well, was drilled in 2007. Water circulation between the first and third wells was tested in early 2008 and a proof of concept electricity generating plant of 1MW is hoped to be completed by the end of 2008. The first production electricity plant is expected to be a 50MW system that is scheduled for completion in 2012. As you can see from this brief history, building an EGS power plant is not like building a gas-fueled power station. We realistically can only expect a limited contribution to electricity generation from EGS before 2030.

Worldwide there is an abundance of geothermal resources. Sufficient to provide all our energy needs for thousands of years — at least in theory. Using geothermal energy produces very little greenhouse gases although there can be other toxic emissions in some circumstances. It generally has a very low environmental impact and requires less land area for large-scale electricity generation than wind and solar power. It is available 24 hours a day so can provide baseload power and has no fuel cost.

10 — Biomass — Plant Power!

Biomass is biological material from recently living plants and animals that contains stored energy from the sun. Examples of biomass fuels are wood, crops, manure, and some garbage. Biomass is a renewable energy source because we can always grow more trees and crops, and we will always produce garbage.

Where Does Biomass Energy Come From?
Plants convert the sun's energy into chemical energy using a process called photosynthesis. When we burn biomass fuels such as wood, this chemical energy is released as heat. Although coal is an ancient product of biomass it is not considered to be a member of the biomass family.

How Do We Use Biomass Energy?
Wood and wood waste is the most common form of biomass and was the most common energy source up to the mid-19th century. Today, wood waste is still burned to produce steam for making electricity, or to provide heat for buildings in many parts of the world. Other forms of biomass such as vegetable or animal garbage can also be burned in waste-to-energy plants using a high-temperature incinerator to produce heat and electricity. About 80% of typical garbage can be burned in waste-to-energy plants.

As well as burning, biomass can be converted to other forms of energy like methane gas or transportation fuels like ethanol and biodiesel often called biofuels. In landfills, rotting vegetable or animal garbage releases methane gas — also called landfill gas or biogas. This methane can be collected and used as a fuel like natural gas.

Crops like corn and sugarcane can be fermented to ethanol, which can replace petrol in petrol engines. Sugarcane and sugar beets are the most common ingredients for ethanol in most parts of the world. The sugar is fermented to create a clear and colourless alcohol (ethanol). Brazil is the world's largest producer and makes most of its ethanol from sugarcane. Corn starch can be fermented to sugar using yeast. The sugar is then fermented into ethanol. Newer products like cellulosic ethanol can also be made from inedible cellulose fibres such as branches and plant stems. Cellulosic ethanol is still in the commercial development stage. Ethanol can be used as a total or partial replacement for petrol in motor vehicles.

Biodiesel can be produced from left-over food products like vegetable oils, animal fats or greases as well as from oil crops such as rapeseed or soybean. The available quantity of waste oil is very small compared to total diesel consumption and biodiesel from oil crops can be expensive. Biodiesel can be used as a total or partial replacement for petroleum diesel in standard diesel engines. We discuss biofuels in more detail in Chapter 22 in Part Three.

How Much Does Biomass Energy Cost and How Much Do We Use?
The cost of energy from biomass can vary considerably depending on the supply of fuel and the type of energy produced, typically heat or electricity. The range can be from $0.02 to $0.15/kWh. So under some circumstances it can be competitive with fossil fuels but not always.

The cost of producing biomass motor vehicle fuels (biofuels), ethanol and biodiesel, varies depending on the supply of raw material and the scale of production. In some locations ethanol and biodiesel can be produced more cheaply than the equivalent petroleum products although this is not common. Ethanol contains only two-thirds of the energy of petrol and biodiesel contains about 90% of the energy of petroleum diesel. To run our cars on pure ethanol would mean we would need to use 1.5 litres of ethanol to travel the same distance we would travel using a litre of petrol, so comparing costs between the two needs to take this into account. In many countries biofuels are more expensive so governments offer subsidies to compensate for the increased production cost and to encourage the use of biofuels.

Worldwide over 10% of total primary energy comes from biomass. For electricity generation less than 1% comes from biomass. The amount of biomass as a percentage of the total varies significantly around the world. For example, in Africa 48% of primary energy comes from biomass whereas in the OECD countries biomass makes up only 3% with China around 14%. Today biofuels provide 1% of all transport fuels and use 1% of all the available arable land. This could rise to 10% by 2030.[1]

How Much Greenhouse Gas Does Biomass Produce?
Unlike other renewable energy sources such as wind, solar, hydro and geothermal, burning biomass fuels does produce greenhouse gases, as does burning ethanol and biodiesel in motor vehicles. In terms of carbon dioxide, this is mainly compensated by the growing of new biomass crops that take up carbon dioxide during photosynthesis. Methane is a much worse greenhouse gas than carbon dioxide, so collecting and burning it from landfills rather than letting it escape to the atmosphere significantly reduces the greenhouse gas effect. Overall, using biomass fuels is a low, but not zero, contributor to greenhouse gases but is largely carbon dioxide neutral.

This is not the case, however, for ethanol made from corn. Because natural gas is used in the production process, corn ethanol will produce about half the total greenhouse gas emissions of petrol (often referred to as the 'well-to-wheel' emissions) or about 1.2 kg CO_2-e/litre. Cellulosic ethanol and ethanol made from sugarcane are much better and will reduce petrol emissions by as much as 86% to about 0.3 kg CO_2-e/litre.[34] We discuss well-to-wheel emissions in more detail in Chapter 22.

The Downside and Upside of Biomass Energy
The major disadvantage with biomass is that it uses arable land that may be needed for food production. As discussed above, biofuels already

use 1% of all the world's arable land and this is expected to increase significantly. This problem may be made worse by climate change, which could reduce the availability of arable land in some countries. Second generation technologies like cellulosic ethanol may address this concern by using existing plantations of trees and shrubs or waste from existing agriculture production.

One of the greatest advantages of biomass is the reduced demand for non-renewable fossil fuels, particularly fuels from crude oil, while at the same time generally producing fewer pollutants — and it's renewable. Biomass energy is stored solar energy that is available 24 hours a day, unlike wind and solar power. It can use biological material that would otherwise go to waste, thus saving disposal cost. Burning landfill gas to produce electricity and heat reduces the amount of methane escaping into the atmosphere.

11 — Hydrogen — the Great Hope or Fool's Gold?

We have probably all heard that hydrogen could be the energy of the future for motor vehicles. There is plenty of hydrogen in the universe. Stars, including our own sun, are largely made of it. Even so, hydrogen gas does not naturally exist on Earth in any quantities although it is plentiful in compound form such as water (which is hydrogen combined with oxygen) and is also plentiful in biomass.

Hydrogen gas needs to be produced from another substance if we want to use it on Earth. This means that hydrogen, like electricity, is not really an energy source but an energy carrier. The manufactured hydrogen can store the energy and can be relocated to where the energy is needed. Hydrogen is a gas at normal temperature and pressure and has the highest energy content of any fuel by weight but the lowest energy content by volume, which means it is light but bulky.

Where Does Hydrogen Energy Come From?

The cheapest and most common way of producing hydrogen is from natural gas. The hydrogen is separated for the carbon in a process called steam reforming. It can also be produced from coal syngas (see Chapter 4). Hydrogen can be released from water by passing an electric current through the water in a process called electrolysis. This is much more expensive than producing hydrogen from natural gas but does not generate greenhouse gas emissions, so long as the electricity came from a no emissions source. Hydrogen can be produced in bulk at large central facilities or at small plants for local use. Currently about 96% of hydrogen is produced from fossil fuels and only 4% from electrolysis.[35]

How Do We Use Hydrogen Energy?

Today hydrogen is largely used in industrial processes in the chemical and petroleum industries and also in the food processing industry. NASA uses hydrogen as an energy fuel for the space program. Hydrogen can also be used as a fuel in internal combustion engines but it needs much larger storage tanks than for petrol or diesel. Hydrogen can be stored and transported either as a liquid in cryogenic tanks or as a compressed gas.

The future interest is in using hydrogen as a replacement for fossil fuels in motor vehicles or for generating electricity. Box 7 discusses how a hydrogen fuel cell produces electricity. Using a fuel cell and an electric motor in a motor vehicle can be a replacement for the internal combustion engine. Small fuel cells can also be used to power electronic equipment like computer laptops while large stationary cells can be used to generate electricity in locations remote from the grid. Fuel cells are still at the experimental stage and not yet widely used in commercial systems despite significant research and development expenditure, particularly from governments looking for a replacement for petroleum products for energy security reasons.

Of course, to use hydrogen as an effective motor vehicle fuel requires some kind of hydrogen distribution infrastructure and hydrogen fuelling stations. Several issues need to be addressed including hydrogen storage, refuelling time, vehicle driving range, cost and safety. Research programs are underway to address these issues. There is also the issue about whether the hydrogen production should be done at home (using electricity) or at a centralised location with public fuelling stations. Although hydrogen as a replacement for fossil fuels holds promise, only time will tell whether hydrogen ever becomes an attractive alternative for motor vehicles. We discuss motor vehicle fuel options in Chapter 22 in Part Three.

Box 7

How a Hydrogen Fuel Cell Works

Hydrogen fuel cells make electricity from hydrogen and oxygen. A chemical reaction takes place in the fuel cell between the hydrogen and oxygen to produce free electrons like in a battery. There are many different types of fuel cells but they all work on similar principles. The most promising for motor vehicle use is the proton exchange membrane (or polymer electrolyte membrane) (PEM) fuel cell which uses a polymer (plastic) membrane that separates the positive and negative sides of the cell. PEM fuel cells are favoured for motor vehicles because of the moderate operating temperature, fast start-up and quick demand response needed for vehicles. The PEM fuel cell uses hydrogen gas from an external source and oxygen from the air to produce the required chemical reaction to generate the electricity.

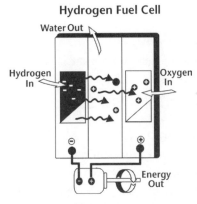

A fuel cell using pure hydrogen emits only heat and water so does not pollute the environment while producing electricity. Fuel cells can be 80% efficient, which would mean that for every 100 units of energy in the hydrogen, 80 units are converted to usable electricity. In practice the efficiency is often much less. For most practical applications fuel cells consist of a stack of individual cells to generate sufficient power.

Image Source: Energy Information Administration

How Much Greenhouse Gas Does Hydrogen Produce?

Fuel cells generating electricity using pure hydrogen produce no greenhouse gas emissions.[20] For motor vehicles using hydrogen fuel cells, the full well-to-wheel emissions depends on how the hydrogen was made. If the hydrogen was made from natural gas then the greenhouse gas emissions would be just over half those for conventional petrol vehicles. If the hydrogen was produced using electrolysis then the well-to-wheel emissions depend on how the electricity was generated. If the hydrogen was produced using average emissions electricity (about 0.6 kg/kWh) then the well-to-wheel emissions would be greater than for conventional engines. If the hydrogen was produced from electricity

[20] Well-to-wheel emissions include the full chain of emissions from production of the fuel (the 'well') to fuel use in the vehicles (the 'wheels').

from solar or wind power then the well-to-wheel emissions would be very close to zero.

Similarly, the well-to-wheel emissions produced in motor vehicles using hydrogen internal combustion engines depend on how the hydrogen is produced — very high if from natural gas, very low if from low average emissions electricity. In addition, if the hydrogen is burned with pure oxygen then no greenhouse gases are produced in the combustion. If the hydrogen is burned with air, emissions of nitrous oxides are possible.

More information on greenhouse gas emissions in motor vehicles using hydrogen can be found in Figure 5 in Chapter 22.

The Downside and Upside of Hydrogen Energy

The big downside of hydrogen for motor vehicles is that it is still experimental, with many technical challenges still to be addressed in storage and distribution. There is no existing infrastructure for refuelling motor vehicles and fuel cells are very expensive today but may become cheaper over time. The other downside with hydrogen as an energy storage method is that it takes much more energy to make the hydrogen than can be recovered. So producing hydrogen energy from electricity using electrolysis and converting it back to electricity in a fuel cell has a 'round-trip' energy efficiency of about 30–50% compared with batteries at about 70–80%.[36]

Hydrogen has the potential to provide a renewable replacement for non-renewable fossil fuels. It is environmentally clean if produced using electrolysis (providing the electricity used is from a clean source) and if used in fuel cells. It is still cleaner than fossil fuels if burned in an internal combustion engine so it can assist with reducing traffic pollution although it will not do much for greenhouse gas emissions (see Figure 5 in Chapter 22). Fuel cells are reliable and quiet as they have no moving parts and remove the need for batteries in conventional electric vehicles.

Part Two
The Changing Climate

The climate is changing for energy. Changes in the political, economic and engineering climate that surrounds energy are driven by dwindling non-renewable resources (particularly oil) and our concerns for the environment. For over 30 years, scientists have been concerned at the levels of carbon dioxide in the atmosphere and the possible effects on the Earth's temperature — often referred to as global warming.

The scientists have been particularly concerned that the carbon dioxide levels that are rising at an alarming rate are caused by burning fossil fuels to create heat and energy. At the same time, in almost a perfect storm, petroleum geologists and engineers have been concerned that the supply of new oil, our principal energy resource, is running out. We are using more oil than we are finding in new reserves by a factor of 4:1.

In Part Two we will explore peak oil and global warming (or climate change) in greater depth. We will explore some of the technological developments that are taking place in the energy field to address our reliance on oil and the concerns about the environment. We will also look at some of the political issues and possible economic responses to encourage change.

12 — A Peek at Peak Oil

We have probably all read something about peak oil over the last few years. It doesn't seem to get the media coverage of climate change and global warming but, as we will see, it is probably just as critical for our energy use and is likely to coincide with the impact of climate change.

What Is Peak Oil?

Peak oil is when the global oil production starts to decline year after year. This is roughly when about half the total available oil is used. At this point, oil production will fall and 'cheap' oil will start to become much more expensive.

To produce oil we have to find it first. Oil tends to be found in defined regions like the Persian Gulf or the Gulf of Mexico. Typically in any oil region, the big fields that have been found are developed first. Once production from the bigger fields has peaked then generally smaller ones are developed to compensate for the decline in production from the bigger ones. Eventually the new production fields get smaller and smaller and total production from the region gets past its peak and begins to fall. This has happened in a number of regions throughout the world including in the UK, Australia and the US. Worldwide, the size of new oil discoveries peaked in the 1960s when the average size of a new discovery was over 500 million barrels (Mb). This has been falling ever since to around 20 Mb today.

How Do We Know When Peak Oil Will Happen?

An estimate of when the world will hit peak oil involves considering the size of the reservoir of remaining oil in the ground and our rate of production or extraction of that oil. The historical production rates are quite accurately known throughout the world and in 2006 it was 29.8 billion barrels or 81.7 Mb per day. Future estimates of production are, of course, less certain. The size of the 'reservoir' is even more uncertain. Remaining world oil reserves are the total recoverable oil that has been discovered but not yet used.

In reality no one knows for sure how big an oil reserve is. Oil reserves are not like the fuel tank in a car which is a known size so when our fuel tank is half empty we know exactly how much fuel is still in the tank. Oil reserves are hidden from sight and only sampled by drilling wells into the reserve and studying the local geology so they cannot be measured accurately — only estimated (see Box 8).

It is also important to understand what is included in 'oil' when discussing oil reserves. Oil falls into two categories, conventional oil and unconventional oil. The definitions of these can vary, but conventional oil generally means oil in liquid form that can be extracted by traditional oil well methods and includes natural gas liquids. This covers about 97% of the world's oil production. Unconventional oil includes biofuels, oil sands/bitumen, ultra-heavy oil and coal and gas to liquids and we will discuss these in more detail later in this chapter.

Box 8

Estimating the Size of an Oil Reserve

The size of a reserve is based on an estimate of the probability of oil existing and being extractable using current methods under current economic conditions. A conservative estimate of the size of a reserve might use a 90% probability which is the amount of oil that has a better than 90% chance of being extracted. A midpoint estimate might use a 50% probability so this amount has a better than 50% change of being extracted. Another way to look at a 50% probability is that the estimate is equally likely to be too high or too low. An optimistic estimate might use a 10% probability so if there is a better than 10% chance of extracting the oil it is included in the reserve size.

A reserve might have a size of, say, 150 Mb at 90% chance but a size of 500 Mb at 10% chance with a size of 260 Mb at 50%. The actual probability used varies between reserves and regions and is often not clearly identified so there is some uncertainty in the reported sizes of reserves.

Figure 2

A Peak Oil Scenario

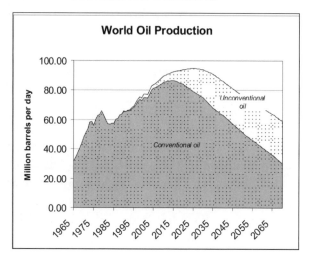

Note: This is just one possible scenario. There are many variations put forward by various experts.

What Do the Experts Say About Peak Oil?

Some petroleum geologists would say that just considering the remaining known conventional oil reserves is a pessimistic assessment of the total available oil resources because it excludes improvements in oil recovery, oil yet to be found and unconventional oil such as oil sands. Some of the peak oil advocates — those who think peak oil is going to happen sooner rather than later — tend to consider only conventional proven oil reserves on the basis that unproven and unconventional sources are uncertain in terms of quantity and efficiency. The peak oil sceptics tend to include all oil resources — both proven and anticipated.

Table 5 below looks at the estimate for remaining reserves of conventional oil from varies expert sources. The sources used are BP,[37] US DOE Energy Information Administration (EIA),[38] Energy Watch Group (EWG),[39] the Association for the Study of Peak Oil and Gas (ASPO)[40] and Cambridge Energy Research Associates (CERA). [41] It is fair to say that EWG and ASPO are peak oil advocates whereas CERA is a peak oil sceptic.

Table 5
Comparisons of Expert Assessments of Reserves and Peak Years

Source	Remaining Oil[a] Reserves (billions of barrels)	R/P Ratio[b] Years	Peak Year	Average Annual Change[c] 2004–2030
BP	1,208	40.5	n/a	n/a
DOE/EIA	1,120	37.5	>2030	+1.1%
EWG	854	28.6	2006	-3.0%
ASPO	n/a	n/a	2011	-0.7%
CERA — conventional	1,245	41.7	>2030	+0.7%
CERA — total oil resources	3,743[d]	125.5	>2030	+2.2%

[a] All values are for proven conventional oil reserves except the total oil resources for CERA.
[b] R/P is the ratio of reserves to current production.
[c] Average annual change in oil production.
[d] This is CERA's estimate of the total remaining global oil resource base not the remaining reserves.

The big difference between EWG's estimate of conventional reserves and the other sources is the amount of reserves left in the OPEC[21] countries. In the mid-1980s many of the OPEC members significantly increased their estimates of reserves by some 300 billion barrels without actually finding 300 billion barrels in new discoveries. OPEC members just increased their confidence of extracting more oil from their existing fields. OPEC production quotas are set according to reserves, so increasing their reported reserves allowed the members to defend their quotas. These reserves are sometimes referred to as 'political reserves' by the peak oil advocates and are often discounted, but the original estimates may also have been too low.

CERA, the peak oil sceptic, believes that total resources should include unconventional oil as well as conventional oil and include exploration potential as well as proven reserves. This trebles the size of the total oil resources! Both numbers are included for CERA in the table. The ratio of reserves to current production (called R/P ratio in Table 5) gives an indication of the number of years that the reserves could last at current production levels if production were to continue at that rate. It is arguably a meaningless number because annual production does not stay flat and declines as oil is taken from a well once it has reached its peak.

[21] Organisation of the Petroleum Exporting Countries.

So a summary from the sources is that no one (including CERA) is suggesting that peak oil will never happen — they just argue about when and the rate of growth in the meantime. CERA believes peak oil will be some time after 2030 and that production will grow to about 100 Mb/day for conventional oil and 130 Mb/day for total oil and stay at that level for a decade or so before beginning to decline and will still be above current production levels in 2070. EWG on the other hand believes that the world has already hit peak oil and that production will decline by over 50% to less than 40 Mb/day between now and 2030. ASPO believes peak oil will happen in 2011 and that production will peak at around 90 Mb/day and fall to 65 Mb/day in 2030. So it seems likely that peak oil will happen sometime in our lifetime or the lifetime of our children. On the positive side, no one is saying that we are about to suddenly run out of oil so we have some time to react.

Why Is Peak Oil Important to the Energy Debate?

Remember in Chapter 3 we discussed crude oil's important place in total energy. About 34% of all our energy comes from crude oil. Of this about half is used for transport fuels and about 15% for electricity generation and domestic and commercial heating and cooking. The rest, about a third, is used in industrial processes. For example plastics, which play such a big part in our lives today, are based on crude oil. As this book is focusing on energy we will not look into oil for industrial processes, but clearly if oil becomes scarce then those industries will be affected and alternatives will need to be found.

Economics teaches us that when a commodity gets scarce and growth in supply is unable to match growth in demand then the price goes up. We are seeing evidence of this already as the price of crude oil has increased from around $30 a barrel in 2004 to over $70 in 2006 and passing $140 in 2008 although this latest price rise could be caused by geopolitical issues rather than scarcity.

In terms of demand growth for oil, according to the World Bank[42] the world population is expected to increase from 2005 to 2015 by over 11% so there is likely to be a corresponding increase in energy demand which could account for an additional 9 Mb/day of oil. In fact the situation is likely to be much worse. The key developing countries of China and India represent 37% of the world's population. According to BP, China and India's demand for oil has increased by 84% in the last 10 years to 10.3 Mb/day or just 12% of the world's total now. That means 37% of the world's total population who live in these fast developing countries currently only use 12% of the world's oil consumption. If, over the next 10 years, the Chinese and Indian demand for oil continues at the rate of the last 10 years their demand would increase to around 19 Mb/day which would be about 20% of world demand. This would still be well below their population percentage and would imply that oil demand may grow more quickly than population increases.

Only the more aggressive oil production growth forecasts of CERA are likely to meet this anticipated growth in demand even if the developed world held its oil consumption at current levels. We either hope that CERA is right and we can keep consuming oil per head at our present rate, at least for the next 25 years, or face up to substantial increases in fuel prices. Alternatively, we look for ways to reduce our conventional oil consumption. Even CERA would admit that we will have to do that at some time anyway. CERA's graphs of future production show declining output after 2045.[41]

What Are the Alternatives to Conventional Oil?
CERA's more aggressive production growth forecasts rely on using unconventional oil sources such as oil or tar sands, oil shales and heavy oil (see Box 9) as well as enhanced oil recovery (getting more from existing wells) and exploration (finding new oil fields). CERA's argument is that technology development and increasing oil prices will bring on another 2,500 billion barrels of oil resources over the next 20 years or so. Non-conventional oil substitutes for conventional oil make up almost half of this. In 1999, BP increased its estimate of world proven reserves by 163 billion barrels from Canadian oil sands (this figure is not included in Table 5).

In terms of significant alternatives to conventional oil, natural gas is a strong candidate. Natural gas is already widely used for producing electricity and heating and can take over oil's role in these areas. Half the oil we use goes to making transport fuel. As we saw in Chapter 2, compressed natural gas (CNG) is already used as a replacement for oil in transport vehicles like buses and trucks that do not travel far away from their home base.

According to BP, at the end of 2006 the proven reserves of natural gas were 181 trillion cubic metres or about 1,200 billion barrels of oil equivalent — similar to the estimate for conventional oil reserves. The ratio of natural gas reserves to production, in other words the number of years that the reserves would last at current production levels if production were to continue at that rate, was 63 years. When we looked at oil in Table 5, the R/P ratio was about 40 years for proven reserves, so using this measure and assuming a steady demand for natural gas, natural gas reserves will last longer than oil.

EIA is predicting natural gas consumption will increase more quickly than oil, which will reduce the number of years supply. Jean Laherrere, a member of ASPO, estimates that peak gas will be reached in about 2030 at a production level about 40% higher than today.[43] Remember that oil peaks when about half the total available oil is used. For natural gas the peak happens when about three-quarters is used so the rate of decline after peak gas will be much faster. At the very least, natural gas could stretch the time to peak oil and falling oil production and allow us to transition to alternative energy sources.

What Are the Energy Options if (When) Oil Really Becomes Scarce?
Oil is not going to become scarce suddenly even when we do hit peak oil. Production will fall and taper off and it is probable that we will never run out of oil completely. It will just get more and more expensive and demand will fall as a result. So we have time to react. True, EWG, a strong peak oil advocate, might say we only have a few years. ASPO might say we only have a decade. CERA, a strong peak oil sceptic, would probably say we have 40 years but it seems that learning to live with less oil is inevitable.

The oil used for domestic and commercial heating and cooking (about 8%) and the oil used in industry for water and steam heating can be replaced by natural gas reasonably readily in many parts of the world, although at some conversion cost. As natural gas also becomes scarce and more expensive, then electricity, solar-thermal and geothermal sources can take over these heating functions. Improved building design including improved insulation can also reduce the need for energy for space heating and cooling.

Box 9

Sources of Unconventional Oil

There are huge resources of unconventional oil such as oil sands in Canada, heavy oil in Venezuela and oil shales that can be processed to produce synthetic crude oil. Unfortunately it is much more difficult and expensive to extract usable oil from these resources than it is to pump conventional oil out of an oil well, so they are not as attractive today. As the price of oil rises these unconventional sources will become more financially viable.

Oil sands consist of a mixture of bitumen[a] and sand or clay. Once the bitumen is extracted from the sand it can be processed into synthetic crude oil. There are two ways of extracting the bitumen, depending on how deep the oil sands are. If they are near the surface they can be mined using open-pit mining. The oil sand is then mixed with large amounts of water so that the bitumen floats to the top and the sand settles to the bottom. If the oil sands are too deep for open-pit mining, the bitumen can be heated underground to reduce the viscosity (thickness) and the liquid bitumen pumped to the surface. Both these processes are complex and expensive and not particularly environmentally friendly. EIA estimates that by 2015 oil sands will contribute 2.3 million barrels oil equivalent per day (2.3 Mboe/day) or 2.4% of the world total oil production.[38]

Another unconventional source is oil shale. Oil shale is not really a shale and doesn't really contain oil. It is petroleum source rock that can be converted to synthetic crude oil by heating it to a very high temperature. The rock is mined using open-pit or underground mining and crushed before heating. Again the process is costly, not particularly environmentally friendly and produces more greenhouse gases than conventional oil. EIA is not forecasting any oil shale production before 2030.

Other unconventional oil sources include biofuels which we discussed in Chapter 10 and coal- and gas-to-liquid (CTL and GTL). Coal can be converted into liquid fuels by several different methods. It can be converted first to syngas (see Chapter 3) which then can be condensed into liquids that can be processed into petrol and diesel. Alternatively it can be liquefied directly and further processed into liquid fuels. Either process involves heating very large quantities of coal to high temperatures with the associated production of additional greenhouse gas emissions. Natural gas can also be converted into liquid fuels — mainly diesel called GTL diesel. The advantage of doing this rather than using the natural gas directly as a diesel replacement is the cost of compressing and transporting the natural gas. EIA is forecasting that by 2015 CTL and GTL will contribute 1.1 Mboe/day or just over 1% of the world total oil production.[38]

[a] Bitumen is a very thick, black, sticky liquid. It is often used for paving roads.

The oil used for electricity generation (about 7%) can also be readily replaced by other sources in the shorter term, particularly natural gas. There are many alternative energy sources for electricity generation discussed in Chapters 4 to 11, amongst them coal, nuclear, solar, wind, hydro, geothermal and biomass, some of which are available everywhere. Modern electricity grids can interconnect all these sources, making the demise of oil and gas a relatively minor disruption to electricity generation. Any talk of large-scale blackouts caused by peak oil are probably exaggerated except in third world countries that may not be able to switch energy sources quickly enough.

The area most exposed to oil is transport fuels. Today, 95% of our transport fuel comes from oil, with the balance from biofuels and natural gas. This is where scarce oil will hit the hardest. In Chapter 3 we discussed how we could reduce oil usage by using more fuel-efficient vehicles such as hybrid-electric vehicles, driving more carefully and keeping our vehicles in good mechanical condition. This will help for a while as the cost of oil rises but it will not fully deal with the longer term problem of falling oil production.

We have also discussed several replacement energy sources for transport in Part One of this book. These include biofuels, natural gas, coal-to-liquid, gas-to-liquid, electricity from batteries and fuel cells, and hydrogen. Each of these has its own issues that do not make them straightforward replacements for oil. It may also take 10–15 years to replace the existing fleet of motor vehicles to be able to use some of these replacement fuels. A full discussion of future transport options is included in Chapter 22. Technology improvements over the next decade may make some of these options more attractive than others and we will deal with this in greater detail in Chapter 14 after we have discussed climate change.

13 — Feel the Heat!

Climate change is one of the most discussed issues in the public media. This is really a book about energy so we will not go into climate change in any great depth. Having said that, because climate change has significant implications for our energy generation and usage, it is important that we understand the relevance of climate change to the world of energy.

What Is Changing the Climate?
Greenhouse gases are a group of gases in the atmosphere that can trap heat near the Earth's surface. As these gases increase in the atmosphere the extra heat they trap can warm up the Earth in what is commonly referred to as global warming. This warming places pressure on the Earth's climate system which can lead to climate change.

What Is the Greenhouse Effect?
In Chapter 6 when we looked at solar power, we discussed energy from the sun. When the sun's radiation hits the Earth about 30% is reflected back into space and 70% is absorbed, warming the land, oceans and atmosphere. The heat energy absorbed by the land and oceans is radiated back into the atmosphere. Some of the heat escapes into space and some is trapped by greenhouse gases. The most powerful greenhouse gas is water vapour which accounts for as much as two-thirds of the total greenhouse effect. By trapping heat near the Earth's surface and

re-radiating it back to Earth the greenhouse gases maintain a suitable temperature range for life. Without them, the Earth would be very cold, about the temperature of the freezer compartment in a refrigerator, so greenhouse gases are essential for our survival.

However, this is a finely balanced process. What maintains the temperature at the level we need is the right amount of greenhouse gas molecules in the atmosphere. Reduce them and the temperature could fall. Increase them and the temperature could rise, causing global warming.

What Are 'Greenhouse Gas Emissions' and Where Do They Come From?
The main greenhouse gases in the atmosphere are water vapour, carbon dioxide, methane, nitrous oxide, and ozone as well as some fluorinated gases such as hydrofluorocarbons (HFCs) which are sometimes used as aerosol spray propellants. Although water vapour has the greatest greenhouse effect (see above), human activity is not thought to have much impact on the amount of water vapour in the atmosphere (which we see largely as clouds). So when we refer to greenhouse gas *emissions* we are referring to those greenhouse gases that are created by us — namely, carbon dioxide, methane, nitrous oxide and three groups of fluorinated gases (sulphur hexafluoride, HFCs, and PFCs).

Carbon dioxide accounts for about 70% of greenhouse gas emissions. Carbon dioxide is emitted when fossil fuels such as oil, coal and natural gas are burned. This might be to make electricity or to run our motor vehicles. It is also increased by the clearing and burning of vegetation. Once released, carbon dioxide can have an effective lifetime in the atmosphere of hundreds of years. According to the Intergovernmental Panel on Climate Change (IPCC),[22] before the Industrial Revolution (around 1750) the concentration of carbon dioxide in the atmosphere was 280 parts per million[23] (ppm). In 2005 the concentration had risen to 379ppm which exceeded by far the natural range over the last 650,000 years (180 to 300 ppm) as determined from ice cores.[44] Carbon dioxide disperses quickly around the world, so controlling the concentration of carbon dioxide is a worldwide problem for all of us, wherever we live.

---

[22] IPPC is a scientific body tasked to evaluate the risk of climate change caused by human activity.
[23] This means 280 molecules of a greenhouse gas per million molecules of dry air.

Methane contributes about 20% to emissions and can come from escaping natural gas, decomposing waste in swamps, garbage dumps or landfills and the digestive processes of farm animals such as cattle and sheep. Methane is a much more powerful greenhouse gas by mass than carbon dioxide but is relatively short lived at about 12 years.

Nitrous oxide emissions come from industrial processes, burning vegetation and the effects of agriculture from using fertilisers containing nitrogen. It is much rarer than methane but is even more potent by mass and can last 120 years.

Greenhouse gas emissions have grown by 70% over the last 35 years. The IPCC believes that the best estimate of the total concentration of all long-lived greenhouse gases in 2005 was 455ppm CO_2-e.[24]

How Much Is the Earth Warming and What Are The Implications?
Figure 3 below shows a line plot prepared by NASA[25] of the global mean land-ocean temperature index from 1880 to now. As we can see, over the last 100 years the average air temperature near the Earth's surface

Figure 3

Global Annual Mean Surface Air Temperature Change

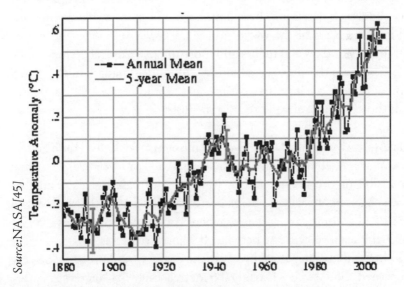

[24] Greenhouse gases are recorded by their carbon dioxide equivalent impact (CO_2-e).
[25] The US National Aeronautics and Space Administration.

has risen 0.7°C and over the past 30 years the temperature has increased by 0.2°C each decade. The IPCC believes this increase in temperature since the mid-20th century is very likely (>90%) due to the greenhouse gas emissions created by us.

The IPCC projects that for the next two decades the temperature will continue to rise by 0.2°C per decade. Even if we kept the concentrations of all greenhouse gases at year 2000 levels (which seems very unlikely) the temperature would still rise at 0.1°C per decade, so further global warming is inevitable. The IPCC actually looked at a number of scenarios involving the rate of population increase, rate of economic growth and the introduction of new and more efficient technologies. In the best case scenario, the IPCC's best estimate of the most optimistic (least) temperature increase by the end of the century (2099) is 1.8°C. In the worst case scenario, pretty much where we keep doing what we are doing now, their best estimate is 4°C by 2099.[44]

A rise in the average temperature of a few degrees might not sound much. After all, the temperature can vary by more than that day to day without any great problem. But even the rise of 0.7°C over the last 100 years has created some alarming changes in climate. Arctic temperatures have risen and the extent of the Artic sea ice has shrunk. Average sea levels have risen. There have been widespread changes in rainfall in some parts of the world. There are fewer cold days and nights with more hot days and nights and more intense tropical cyclones. The IPCC believes that further warming will induce changes in the global climate system during this century that would very likely be greater than those we have already seen in the 20th century.

How Much Would We Have to Reduce Emissions to Make the World Safe?
As the average temperature rises, so will the sea levels from thermal expansion of the oceans and melting of land-based glaciers and ice sheets. Melting, floating icebergs don't actually change the sea level. In the IPCC's worst case scenario, where the temperature rises 4°C by 2099, the sea level will rise between 0.3 and 0.6 metres.

So how safe is safe? If we live near the coast we will probably be very concerned about sea levels rising 0.6 metres. But a 4°C increase in average temperature won't be good for many species living in polar or high mountain areas either. The IPCC believes that 20–30% of plants and animals are likely to be at increased risk of extinction from a rise of just 1.5–2.5°C.[46]

If we accept that global warming has been caused by our greenhouse gas emissions then we need to at least stabilise the concentration of greenhouse gases in the atmosphere if we are to slow the rise in temperature. To stabilise greenhouse gases realistically, we have to first let emissions reach a peak and then get them to decline (see Figure 4). The lower we set the stabilisation level the more quickly we need to reach the peak and the faster the decline. But the temperature and sea level rises don't stop once we have reached peak emissions. Sea levels may not reach equilibrium for many centuries. According to the IPCC we may eventually stabilise temperatures at 5–6°C above pre-industrial levels with sea levels up 1–4 metres! So what is a 'safe' level of stabilisation?

Figure 4
Possible Emissions Path to Stabilise Greenhouse Gases at 550ppm CO2-e

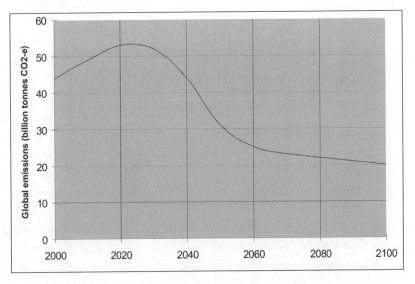

To stabilise greenhouse gas emissions at around 450ppm would require us to peak our emissions output before 2015 and then reduce the emissions from there to less than 50% of the 2000 level by 2050. This is probably unrealistic given the real difficulties of making the required sharp reductions in emissions in the time frame with the current and foreseeable technologies (see Part Three for more details). With a fast expanding China and India playing catch-up with the West and increasing their demand for fossil-fuel energy per capita (see Chapter 12) we are unlikely to achieve such an aggressive target.

A more realistic target may be to stabilise concentrations at around 550ppm. This would require us to peak our emissions output by 2030 and then reduce emissions to up to 30% below the 2000 level by 2050. [46] Reversing the historic growth trend and achieving cuts of 30% is a major challenge over the next 40 years, so the sooner we start the better. Even at this challenging target, the IPCC predict the average global temperature will increases by around 3°C above pre-industrial levels and sea level will eventually rise more than 0.6 metres. So reducing emissions is about mitigating the impact of climate change not eliminating it. If we want to reduce the impact even further we will need to reach peak emissions earlier and reduce the output from there even more steeply.

How Would We Cut Emissions?

To reduce emissions we need to shift from high-carbon to low-carbon goods and services and this will incur costs. As we can see from Table 6, energy is the largest contributor to greenhouse gas emissions, so any meaningful reduction in emissions will have a big impact on our choice of energy sources and how we use energy.

In Part One of this book we discussed the amount of greenhouse gas emissions that came from various energy sources. When we looked at electricity generation, it was clear that the sources with the highest emissions intensity (the amount of greenhouse gas emissions produced per kWh) was much higher for the fossil fuels than from any other source. These are the clear targets when looking for ways to produce fewer emissions. But switching to cleaner energy sources isn't the only way we can reduce emissions. According to the Stern Review,[26] produced by the UK Government Treasury, [47] greenhouse gas emissions can be cut in four ways:

---

[26] The Stern Review was released by economist Nicholas Stern in October 2006 and discusses the effects of climate change and global warming on the world economy.

Table 6

Source of Greenhouse Gases in 2000

2000 Greenhouse Gas Emissions Source	Emissions (billion tonnes of CO_2-e)	Emissions (billion tonnes of CO_2-e)	Percentage of Total
Energy emissions:		27.8	63
Electricity and heat	11.6		26
Manufacturing and construction	4.7		11
Transportation	5.9		13
Other fuel combustion	4.0		9
Other	1.6		4
Non-energy emissions:		16.1	37
Industrial processes	1.4		3
Agriculture	5.7		13
Forestry	7.6		17
Waste	1.4		3
Total	**43.9**		

Source: **WRI — CAIT Version 5.**[2]

1. Reducing demand for emissions-intensive goods and services;
2. Increasing efficiency, which can save both money and emissions;
3. Action on non-energy emissions, such as avoiding deforestation (land clearing); and
4. Switching to lower-carbon technologies for power, heat and transport.

Because this is a book about energy, we will focus on the energy related emissions. Given the proportion of emissions (nearly two-thirds) that comes from energy it is hardly surprising that Stern believes that a large-scale uptake of a range of clean power, heat and transport technologies is required to radically cut emissions. Stern says that the power sector will have to be at least 60% decarbonised by 2050 to stabilise greenhouse gas concentrations at or below 550ppm. Even with a very strong expansion of the use of renewable energy and other low-carbon sources like nuclear power, fossil fuels may still produce over half of the total energy supply by 2050. This means that extensive use of carbon capture and storage (CCS) will be needed to 'decarbonise' fossil-fuel (primarily coal) sourced energy. We will discuss CCS and other developing technologies in more depth in Chapter 14 and in Part Three we will look at the future of energy to address both climate change and peak oil.

In Part One we discussed several ways to increase energy efficiency in electricity use, transport and buildings such as improved insulation and passive and active solar and geothermal heating and cooling. The IPCC believes that energy-efficiency options for new and existing buildings could considerably reduce greenhouse gas emissions and we will discuss some of these in the next chapter.

What Will it Cost the Economy to Stabilise at 550ppm?

Both the IPCC and Stern looked at this question in some detail. To come up with the answer they both considered the costs and benefits of climate change mitigation. That is the costs and benefits of reducing the severity of climate change. The IPCC estimated the reduction in annual global gross domestic product (GDP) to stabilise concentrations at around 550ppm at 0.6% by 2030 and 1.3% by 2050. This is equivalent to a reduction in average annual GDP growth rate of less than 0.1%.[46] Stern was very similar at around 1% by 2050. Not everyone agrees with the IPCC and Stern about the causes and effects of climate change. But if the net cost of mitigation is relatively low, as implied by these estimates, it may well be a cheap insurance policy given the potential risks.

14 — Technology to the Rescue?

In Chapter 12 we discussed peak oil and how we might learn to live with less (or even no) oil over the next few decades. In Chapter 13 we discussed reducing greenhouse gas emissions to mitigate the impact of climate change. The recent climate change reports we discussed from the IPCC and Stern both emphasised the need for technology developments to achieve the required reductions in greenhouse gas emissions. In this chapter we will look at some of these developing technologies that will help with these major issues that we face, including addressing some of the limitations of renewable energy resources. The technology descriptions will be of interest to some readers but may seem a bit too technical for others. It is more important that we understand what the technology can deliver for us and why we need it than have a detailed understanding of how it works.

Although peak oil and global warming are worldwide issues, some of these technology solutions will be more attractive and practical in some regions than others.

Can We Keep Burning Fossil Fuels and not Fry the World?

As we have discussed so far, the problem with fossil fuels (coal, oil, natural gas) is that when we burn them they give off carbon dioxide — the biggest contributor to greenhouse gas emissions. Today we burn fossil fuels when we make electricity, heat our homes and drive our motor vehicles. As we discussed in Chapter 12, there are some replacement fuels that can take us part way but we will probably need to keep burning fossil fuels for many decades to come to satisfy our growing demand for energy. Most of the IPCC scenarios project that fossil fuels will continue to dominate the primary energy supply until at least the middle of the century. The key is to find a way to process these fuels to eliminate or reduce the amount of greenhouse gas emissions that gets released into the atmosphere.

We have already discussed turning coal into syngas in a process called coal gasification (see Chapter 4). This process involves subjecting the coal to high temperature and pressure before conversion to heat and syngas. This reduces the emissions of sulphur, nitrous oxide and mercury, which makes the resulting syngas a much cleaner fuel (more like natural gas) than burning the coal directly. This process can be used to produce electricity by using the syngas in a gas turbine and the heat in a steam turbine in a CCGT unit. The process is often referred to as integrated gasification combined cycle (IGCC). IGCC aims to improve the efficiency of converting coal to electricity and also makes it possible to separate out the carbon dioxide before burning the fuel.

Oxy-fuel combustion is another technology under development that can be retrofitted to existing coal power plants to assist with collecting the carbon dioxide. Pulverised coal is burned in a mix of oxygen and recirculated waste gases to create a high concentration of carbon dioxide in the power plant flue gases. This carbon dioxide can then be captured (see Box 10).

There is a technology under development called carbon capture and storage (CCS) (see Box 10) that aims to reduce carbon dioxide emissions for fossil-fuel power plants and coal or gas to liquid plants. It has the potential to reduce greenhouse gas emissions from fossil fuels to levels close to those from renewable energy sources but at a cost to electricity prices that is less than some renewable sources. This makes CCS very attractive as a transition technology from fossil fuels to renewables.

The IPCC predicts that by 2050, 30–60% of the carbon dioxide emissions from electricity generation can be captured using CCS and that CCS will contribute 15–55% to the cumulative mitigation effect up to

Box 10

Carbon Capture and Storage (CCS)

CCS involves capturing the carbon dioxide before it is released into the atmosphere and putting it into long-term storage. The storage can be deep in underground reservoirs or coal seams or in the ocean. Deep ocean storage is only in the research phase and there are significant concerns about the impact on marine life. Storing carbon dioxide in underground reservoirs is already done in the oil and gas industry to enhance oil and gas recovery (EOR). Compressed carbon dioxide is injected into depleted oil and gas reservoirs to force out the remaining oil and gas, leaving the carbon dioxide permanently stored in the cracks and pores within the rock layers that trapped the oil and gas for millions of years. Carbon dioxide can also be stored in underground saline (salt water) reservoirs.

The carbon dioxide capture can either be before the fuel is burned or after. Where the capture is post-combustion (after), the carbon dioxide is separated from the other flue gases before they are released to the atmosphere. This technology is already in use for natural gas and can be fitted to existing non-CCS power plants. Where the capture is pre-combustion, the coal is first turned into gas and the resulting hydrogen and carbon dioxide gases are separated and the hydrogen gases are used as fuel for a gas turbine. This process is already used in fertiliser and hydrogen production.

CCS is most effective in large plants that generate lots of carbon dioxide emissions. These include large thermal and cogeneration (CHP) plants, major energy using industries and chemical plants for producing cement, coke, ammonia or hydrogen. There is a cost, however. CCS systems need roughly 10–40% more energy than today's equivalent plants, depending on the fuel source and the process used. The most costly is coal with post-combustion. The additional energy is mainly used in the capture and compression processes.

Once the carbon dioxide is captured it is compressed and transported to the storage site or enhanced oil recovery site. Where the distance between the plant and the storage is less than 1,000 km, pipelines can be used. Large plants are usually concentrated close to major industrial and urban areas. The IPCC believes that many of these plants are within 300 km of potentially suitable storage sites.[48]

2100. This will increase the electricity generation cost by about $0.01-0.05/kWh using today's fuel prices. Based on Table 2 in Chapter 1 this will increase the cost of generation from coal by about 70% but it will still be cheaper than many renewable sources although not as cheap as nuclear power. The IPCC calculates the carbon dioxide avoidance cost for coal with CCS at between $30 and $70 per tonne of carbon dioxide avoided. This is reduced to $10-40 where enhanced oil recovery (EOR) is possible during the storage. It is not clear how often this will be possible, and without it a carbon price[27] below $30 is not going to cover the cost of CCS for many plants and therefore not encourage the use of CCS.

So far there are no large-scale CCS power plants in operation and none are expected before 2015, although there are several working pilot plants around the world. If production plants are built or existing plants upgraded, these available CCS technologies could reduce the carbon dioxide emissions for fossil fuel plants by 80–90%.[48] This would bring the emissions intensity in line with renewable energy sources (see Table 3 in Chapter 1).

The upside of CCS, if it can be made to work cost-effectively, is that it will allow us to keep using coal (our principal energy source for electricity generation) for the next few decades and still meet greenhouse gas emissions targets needed to mitigate climate change. The downside is the possibility of some of the carbon dioxide leaking out of the underground storage back into the atmosphere. If the leakage was relatively small it would just reduce the effectiveness of the whole process of reducing emissions from the atmosphere with no damage to the environment. If the leakage was large and sudden it could be fatal to animals and people in the vicinity of the leak. This means that storage sites would need monitoring for very long periods. A large leakage from an EOR site is extremely unlikely (see Box 10).

What About the Next Generation of Nuclear Power Plants?

In Chapter 5 we discussed how nuclear power had the great advantage of being able to produce baseload power with relatively low greenhouse gas emissions but had some environmental and safety concerns. The next generation of nuclear power plants are being designed to address some of these concerns (see Box 11).

Generation III+ reactors use fuel which is proliferation resistant (it is hard to use for nuclear weapons) and which produce less long-lived waste. Unlike most Generation II reactors, they are gas cooled and don't use water or steam and are more fuel-efficient. Generation III+ reactors are expected between 2010 and 2020.

Generation IV reactors are those expected to be available after 2030.

---

[27] Carbon price is the price that polluters will pay for the right to emit one tonne of CO_2-e greenhouse gas (see Chapter 16).

The goals for these reactors are:
- Minimal nuclear waste,
- Reduced risk of theft of weapons-usable material,
- Enhanced safety and reliability, and
- Highly economical.

Box 11

Next Generation Nuclear Reactors

High temperature gas-cooled reactors (HTGR) are Generation III+ reactors that are helium-cooled and use graphite as a neutron moderator (which we will discuss below). The light water reactors (BWR and PWR) discussed in Box 3 in Chapter 5 use pellets of uranium oxide fuel whereas HTGRs use tiny spheres with a core of enriched uranium coated in ceramic. Thousands of these tiny spheres are pressed together and coated with graphite. In pebble bed modular reactors (PBMR) the pressings are in the shape of tennis-ball size spheres called 'pebbles' while in gas turbine modular helium reactors (GT-MHR) the fuel is in small cylindrical rods. The nuclear reaction in the fuel heats the helium, which is used to drive a gas turbine which avoids the steam management system in LWRs and is more efficient. The fuel is proliferation resistant (it is hard to use for nuclear weapons) and produces less long-lived waste.

Fast neutron reactors are expected to play a major part in the next generation of reactors. In thermal reactors (such as light water reactors) moderators are used to slow down the neutrons produced in the fission process (see Chapter 5). In fast reactors, the fission chain reaction is sustained by fast neutrons. Fast reactors can also 'burn' long-lived radioactive waste produced from conventional power reactors. Generally, fast reactors cannot be water cooled (as in LWRs) because water acts as a neutron moderator. Some of the reactor types which hold the greatest promise are the gas-cooled fast reactor (GFR), the lead-cooled fast reactor (LFR), the molten salt reactor (MSR) and the sodium-cooled fast reactor (SFR). These reactors could be used to produce hydrogen as well as electricity (see Chapter 11).

If the goals of Generation III+ and IV reactors are met, and if the public concerns about nuclear power can be addressed, then nuclear power will continue to play a significant, and probably growing, role in reducing greenhouse gas emissions over the next half century.

Will the Oceans Provide the Answer?
The potential to capture energy from tides and waves is huge. Tides are

caused by the gravitational pull of the moon and sun, and the rotation of the Earth. Near shore, water levels can vary by 12 metres or more in some places. The advantage of using tides as a renewable energy source is that, unlike wind and sunshine, they are very predictable and they work day and night all year round. Waves are caused by the wind blowing over the surface of the ocean. The total power of waves breaking around the world's coastlines is estimated to be 2–3 million MW. Waves, of course, are less predictable because they rely on the wind.

The simplest tidal plants involve a dam or barrage across an inlet where the tide flows in and out. Sluice gates on the barrage allow the tidal basin to fill on the incoming high tides and to empty through a turbine system on the outgoing tide. These systems can be made to be two-way so that electricity can be generated on both the incoming and outgoing tide. There are two commercial barrage tidal plants in operation, one in France and one in Canada. The downside with tidal barrages is they are expensive to construct, they change the tidal level in the basin and change the turbidity (cloudiness) in the water. They can also affect navigation and recreation as well as plants and animals in the estuary. The upside is the tidal turbines are under water and away from view unlike off-shore wind farms.

There are two other ways to harness tidal power by using the tidal stream to power a turbine. One involves mounting vertical axis turbines in a tidal fence across a channel. The other is to use horizontal axis turbines like wind turbines that are located in a strong tidal current. Strong tidal currents occur where the natural flows are concentrated between obstructions such as headlands or entrances to bays or rivers. Water is much denser than air (about 800 times denser) so the turbines can capture much more energy than wind turbines but the turbines need to be much stronger and consequently much more expensive. The International Energy Agency (IEA) has estimated that energy from tidal currents could yield in excess of 10 billion kWh/yr (about 1.5 nuclear power plants) but would cost in the range of $0.45–1.35/kWh, which would probably make it too expensive compared to other alternatives.[49] Tidal turbines are still in the development stage, with several trials being conducted around the world.

Wave energy can be harnessed by several methods. One is to focus the waves into a narrow channel to increase their power and size. The waves can then be focused into a reservoir or used directly to spin turbines. Another is to use the mechanical energy from a rising and falling floating body or buoy on the surface of the waves to drive a generator. The challenges with wave power are to convert the wave motion into electricity efficiently and to build devices that can handle storm damage and corrosion from salt water.

The clear upside with ocean power is that it is renewable and, in the case of tidal power, predictable and would help with minimising greenhouse gas emissions. The downside includes the economics, the harsh conditions and the possible impact on the marine environment. The only commercially tested method is barrage tidal power. The other systems are still in development and testing with uncertainty as to the future commercial viability.

Can We Run the Grid on Solar Power Alone?

In Chapter 6 we covered solar power in some detail. As we saw, solar power's big advantage is that it produces no greenhouse gases during electricity production but the problem is the sun only shines for so many hours a day and those hours can vary significantly depending on our distance from the equator and the time of year — summer or winter. Solar energy capture is also impacted by overcast weather. We expect our grid electricity to be available 24 hours a day 7 days a week. In fact, in first world countries we get very upset when the electricity is unavailable for more than a few minutes, so solar presents some challenges for grid electricity. The peak time for grid electricity use for domestic and commercial use, particularly in winter, is often between 3pm and 8pm. In many parts of the world the availability of usable sunlight doesn't coincide with electricity demand. This means we either need a way of storing the solar energy for later use or use a non-solar energy source when the sun isn't shining.

There are two ways of using solar energy to generate electricity, solar photovoltaic (PV) and solar-thermal. We have already discussed how each of these produce electricity. PV is mainly used for buildings, both residential and commercial, and although these PV building mounted systems are often connected to the grid and can add power to it, their main use is for generating electricity for local consumption inside the building. In this section we will focus on how developing solar-thermal technologies can extend the usefulness of solar power for large-scale grid electricity sometimes referred to as concentrated solar power (CSP). CSP systems can be integrated into conventional thermal power stations alongside fossil-fuel-powered steam generators to reduce greenhouse gas emissions. Concentrated PV plants are also being developed, but we will use CSP to mean thermal plants not PV.

Today, to supply solar generated electricity to the grid costs between six and ten times more than existing non-renewable technologies and three to six times more than other renewable technologies (see Table 2 in Chapter 1). The daytime-only availability of solar power and reduced output in cloudy conditions limit its usefulness for baseload grid supply unless the energy can be stored in some way. Solar-thermal CSP systems can heat fluids to very high temperatures so they can be stored for several hours or even days to generate electricity when the sun is not shining.

There are several research projects underway involving large CSP systems. Research is being performed to improve the efficiency of the solar collectors and the heat transfer fluids and heat storage systems. One of the more promising systems involves a solar parabolic trough collector where a long curved mirror trough concentrates the sun's rays onto an absorber tube containing molten salt heat transfer fluid. The trough can track the path of the sun to maximise the amount of solar energy collected. A practical parabolic trough collector power station would use a large number of long troughs. A large-scale parabolic trough collector demonstration plant has been in use in California for over 20 years using oil as the heat transfer fluid and natural gas as an auxiliary energy source.

High temperature (over 300°C) molten salt fluid can create steam through a heat exchanger to drive a generator turbine. The salt fluid can be stored in tanks to provide heat when the sun is unavailable.

Other collector systems use adjustable flat mirrors that track the sun and focus the sunlight onto an elevated absorber tube. These Fresnel collectors can reduce costs by about 20%. Other approaches to heating the transfer fluid include high solar towers with parabolic mirrors focusing the sunlight onto the top of the tower where the fluid is heated. Solid heat storage systems (for example, concrete) are also being considered. There are a number of technical issues still to be addressed in all these systems in fluid development, increasing the length of time the heat can be stored and the cost efficiency compared to fossil-fuel power plants.

The downside with CSP systems is they need a large area of collectors to generate enough power for a reasonably sized power station. At least 50,000 square metres (five hectares) of land would be required to produce 1MW of continuous electrical power using parabolic trough collectors and thermal storage. So a CSP power plant delivering 500MW could require 2,500 hectares or 25 square kilometres of reasonably flat open land for collectors (about 2,500 football fields). This land has to be dedicated to collectors and is not available for other uses, unlike wind turbines that have a relatively small dedicated footprint (base area) (see Chapter 7). This means that if a large-scale CSP system is to be used to supplement or replace an existing coal power station in the same location then a large area of flat land will be needed adjacent to the existing power station.

The upside in thermal storage CSP systems is they could increase the capacity factor of solar systems from around 25% to 60% or 70% with an associated reduction in the cost per kWh of the electricity generated. The US government National Renewable Energy Laboratory (NREL) believes that future generation CSP systems with advanced storage could produce electricity at $0.07/kWh, which would be comparable with fossil fuels using CCS.[50]

Since a new stand-alone large CSP plant would probably need to be built in areas some distance from large population, there would be additional costs of transmitting the electricity to where it is needed. If solar-thermal storage cannot be extended beyond one to two days the plant would need to be built in an area of very high sun availability to provide all solar power continuously throughout the year, but even then a long-lasting cloud event could cause the power station to shut down.

CSP systems are still in the demonstration phase, with several small plants built and in development around the world; many with less that one hour of thermal storage or using fossil-fuel backup heating. There are no commercial all solar-thermal systems currently in production for supplying continuous power to the grid. The most likely commercial use in the near term is as peak or intermediate-load stations (see Chapter 1) or in combination with fossil-fuel-powered steam generation to supplement the solar-derived steam when the solar is not available.

CSP systems with thermal storage could provide a valuable contribution to reducing greenhouse gas emissions in some low latitude areas with high sun availability like south-west US, southern Europe, North Africa and parts of Australia but it is probably not going to be competitive with alternatives in northern Europe or most of North America.

What About the Next Generation of Solar PV Cells?

We can expect substantial investments in improving the efficiency of PV cells. Nanotechnology[28] is being used to produce thin film solar cells that are 100 times thinner than traditional silicon wafer cells at substantially lower cost per watt.[51] These cells are printed in rolls and could revolutionise the manufacture and cost of solar PV cells. As with all new technologies, it may take many years before these PV cells are widely used in commercial products.

How Can We Store Grid Electricity?

As we discussed in Chapter 1, the demand for grid electricity is not constant throughout the day or even throughout the year. Electricity storage allows the energy supply (the generators) to operate somewhat more independently from the energy demand. The concept of storing electricity is to use the excess capacity generated during low demand periods to charge an energy storage device that can be used to supply electricity during high demand. In the chapter on hydropower, we discussed such an energy storage system called pumped storage. We have discussed how both wind and solar power are not available all the time. Using an energy storage system can help match the output from these intermittent sources with the demand for electricity.

Pumped water storage, where off-peak electricity is used to pump

---

[28] Nanotechnology refers to a field of science and technology that controls matter on the atomic and molecular scale.

water from a lower reservoir to a higher reservoir, is the most effective commercially viable way of storing grid electricity today (Box 5 in
Chapter 8). During peak times the water in the higher reservoir is used
to drive a turbine and generator. It has the big advantage that it can
store a large amount of usable energy for a very long time (compared
to solar-thermal systems). The big disadvantage is that it requires the
right type of environment to put two large reservoirs one above the
other and the availability of large amounts of water. Pumped water
storage systems are also very expensive to build. This means that not
all countries are able to use it, so what alternatives are available or on
the horizon?

Compressed air can also be used as a storage medium. This is referred
to as compressed air energy storage (CAES). For grid electricity, off-
peak (low cost) power is used to drive an electric compressor to pump
air into a sealed underground cavern to a high pressure. The pressurised
air is then kept underground and can be used to generate power at peak
times by extracting the compressed air from storage and mixing it with
natural gas and burning to produce hot combustion gases that drive a
turbine. The turbine uses only 40% of the gas used in a conventional
gas turbine to produce the same amount of electricity. This is because
in a conventional gas turbine, two-thirds of the energy from the gas is
used to compress air at the time of generation. This is not needed with
the pre-compressed air produced using low cost electricity.

The upside of compressed air storage is it can be used for large-scale
grid storage and can store energy for a long period. It can also be used
for a fast start-up peaking station. The downside is finding suitable underground storage areas and it still needs to use natural gas fuel. There
are very few compressed air storage systems in production although
one has been in use since in 1978. With the advent of demand for storage for wind and solar generated electricity this method may become
more attractive but it will still require burning some natural gas.

Another energy storage system we discussed in Chapter 1 was batteries. Batteries come in many forms and most, like lead-acid batteries
(similar to the ones used in cars), store relatively little energy and are
generally unsuitable for storing the high energy demands of grid electricity although they have been used in some cases.

Other batteries like flow batteries potentially have much larger storage capacity and are being considered for storing grid electricity at the source of generation. A flow battery uses chemical solutions which flow through a power cell where the chemical energy is converted to electricity. The chemical solutions are stored in tanks outside the cell and pumped into and out of the cell during operation. The cell can be used to provide electricity during peak periods and the chemical solutions can be recharged during off-peak times. The total amount of energy stored is related to the size of the tanks used. Various chemical combination can be used in flow batteries.

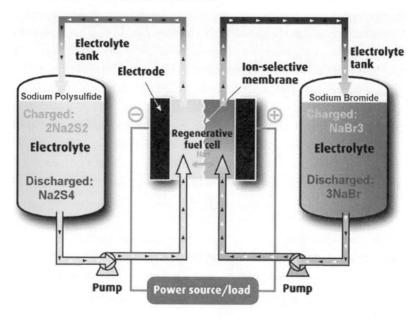

Example of a Flow Battery (courtesy of Regenesys Technologies)

Zinc-bromide flow batteries have been available and tested for some time. Other flow battery types include sodium-bromide, vanadium-redox and cerium-zinc and are in various stages of development. The upside of flow batteries is that they are very flexible and scalable as to storage and power output. The downside is that they are relatively complicated and the technology is still in the development stage, with no large-scale production system yet built.

A different type of battery that may be useful for grid electricity storage is called the sodium-sulphur (NaS) battery. This battery has a high energy storage capacity with a 6MW unit installed in Japan. This battery may be useful in increasing the capacity factor of wind farms where the battery can be charged during periods of good wind but low electricity demand and then provide electricity during low wind and high demand. There are some safety concerns as the batteries need to operate at over 300°C and sodium can be highly corrosive.

Other developing short-term storage technologies can be used with power grids to ride through momentary outages and reduce voltage sags and surges. These technologies such as flywheels and superconducting magnetic energy storage are intended for electricity utilities to improve power quality and reliability and we will not discuss them in this book.

How Can We Store Off-Grid Electricity?

The use of off-grid electricity is growing as more solar PV panels are used on buildings and on roadsides. Electricity storage is needed with solar panels to provide electricity at night. Generally these applications require much lower storage capacity than is needed for grid electricity, which means different technologies can be used.

One of the oldest and cheapest electricity storage solutions is lead-acid batteries. They are widely used in motor vehicles, particularly for starting an internal combustion engine but also for traction using electric motors in golf carts, forklift trucks and, more recently, some plug-in electric and hybrid cars. They are also used for backup power supplies for telephone exchanges and computer centres and off-grid residential and commercial electric power systems. Most residential and commercial solar PV systems use lead-acid batteries to hold the surplus power produced during the sunlight hours so that power is available during the rest of the day (see Chapter 6).

Rechargeable nickel-cadmium batteries are commonly used in portable consumer electronic devices like cordless phones. They have a higher energy density (energy for size ratio) than lead-acid batteries and they can be discharged and recharged many times before needing replacement. A newer and higher energy nickel battery is the nickel metal hydride battery which is used in most electric and hybrid cars such as the Toyota Prius as well as consumer electronic devices.

Lithium-ion batteries are also used in consumer electronic devices such as laptop computers and mobile phones. They have an even higher energy density than nickel batteries. However they are expensive for high energy use like storing off-grid electricity. Development work is being done to reduce the manufacturing cost to capture the larger energy markets that require several kWh of storage such as residential solar systems and the next generation of plug-in electric and hybrid cars where the energy to weight ratio will become increasingly more important to reduce the total energy consumed.

How Can Technology Help Us Use Less Energy in Our Buildings?

The IPCC identified that the greatest contribution to mitigating climate change could be made in buildings. This included more efficient lighting, electrical appliances and heating and cooling devices, passive and active solar design for heating and cooling, and using technologies like smart meters and integrating PV cells into the building. We will discuss some of these here, particularly the readily available solutions that can help us save energy now.

In Chapter 1 we briefly discussed smart meters. Smart meters allow us to monitor our electricity usage in real time throughout the day. The meter will monitor our usage and, if required, transfer the information for monitoring remotely. They often have an in-home display which shows the current energy being used and the current tariff charged.

Knowing how much electricity we are using at different times of the day, and what the tariffs are during those times, can help us change our usage to reduce our electricity costs. For example, we could use the dishwasher or washing machine during a low tariff period instead of a high tariff period. Whereas this doesn't, of itself, mean we use less energy, if we can use the energy at a time when it might otherwise be wasted then less energy is needed overall to provide our electricity requirements.

Smart meters can help us match our electricity consumption more closely with generation and reduce the overall peak demand on the grid. This can reduce the electricity supplier's overall energy usage, greenhouse gas emissions and our electricity cost. Peak demand in California has been reduced by 12–35% by using smart metering technology.[52]

Compact fluorescent lamps (CFL) are a type of fluorescent lamp designed to replace an incandescent lamp. They fit into the existing light fittings that we have in our homes and work places. They use significantly less energy for the same light output than incandescent lamps, often 75–80% less. This is because incandescent lamps produce a lot of heat as well as light. A typical residential property uses almost 10% of its electricity for lighting, so compact fluorescent lamps can reduce our electricity usage by around 7%, with the associated reduction in greenhouse gas emissions. CFLs also last a lot longer than incandescent lamps, about 6–15 times longer, but they can cost 10 times more than an incandescent lamp. Some countries are considering withdrawing incandescent lamps from sale to ensure we all switch to compact fluorescent lamps.

Another form of building lighting we will see more of in the future is the light-emitting diode (LED). An LED is made from a semiconductor that emits light. It is even more efficient at converting electricity into light than the CFL, lasts longer and is more robust.

We discussed standby power in Chapter 1, where many electronic devices continue to use electricity even when we are not using them. Although the amount of power used in standby mode is small, between 0.5 and 10 watts, the number of electronic devices in our homes is large. Typically 20 such devices are left on permanently in each household and standby power contributes between 5% and 10% to our electricity bill.

The International Energy Agency (IEA) claims standby power also contributes about 1% to greenhouse gas emissions.[53] It is not always convenient to turn these devices off at the wall socket so we need the manufacturers to work at minimising the standby power used. Technology has made it possible for manufacturers to reduce standby power by as much as 90%. Back in 1999, the IEA proposed the One Watt Plan, whereby every device will consume no more than one watt of standby power by 2010. A device using one watt of power left on permanently uses 9 kWh a year. Since then various countries have introduced regulations to minimise standby power, with the US mandating one watt for many electronic devices purchased by government.[54]

Water heating can make up a significant part of our electricity and gas usage in buildings, and hence our greenhouse gas emissions. By some estimates as much as 30% of the energy we use in our home goes to heating water. Solar water heating or using a heat-pump can reduce the amount of electricity or gas we use for heating water by more than half, depending on the system and where we live. Additional savings can be made by reducing the demand for hot water by using more water-efficient washing machines, dishwashers and other water-saving fixtures. We discussed solar water heating in Chapter 6.

Another significant user of energy in our homes and work places is space heating and cooling. About 30–40% of our energy use in the home is for heating and cooling and possibly even more in colder climates. A number of modifications can be made to existing buildings to improve their thermal insulation such as sealing air leaks around doors and windows and in floorboards, putting insulation in wall cavities and the roof and using multiple glazing in windows. Passive solar heating such as sun-facing windows, solar air collectors and thermally massive walls can significantly reduce the need for heating in cold climates.

Heat pumps transfer heat from a cooler medium such as the outside air or ground in winter to a warmer medium such as the warm air or hot water used to heat a building. In summer the pump can work in reverse for cooling the building. In cold climates, ground sourced heat pumps are the most effective for heating. Heat pumps are particularly cost effective for cooling in warm climates. Air-to-air heat exchangers can lower heating and cooling costs by recovering heat or coldness from the ventilation exhaust air and returning it to the building.

Electric heat pumps work like a refrigerator in reverse, absorbing heat from the air and transferring it to the water. Heat pumps can also use solar panels to provide the heat source or use the waste heat from air-conditioners and refrigerators. Different systems work better in different climates but they are all more energy efficient than using electricity or gas to directly heat the water.

Upgrading our heating and cooling systems with modern technology combined with improving the thermal insulation in our buildings can save over 40% of the energy used for heating and cooling. This can be the greatest contribution we can make as consumers to reducing our greenhouse gas emissions. We will cover the future of energy in building in greater depth in Chapter 23 in Part Three.

How Can Technology Help Us Use Less Oil in Our Transport?
The motor industry is continuously applying technology to improve the fuel economy in its vehicles by reducing vehicle weight with lightweight materials, reducing wind resistance and using more efficient engines and transmissions. This is partly because we are demanding better fuel economy from our vehicles to offset rising fuel prices and partly because some governments are mandating it. They are developing cleaner and more fuel-efficient light duty diesel engines which have become popular in Europe to replace petrol engines in cars. We discussed hybrid and plug-in vehicles in Chapter 3 and we can expect significant technology improvements in power and battery reliability.

Biofuel research continues to seek better ways to produce synthetic fuels to reduce crude oil consumption and greenhouse gas emissions. In Chapter 10 we discussed cellulosic ethanol which reduces the use of food crops to produce biofuels. Research is also finding ways to make biodiesel from algae using bioengineering.

Another motor fuel alternative is hydrogen, which can be produced from fossil fuels or renewable resources such as from water or plant material. Hydrogen can be mixed with natural gas and burned in an internal combustion engine as a direct replacement for petrol or diesel or used in a fuel cell to generate electricity. Such vehicles are not yet commercially available and significant improvements in hydrogen storage and distribution are needed before hydrogen is widely used as a replacement for petrol or diesel in motor vehicles (see Chapter 11).

Compressed air can also be used as an energy source in light vehicles. Using compressed air to drive a motor has been in use for over a century but the increasing price of petrol and diesel and the concerns about greenhouse gases are encouraging development in commercially available light motor vehicles running on compressed air. The air is stored in a pressurised tank on the vehicle similar to the tanks used for CNG and is recharged with a high pressure air compressor at a fuelling station or at home using electricity. A car tyre air compressor will not be up to the job of providing the pressures needed for compressed air cars.

Aviation is one of the fastest growing transports and continues to be a challenge for more fuel economy and reducing greenhouse gas emissions. Renewable fuels such as biodiesel, synthetic kerosene and hydrogen could be suitable for aviation although fuel cost will be a barrier. Scheduling and operating technology could be applied to reduce fuel wastage from excessive taxi-times, holding and stacking, flying at optimum altitude and flying the minimum distance between departure and destination.

We discuss the future of transport energy in more detail in Chapter 22 in Part Three.

Are There any Magic Technology Bullets to Solve our Energy Problems?

Over the years there have been plenty of claims of generating free energy from devices like self-running magnet motors usually involving unknown sources of energy in electromagnetic fields. These systems are generally perpetual motion machines. Any system that can output more energy than is put into it will be defying the laws of physics. The products are often convincingly demonstrated by their enthusiastic inventors. Some of them even find hopeful financial investors but never seem to reach production or the attention of mainstream manufacturers. If a product seems too good to be true, it probably is — particularly if it defies the laws of physics.

So Will Technology Come to the Rescue?

Technologies do exist that can make a difference over the next 10 to 50 years. However, none of these technologies can make sufficient differences on their own. We will need to explore all of them and hopefully install some of them to achieve the demands of the next half century. Table 7 gives a summary of some of the technologies we have discussed in this chapter and shows the stage of development and likely cost impact.

Many of these technologies still need significant financial investment to make them commercially viable products. Private industry will probably not do this on its own without encouragement. We need our governments to assist in their development, either through tax concessions, grants or other financial assistance. We will discuss this in greater depth in the next chapter.

Table 7

Summary of Potential New Technologies

Technology	R&D Phase	Pilot Plants or Prototypes	Commercial Testing	When Available	Likely Cost Impact[a]
Generation III+ and IV nuclear plants	Yes	III+ under construction	III+ evolution from II & III	III+ 2010 on IV 2030 on	+20–50%
Carbon capture and storage (CCS) for power stations	Yes	Under construction	Technology already in use	2015+	+25–100%
Concentrated solar power (CSP) thermal + storage	Yes	Yes	Yes without storage	Now without thermal storage	+100–150%
Tidal power	Yes	Yes	Barrage now	Tidal turbines 2010+	10–20x
Wave power	Yes	Planned	No		
Compressed air storage (CAES) for grid electricity			Yes	Now if sites available	$0.02–0.05/ kWh[b]
Flow batteries	Yes	Yes	Zinc bromide		$0.05–0.90/ kWh[b]
Sodium-sulphur (NaS) battery	Yes	Yes	In process		$0.09–0.30/ kWh[b]
Hydrogen cars	Yes	Yes	In process	Limited by refuelling infrastructure	
Compressed air cars	Yes	Yes	No		

[a] Likely cost impact over existing commercial technology (for example, coal and gas power stations without CCS). +100% and 2x mean twice the cost. +200% and 3x mean three times the cost.
[b] Capital cost of electricity storage per cycle — source Electricity Storage Association.[55]

15 — We Can't Escape the Politics

We have already discussed two political issues, global warming and peak oil, both of which have been keenly debated around the world. Other political issues we will cover here are energy security, government responses to address global warming including emissions trading schemes and the developing world's growing demand for energy. We will also cover the environment lobby and that thorny issue, nuclear power. But let's start by looking at a brief history of how we got where we are now.

So How Did We Get to Where We Are Today?

Prior to the Industrial Revolution in the mid-18th century, the primary fuel used by man was wood, which really only involved heating and cooking. The only powered machines were wind and water powered wheels used for milling, sawing and pumping water and horse, cattle or man drawn carts, barges and ploughs. Greenhouse gas emissions were relatively non-existent.

In the second half of the 18th century James Watt developed the steam engine primarily fuelled by coal. These engines were used to drive the textile mills and iron foundries which led to rapid economic expansion. Later came steam driven, coal burning locomotives and railways. Coal was used to replace wood for domestic heating and for producing oil and gas for lighting. Greenhouse gas emissions and other industrial pollutants started to increase.

The 19th century saw the steady development of electrical devices including batteries, electric lamps, electric generators and motors. By the end of the 19th century we had electric street lighting, electric tramways and, of course, power stations using coal and oil as well as hydropower. The modern history of petroleum also started in the mid-19th century. It was first used for heating and lighting until the mass production of motor vehicles at the end of the 19th century. Over the next half century, these vehicles running on petrol and diesel drove a massive increase in oil production until it became our major source of primary energy — and a major contributor to greenhouse gas emissions. The greenhouse effect from atmospheric gases was first investigated towards the end of the 19th century.

The 1950s saw the first nuclear reactors for generating electricity. It was also a time of growing concern about industrial and motor vehicle pollution and smog resulting in legislation to control emissions, particularly in urban areas. The theory of peak oil was first raised in 1956. From the end of the 1950s, greenhouse gas emissions started to rise sharply from accelerated economic activity resulting in greater energy use.

The first 'oil shock' was in 1973 when OPEC introduced an oil embargo as a result of war between Arab countries and Israel, which made governments more concerned about energy security. This encouraged the car makers to improve fuel economy — and, in effect, reduce their greenhouse gas emissions, although no one talked much about greenhouse gas emissions then. The oil shock also led to an interest in alternatives to oil such as nuclear, wind and solar power supported by government incentives. The nuclear interest was cut short by the accident at Three Mile Island in 1979 (see Chapter 5).

Further oil shocks took place in 1979 and 1980, caused by a revolution in Iran and the invasion of Iran by Iraq, severely impacting oil production in both countries. This encouraged oil consuming countries to look for alternative sources of supply of oil and gas, away from the Middle East. World over-production then followed, leading to a fall in oil prices from 1981 to 1997, almost back to the levels before 1973. It also reduced some of the enthusiasm for the motor vehicle efficiencies that had taken place in the 1970s and 1980s. So-called gas-guzzling sports utility vehicles (really upmarket four-wheel-drive light trucks) started to become popular for taking the children to school.

Global warming, caused by burning fossil fuels, first became a public issue in 1988 when a NASA scientist briefed the US government about it, creating a political and scientific furore. The United Nations formed the IPCC in 1988 to report on climate change and it has produced four reports over the last 20 years, the first in 1990 alerting the world to global warming through human activity. In 1992, the Rio Earth Summit was held aimed at reducing greenhouse gas emissions in order to combat global warming. In 1997, an agreement called the Kyoto Protocol was made between developed and developing countries to reduce emissions of greenhouse gases. At the time global warming received relatively little public interest in many countries.

From 1998, oil prices had started to rise again, and by 2008 had passed the peak level of 1981 in real dollar terms.[29] Once again the motor vehicle industry became more mindful of fuel economy, partly driven by government rules in some countries looking for ways to reduce greenhouse gas emissions. Hybrid cars started to become more popular. There was increased interest in biofuels as substitutes for oil products, partly driven by the price of oil and the need for energy security, and partly driven by the potential reduction in greenhouse gas emissions. As we will see, this last aim for biofuels has had limited success.

Despite repeated warnings from the IPCC over more than 15 years, progress on addressing climate change had been slow, with a great deal of scepticism from the US and some other countries including Australia. But around 2005 the world started to wake up to the issues of both global warming and peak oil and these concerns began to make headline news. At last the attention of mainstream media and many governments had been galvanised on both subjects. There was a renewed interest in nuclear power as a low-carbon energy source. The world also started to wake up to the reality that some climate change mitigation solutions came at a cost. For example, biofuels started to compete with food crops with the consequent risk of increased food prices.

[29] Real dollar terms means in inflation-adjusted dollars.

But Are the Climate Scientists Right About Global Warming and its Causes?

The IPCC is the main international body raising concerns about climate change. The IPCC believes that the world is warming, and this warming is due to human activity increasing the level of greenhouse gases in the atmosphere. They also believe that if the greenhouse gas emissions continue at the current level then so will the warming, with serious consequences for the environment. The IPCC bases these beliefs on climate change models prepared and analysed by many climate scientists over several years.

Because so much is at stake for both the environment and the economy, climate science has been subjected to intense scrutiny over the last 20 years and some scepticism from both politicians and scientists. Some of the issues raised by the sceptics with some immediate responses in italics are shown in Box 12. Full responses to these issues would be long and relatively involved so we won't discuss them further here. A good description of these various concerns plus many others with fuller responses can be found in The New Scientist Environment in a special report on climate change.[56]

Political scepticism kept countries like the US and Australia from ratifying the Kyoto Protocol. Australia has since had a change of government and has now ratified Kyoto. The fossil-fuel industry has not been a strong supporter of global warming for obvious reasons, with Exxon Mobil financially supporting scientific groups that challenged the global warming hypothesis. Exxon appears to have since shifted its position.[57] Some of the sceptics claim that scientists who support the IPCC view find it easier to fund their research than those who oppose it. A minority report to the US Senate released at the end of 2007 states that over 400 prominent scientists from more than two dozen countries recently voiced significant objections to major aspects of the so-called consensus on man-made global warming.[58]

Despite the scepticism about the impact of human activity on global warming, governments around the world are starting to take it very seriously and to recognise they have a major role to play. If the IPCC is correct, our governments face three key challenges. The first challenge is that severe climate change impacts can only be prevented by early, deep cuts in greenhouse gas emissions. This requires a swift transition to a global low-carbon economy. The IPCC says that a certain degree of climate change is inevitable throughout this century and beyond, even if global mitigation efforts over the next decades prove successful. So the second challenge is that, with climate change already happening, societies worldwide have to adapt to its impacts. The third, and most difficult challenge, is that tackling global warming will mean increases in energy prices which will be unpopular among some of the electorate.

Box 12

Some Issues Raised by Climate Change Sceptics

1. Can we trust the scientists given the difficulty of predicting chaotic systems like the climate? After all, they predicted global cooling in the 1970s. *A few climate scientists back in the 1970s suggested that the cooling effect of dirty air from pollution could outweigh the warming effect of carbon dioxide, potentially leading to an ice age. This was supported by a falling trend in temperatures between 1945 and 1970. This trend has reversed since 1970 (see Figure 3 in Chapter 13).*

2. The Sun has a much bigger impact on the climate than humans ever could. Other planets like Mars and Pluto are also warming so it must be the Sun that's doing the warming, not humans. *Apparently none of the other planets around the Sun are warming and the Sun's energy has been measured for the last 30 years and is not showing any sign of an upward trend.*

3. Human carbon dioxide emissions are tiny compared to those from natural sources. *This is true. But natural emissions are usually balanced by natural absorptions so they do not increase the total amount of carbon dioxide in the atmosphere. The increase in carbon dioxide is probably caused by the human emissions not being absorbed at the same rate as natural emissions.*

4. Water vapour is by far the most important contributor to the greenhouse effect, so how can human carbon dioxide emissions be causing global warming? *This is also true. However, water vapour is relatively short lived in the atmosphere (a few days) compared to carbon dioxide (hundreds of years) so we would not see a long-term build up of water vapour even if human activity was increasing water vapour (which it's not).*

5. The Hockey Stick Graph[a] has been shown to be plain wrong. *The graph was heavily criticised at the time and the US National Academy of Science was asked to*

assess the validity of the data. The Academy agreed with the conclusion that the late 20th century warmth in the Northern Hemisphere was unprecedented during at least the last thousand years.

6. The temperatures actual fell in the 1940s so human emissions can't be causing global warming. *The drop in temperature appears to have been caused by sulphates in the atmosphere from increased industrial activity at the end of the Second World War. These sulphate aerosols scattered light from the sun, reflecting the energy back out into space, which had a cooling effect on the climate. Clean air programs have significantly reduced the level of sulphates since the war.*

7. The Earth was much warmer 55 million years ago (perhaps 5–10°C warmer) so why should we be concerned? *The warming lasted 200,000 years and caused mass species extinctions. It was believed to be caused by the release of massive amounts of methane or carbon dioxide from thawing methane ice or from a massive volcanic eruption. The methane probably ignited from hot magma producing carbon dioxide. The carbon dioxide concentrations rose to about five times the levels they are today. It was actually an example of catastrophic global warming triggered by the build up of greenhouse gases in the atmosphere.*

[a] This was a graph of Northern Hemisphere temperatures for the last 1,000 years, produced in 1998, which showed a small fall from 1000 AD to the early part of the 20th century and a significant and sharp rise since then.

So What Should Governments Be Doing About Global Warming?

To address these challenges, our governments need both a mitigation strategy to reduce the severity of climate change and an adaptation strategy to adapt to the effects of climate change. We shouldn't see adaptation as a replacement for mitigation. Without adequate mitigation, the adaptation challenge will become ever more difficult. All countries need an adaptation strategy as all countries are likely to be affected, but not necessarily all countries need to be involved in mitigation. However, all major current and future emitting countries need to be involved in mitigation if it is to work.

A mitigation strategy might include:

- Providing incentives to reduce emissions, particularly in electricity generation, industry and transport, by introducing energy bill levies, carbon taxes or cap and trade systems. We will discuss incentives in Chapter 16.
- Encouraging greater energy efficiency in buildings by providing sub-

sidies for solar panels, installing smart meters, and setting minimum energy performance requirements for new residential and commercial buildings as well as for appliances and equipment.

- Encouraging greater energy efficiency in motor vehicles by setting emissions targets for manufacturers' car fleets. The European Union has recently set such a target of less than 130g of CO_2 per km. This requires an average fuel consumption of 5.5 litres per 100 km for petrol engines so it will also help mitigate the effects of peak oil.
- Providing funding to help develop the new technologies needed to develop low-carbon energy sources.
- Setting realistic targets for future greenhouse gas emissions and ensuring that the targets are met. The UK plans a 60% cut in emissions by 2050 (compared to 1990 levels), with an intermediate target of between 26% and 32% by 2020. Such targets would need to be different for different countries depending on what is realistic for them. Low-carbon energy sources are not evenly distributed around the world (see next section on energy security).
- Requiring electricity suppliers to supply a set portion of their electricity from renewables sources. More severe measures might include banning new coal-fired power stations. These kinds of measures can impact technology development which often brings up the issue of whether governments should pick winners.

An adaptation strategy might include:

- Assessing risks from rising temperatures, rising tides, extreme weather patterns on such things as ecosystems, human health, economic development, property and infrastructure.
- Minimising threats and reducing potential damage by constructing dykes, protecting ports and urban coastal areas.
- Assessing the costs and benefits of adaptation.
- Preparing a plan of action before the crises and disasters happen.
- Setting priorities for adaptation action based on when the risks are likely to become significant and the likely future consequences.
- Involving all sectors of the economy: public, private, business, industry and service as well as individual citizens. Plans need to be made at the national, regional and local level to reflect the priorities and responsibilities of each level.

- Managing energy demand while waiting for the technology to deliver low-carbon energy and having an energy security plan.

What Is Energy Security?

Primary energy sources are unevenly distributed between countries, particularly oil, gas and uranium. Many countries are not energy self-sufficient and rely heavily on imports from other countries. However, all countries need access to energy and most see it as an entitlement. Globalisation has made our modern economies interdependent. Much of what we consume has actually been made using energy somewhere else, so we cannot afford to be protective about our own sources of energy. Energy has become a critical resource that needs to be protected for all of us — hence the need for energy security on a global scale.

As we have seen from our previous discussions, the world energy supply is likely to get tighter because of peak oil and gas some time in the next few decades. About one-third of the world's oil supply comes from the relatively politically unstable Middle East — Saudi Arabia, Iran, UAE, Kuwait and Iraq. As the oil supplies dwindle from more stable regions like the North Sea, US, Australia and Indonesia, supplies may have to be sourced from more unstable regions of the world. Growing demand for energy from China, India, the Middle East and the former Soviet Union is putting pressure on supplies. Concerns about greenhouse gas emissions are pushing electricity utilities from abundant coal to less abundant natural gas. In our modern economies we continue to rely on abundant, cheap energy.

We need to diversify our sources of energy to avoid relying on a narrow source of supply that might get turned off — as OPEC threatened to do with oil in 1973. It is a natural temptation for countries that can control a critical resource to use it for political advantage, as has been seen in Russia, Iran and Venezuela in recent years. Oil and gas tend to travel around the world on a few defined sea routes and can be vulnerable to terrorist attacks, especially at points such as the Suez and Panama Canals, the Strait of Hormuz and the Strait of Malacca. Oil and gas supplies can also be impacted by natural disasters like hurricanes Katrina and Rita that struck the Gulf of Mexico in 2005.

Diversifying oil supply from the Middle East will be a significant challenge in the short term. There is a growing interest in home-grown biofuels in some countries to reduce exposure to imported oil. Natural gas can be used as a substitute for oil in many cases as we discussed in Chapter 12. Gas is also more diversified across non-Middle East countries, particularly in Europe and the Asia-Pacific region. Sweden intends to significantly reduce its reliance on imported oil by 2020 by replacing oil with renewable energy and energy conservation to cut total energy use. In an effort to reduce the impact of a disruption to oil supplies, members of OECD's IEA are required to maintain emergency oil reserves of at least 90 days of net oil imports.

Coal production is widely distributed throughout the world but nearly half of it is produced and consumed in China and India. Coal reserves, the amount of coal still in the ground, are not evenly distributed with many countries having to rely on imports for future needs. The biggest importers are Japan and Korea and the biggest exporters are Australia, Indonesia and Russia.[23]

Uranium production, like oil, is concentrated in a few countries, with 30% coming from the former Soviet Union, 25% from Canada and 19% from Australia.[59] With most of the supply coming from politically stable countries, supply security is probably less exposed with uranium than with oil although prices have risen quite sharply for both since 2003.

Although renewable energy resources occur throughout the world, sources such as wind, solar, geothermal, hydro and ocean power are not readily available for every region. Regions in the higher latitudes (closer to the poles than the equator) receive significantly less solar energy than those closer to the equator. Wind turbines only operate effectively in a wind speed above 14 km/h. Regions that are generally calm are unsuitable for wind power and turbines typically shut down in strong winds above 90 km/h. Regions with poor or intermittent access to running rivers cannot use hydropower and the right geological environment is needed for geothermal power.

Energy security is not just about primary energy supply, of course. It is also about changing energy demand. Events like climate change with sustained heatwaves and severe weather events can impact on energy demand and energy distribution stability. Population growth, particularly in developing countries, inevitably means increased demand for energy. We have already seen in Chapter 12 that China and India are likely to increase their oil demand from 12% of the world's consumption to 20% over the next 10 years.

Where Can Governments Get in the Way?

Governments often try to 'protect' retail energy consumers by regulating retail energy prices. This happens for electricity, oil, gas, petrol and diesel. It is usually done by fixing retail fuel price caps which set the highest price an energy supplier can charge its retail (and some business) customers. This can be good for winning votes but has some unintended consequences. Firstly, the supplier will often charge the fixed cap price even though their cost 'of supply varies depending on seasonal demand. This means that we, as retail consumers, have little financial incentive to reduce demand during high cost periods and get no reward for switching usage to low demand periods. Regulating prices can actually disadvantage the customer where there is more than one supplier, as it may restrict price competition between the suppliers. If the regulated price is set too low it can discourage the supplier from investing in improved infrastructure.

Another way that governments try to protect their electors is by providing energy subsidies to hold down energy prices artificially. The environmental lobby has long complained about subsidies for fossil fuels. In turn they would like to see subsidies for green renewable energy. In either case, subsidies can prop up non-competitive technologies and fuel sources. A better solution is to ensure that the energy suppliers have to pay for any external costs[30] such as greenhouse gas emissions and let the market decide which technologies and fuel sources are the most competitive. We will discuss carbon taxes and carbon trading in detail in Chapter 16.

Whereas we want governments to provide funding to help develop the new low-carbon energy sources, we need to ensure that governments aren't trying to pick winners by targeting particular technologies. When governments fund specific targets such as solar power, sometimes better options may get neglected. Funding should be provided for any

[30] External costs are costs to others (such as the general public or the environment) that are not related to the economics of the process itself. For example, air pollution from a factory.

promising new energy developments, irrespective of the primary fuel source.

Another area where governments are at risk of trying to pick winners is with renewable energy targets rather than greenhouse gas emissions targets. Such renewable targets may push the energy suppliers toward wind and solar energy sources when CCS or nuclear power might actually turn out to be the cheaper long-term solution in their region. Because wind is generally cheaper than solar, renewable targets tend to favour wind over solar. If all the external costs are internalised, that is, paid for by the supplier, for all energy sources then the market can choose which technology or energy source it prefers so we wouldn't need renewable energy targets. In fact, they are likely to be counterproductive when combined with an emissions trading scheme.

What Will Be the Impact of the Developing World on Energy Demand?
The world population is expected to grow from almost 7 billion to over 9 billion by 2050. Most of this growth is expected in the developing world. The developing world accounts for 80% of the population yet uses less than half of the world's total energy consumption. By 2050, these regions are expected to make up 86% of the world population.[60]

Energy use is a key component in economic growth. In 2006, the world consumed 10.9 billion TOE[31] of primary energy[37] or 1.6 TOE per person. However there is a big difference in energy use per person between the developed world and the developing world. The developed world (OECD countries) used an average of 4.7 TOE per person. In comparison, the developing world used just less than 1 TOE per person. As the developing world demands a standard of living closer to that of the developed world, with more cars and consumer goods and better heating and cooling, then we can expect the TOE per person in the developing world to rise significantly.

For the developing world to reach the same primary energy consumption per person in 2050 that the developed world currently has, the total world primary energy demand will need to grow almost fourfold from 11 to 43 billion TOE by 2050. This would be a big challenge in a world where we want to stabilise and then reduce greenhouse gas emissions

[31] TOE means tonnes of oil equivalent.

(see Figure 4 in Chapter 13). Of course this assessment assumes that those of us in the developed world will continue to consume 4.7 TOE each, every year. A key part of mitigating climate change is to reduce our total energy consumption through greater efficiency (with minimal economic disruption) so hopefully our energy use per person will be lower in the future without substantial sacrifice to our quality of life.

What Does the Environmental Lobby Have to Say?

Greenpeace International has a very optimistic view about future energy. In their Energy [R]evolution Report of January 2007,[61] Greenpeace states that renewable energy, combined with the smart use of energy, can deliver half the world's energy needs by 2050. This can cut carbon dioxide emissions by almost 50% by 2050. Further, this is based only on proven and sustainable technologies such as renewable energy sources and efficient decentralised cogeneration.[32] It specifically excludes carbon capture and storage (CCS) and nuclear energy. It does seem to include large-scale concentrated solar power (CSP) systems and enhanced geothermal systems (EGS) even though these are not yet proven and sustainable technologies.

These Greenpeace targets assume that 70% of electricity will come from renewable energy sources using decentralised energy systems with local distribution networks rather than high voltage transmission lines. By 2030, nuclear power and lignite (brown) coal will be phased out completely and black coal will be reduced by 40%. By 2050, 40% of total electricity demand will come from variable renewable energy sources (wind and solar). As the variability cannot be fully controlled, this will present some issues with balancing supply and demand. It will almost certainly rely on some of the electricity storage systems we discussed in Chapter 14, many of which, except for pumped storage, will not pass Greenpeace's criteria of being based only on proven and sustainable technologies. Pumped storage will not even be available in some regions.

To get half the total energy from renewable resources and, at the same time, phase out nuclear power and significantly reduce coal and oil usage, the Greenpeace targets rely on a reduction in total world

---

[32] Cogeneration typically means producing both electricity and heat from a single energy source.

primary energy demand by 2050 of 3%. This seems at odds with a world population growth of 37% plus the desire by the developing world (particularly China and India) to lift their standard of living to those in the developed world. Greenpeace acknowledges in its report that energy is central to reducing poverty. The International Energy Agency (IEA) predicts that total energy demand will grow by 55% to 2030[62] and Greenpeace extrapolated this IEA prediction forward to 85% by 2050.

Current world primary energy demand is 10.9 billion TOE or an average of 1.6 TOE per person per year. A 3% reduction by 2050 would reduce energy consumption to about 10.6 billion TOE. By 2050 the world population will have risen to over 9 billion. This means that the average energy consumption per person will need to fall from 1.6 TOE to 1.2 TOE or an average reduction of 25% for everyone in the world. If we are to reduce world poverty and, at the same time, meet the wealth aspirations (that will demand more energy use not less) of the 80% of the world population that live in the less developed regions we could expect energy demand per person to increase not decrease.

The developed world will also be hit hard by the Greenpeace targets. For example, today in OECD North America (US, Canada, Mexico) the current primary energy demand is about 2.7 billion TOE or an average of 6.4 TOE per person per year. This is very high, even by the average for the developed world at 4.7 TOE per person, so there is probably scope for significant improvements, at least in the US and Canada. Under the Greenpeace targets, by 2050 the OECD North America primary energy demand will reduce by 39% while the population will increase by 38%. This will require people living in North America to more than halve their energy usage (not greenhouse gas emissions). This is unlikely to be possible from energy efficiency alone and will probably require significant changes to North American lifestyle that are probably not going to be politically acceptable to the people of Canada and the US. If a proposal is politically unacceptable then it is unlikely to be implemented, except in a dictatorship.

Do We Really Need Nuclear Power?

This chapter is about politics, so what better subject to end it on than one of the most divisive subjects in energy — nuclear power. As we discussed in Chapter 5, there are strong community concerns about nuclear power and its threats to people and the environment. In summary they include long-term storage of the waste, the risk of proliferation of nuclear weapons and the possible danger from a reactor accident. Some would add to these the risks and environmental damage from uranium mining, processing and transport. Financial markets can command a higher interest rate to those borrowing to build nuclear plants because of these perceived risks. Environmental concerns increase the costs of getting permits and in some locations the 'not in my backyard' (NIMBY) lobby often wins out.

Nuclear proliferation generally means the spread of nuclear material, technology or weapons to nations outside the five recognised nuclear weapon states of the US, Russia, the UK, France and China. The more countries (or terrorist groups) that acquire nuclear weapons the more our regional and international security becomes destabilised. The Nuclear Non-Proliferation Treaty between 189 nations aims to prevent the spread of nuclear weapons, achieve nuclear disarmament and facilitate the peaceful use of nuclear energy. Compliance with the terms of the treaty is verified and monitored by the International Atomic Energy Agency (IAEA). Despite this, four additional states, India, Pakistan, Israel and North Korea are thought to possess nuclear weapons in breach of the treaty — although none of these countries are signatories to it.

Most nuclear power plants present a low risk of nuclear proliferation. The risk is higher with online refuelling[33] and fast breeder[34] reactors. Typical reactors produce plutonium in spent fuel. Reactor-grade plutonium is generally not suitable for use in nuclear weapons. Plutonium from spent power reactor fuel could theoretically be used to develop a dirty bomb[35] but there have been no known nuclear explosion using unprocessed reactor-grade plutonium from light water reactor spent fuel. To produce weapons-grade plutonium in a typical power reactor would require operating the reactor in an abnormal way which would

[33] Online refuelling means changing the nuclear reactor fuel without shutting down the reactor.
[34] A fast breeder reactor is a fast neutron reactor that produces more fissile material than it consumes.
[35] A dirty bomb is a crude nuclear device that seeks to disperse radioactive material rather than relying on a nuclear explosion. The likely health impacts of the airborne radioactive dust would be minor. The explosion would be from a conventional source such as dynamite with similar results.

be in breach of IAEA safeguards and readily detected. The reactor spent fuel must be reprocessed before use in a nuclear weapon, which is a significant hurdle for a would-be terrorist group.

Shutting down the nuclear power industry is not likely to influence a country's decision to develop nuclear weapons. Countries that currently possess nuclear weapons developed them separately from civilian power programs. Using safeguards such as inspections, measurements and analysing information, the IAEA can verify that a country is honouring its international commitments to not use nuclear power programs for nuclear weapons purposes. A key objective of the next generation of reactors is to improve proliferation resistance.

Over the years, there has been much analysis of the health and safety issues of nuclear power. The European Commission's ExternE study[63] examined the external costs of electricity generation using a life cycle assessment. The results show that, on a unit of energy produced basis, the health and safety costs of uranium mining and the use of nuclear fuel, including waste disposal, are lower than fossil-fuel-based energy generation. In other words nuclear is safer than coal or gas. Nuclear power generation is actually one of the safest power sources we have. Hydro power has been one of the worst, mostly from dam accidents which have killed tens of thousands of people. Even wind farms have directly killed 35 people, many being industry workers falling from turbines, which is more than have been killed directly by nuclear reactors.[64]

The health and safety performance of nuclear power facilities has improved significantly over time and is expected to improve even further with the new generation of reactors (see Chapter 14). The nuclear and uranium mining industry is stringently and physically controlled by regulations and the IAEA. Nuclear power has a 50 year history so there is some basis on which to be confident that the health and safety risks of nuclear power are no greater than for any other power source, and much less than for fossil fuels.

In Chapter 5 we discussed the problem of final storage of nuclear waste. We won't see production final storage sites until after 2010 but safe disposal of low level and short-lived intermediate level waste has been demonstrated at many sites and the technology exists for long-lived intermediate and high-level waste. Although the volume of nuclear waste is significant it is tiny compared to other industrial waste. The World Nuclear Association provides a detailed discussion on nuclear waste management for those looking for more information.[65]

The decision about nuclear power comes down to one of relative risk. All activity comes with some level of risk. Not switching to low-carbon energy sources may present a significant risk to the environment and possibly to mankind. Individual countries may have to weigh up the potential risks from using nuclear energy against the risks from not reducing greenhouse gas emissions.

In their latest report, the IPCC recognised that nuclear energy could make an increasing contribution to carbon-free electricity and heat in the future, contrary to the views of Greenpeace and Helen Caldicott. The IPCC expects that nuclear power, not solar, wind or geothermal energy, will be the primary source of low-emissions electricity by 2030. Even the originator of the Gaia hypothesis, James Lovelock — once a darling of the environmentalists — claims that much of the criticism of nuclear power is wrongheaded and nuclear energy is the only immediately available source of energy that does not cause global warming.[66]

Many of the environmentalists and conservationists who are only too ready to accept what the IPCC has to say about the impacts of global warming appear to ignore what the IPCC has to say about the solutions to global warming which rely heavily on nuclear power and CCS. We will cover this in depth in Part Three when we look at the future of energy.

16 — Trading, Taxing, Offsets and Other Inducements

In the previous few chapters, we have talked extensively about mitigating climate change. Mitigation will largely come from reducing greenhouse gas emissions and nearly two-thirds of these emissions come from energy use. So in this chapter we will talk about how we could encourage energy producers and consumers to reduce their emissions.

Why Do We Need Schemes Like Carbon Trading or Carbon Taxing?
In Chapter 13 we discussed how greenhouse gas emissions, from the production of goods and services, impose a cost on society through environmental damage. Without some kind of mechanism to recognise this cost, it will not be reflected in the price of products. Those of us who produce the greenhouse gas emissions by using high-carbon goods and services are bringing about climate change. There is an economic argument that says those that create the problem and create the cost should pay for it. We need to implement measures to ensure businesses and consumers factor in the impact of environmental damage when they make production and consumption decisions.

One way to factor in the impact of environmental damage is through a market-based approach called a market mechanism. With a market-based approach, businesses choose which carbon reducing opportunities they exploit at least cost to themselves and the economy. Carbon trading and carbon taxing schemes are both market mechanisms. Both impose a price on emissions which businesses will include in the prices of their goods and services so the consumers ultimately pay for the cost of those emissions. Those businesses that use clean technologies will not have to pay for emissions and can offer their goods and services at lower prices than those that continue to produce emissions.

Non-market-based approaches to greenhouse gas emissions generally use regulations to either require or ban particular technologies or production processes. Examples of non-market approaches include specifying that a certain percentage of electricity has to be generated by renewable energy and banning coal-fired power stations. The costs of complying with these regulations will vary significantly between industries and suppliers, are not immediately obvious to consumers and may not lead to the best solutions.

What Is Carbon Trading?

A carbon trading scheme sets a price on emissions by constraining the total amount of emissions that can be produced. The scheme involves the government issuing permits to businesses that produce emissions. Each permit represents the right to emit a specified amount of greenhouse gas — for example, one tonne of CO_2-e. Businesses must hold enough permits to cover the greenhouse gas emissions they produce each year. The number of permits issued (either auctioned or freely allocated) must be less than the amount required under normal business-as-usual conditions if we are to reduce emissions. In other words there must be fewer permits than the current level of emissions. This is necessary to get a reduction in total emissions and it is the scarcity of the permits that gives them a value.

The most common type of emissions trading system is known as a 'cap and trade' scheme. Under such a scheme, the government sets a target or cap on the greenhouse gas emissions and issues tradable emissions permits up to the cap. The cap is progressively lowered over time to achieve an overall emissions target. Permits can be bought and sold and the price is determined by supply and demand. Governments can choose how they wish to allocate permits, for example, by auctioning them. They may also chose to allocate them for free to some unfairly disadvantaged industries.

Businesses covered by an emissions trading scheme periodically have to surrender permits to the government equal to their emissions. Businesses that have reduced their emissions may have excess permit that they can sell to others or hold over for the next period. Those that have remained high emitters may need to buy additional permits to cover their emissions above the level allowed by the permits they currently hold. Businesses will have different capacities to reduce emissions but they can improve that capacity by investing in emissions reduction technologies.

So we can get a better idea of how a cap and trade emissions trading system might work to advantage, Box 13 contains a worked example. By placing a price on emissions, trading provides incentives for businesses to reduce emissions where this would be their cheapest option. It also allows businesses to continue producing emissions where it would be more costly to reduce emissions than to buy permits. In effect, the buyer is paying a charge for polluting, while the seller is being rewarded for having reduced emissions by more than the target.

The European Union Emissions Trading Scheme (EU ETS), which started in 2005, is the largest example of a cap and trade scheme. The governments of the EU Member States agree on national greenhouse gas emissions caps and, during phase I, allocated mainly free permits to their industrial operators. The governments monitor and validate the actual emissions. Every year, the operators are required to surrender (give back) an amount of permits to the government that is equivalent to their emissions in that year. If they were allocated insufficient permits then they can buy additional permits from other operators, either directly or on the trading markets.

Emissions trading is a means of achieving a certain level of emissions reduction at the lowest possible cost to the economy. It also enables the market, not governments, to decide which new or existing technologies will reduce emissions at least cost. Emissions trading schemes can work both nationally and internationally.

What Is Carbon Taxing?

A carbon tax can be levied on a business for every unit of emissions it produces. The price of emissions is fixed by the tax and the revenue goes to the government. A carbon tax will encourage businesses to re-

Box 13

Worked Example of a Cap and Trade Emissions Scheme

1. Two companies, A and B, each emit 1 million tonnes of CO_2-e each year. The government wants to cut emissions by 5 per cent in the year so it allocates each company permits to emit 950,000 tonnes. Each company has the option of either reducing its emissions by 50,000 tonnes or buying additional permits on the market. The price of the permits will be set by the market but let's assume the price is $20 per tonne.

2. If either company does nothing about reducing its emissions then it will have to buy permits for 50,000 tonnes at a cost of $1 million.

3. If either company can reduce its emissions by 50,000 tonnes for less than $1 million then this would be a good economic decision.

4. But let's assume Company A can actually reduce its emissions for $10 per tonne (half the cost of the permits). It is reasonable for A to cut its emissions by 100,000 tonnes (twice the amount required) to avoid the cost of additional permits and enables it to sell the extra 50,000 tonnes of emissions reductions for $1 million to fully recover the expenditure incurred on reducing the emissions by 100,000 tonnes.

5. Now let's assume that for company B, making reductions is more expensive at $30 per tonne. If B was to reduce its own emissions by 50,000 tonnes it would cost $1.5 million so B decides to buy the 50,000 tonnes of surplus allowances on offer from A for $1 million. This saves B $0.5 million.

6. In fact both A and B save $0.5 million because of emissions trading. A from recovering the cost of reducing its emissions and B from being able to buy the permits cheaper than doing the reduction itself.

7. If the government had forced them both to reduce their emissions by 5% the total cost to the economy would have been $2 million dollars, $0.5 million for A and $1.5 million for B. So the economy has achieved a 5% cut in emissions with a $1 million saving because of emissions trading.

duce their emissions and their tax bill. The cost of emissions is known with certainty but the emissions outcome is less certain. Compare this with an emissions trading scheme, discussed above, where the government sets the emissions reduction target and the market determines the price of each unit of emissions.

The incentive for business to reduce emissions is similar for a carbon tax and an emissions trading scheme. Carbon taxes will reduce emissions by setting a cost for emissions and allowing the market to determine the amount of emissions reduction to reduce the tax paid. Some businesses would continue to emit and pay the tax unless it became cheaper to reduce emissions. The cost of reducing a tonne of emissions is likely to increase as the demand for overall reductions increases. This is because the initial simple, low cost opportunities to reduce emissions will be used up first, requiring more expensive solutions later on. This means that the tax rate will need to be increased over time to encourage further emissions reductions so that the government can reach its overall emissions target.

How Do the Two Schemes Compare?

With carbon taxes the amount of emissions reduction is not guaranteed and can only be controlled by changing the tax rate. With carbon trading the number of permits issued controls the quantity of emissions and the amount of emissions reduction — assuming tight monitoring and policing of the emissions reporting.

With carbon trading the cost of complying to the scheme is unknown in advance and will vary over time depending on market conditions and might ultimately exceed any benefit. With carbon taxing the cost is known for the period ahead (as set by the tax rate) although the taxes will need to be varied to achieve greater emissions reductions as the cost of reducing emissions changes.

With carbon taxes, the revenue flows to the government. With carbon trading some revenue will flow to the government from permit auctions and emissions penalties on businesses with insufficient permits, but much of the revenue flows to the businesses that are able to sell permits at higher prices than their cost of reducing emissions. These are the ones most successful at reducing emissions cost effectively. After all, this is the primary aim of the schemes in the first place. We need the government revenue from carbon taxing and trading to support reducing emissions. This means it must be spent appropriately by the government. We will discuss government incentives shortly.

Unfortunately, there is significant uncertainty in the effectiveness of price controls (taxes) to reduce emissions. This favours carbon trading where at least the emissions levels can be controlled with more certainty. On the other hand, there is significant uncertainty as to what the trading caps should be and what the impact will be on environmental damage. This could favour carbon taxes where at least the total cost is known and can be controlled. The administrative costs are also probably cheaper for taxes than trading schemes and trading schemes are probably impractical at the household level.

There are hybrid systems that try to get the best of both schemes by capping the maximum and minimum permit price (to increase price certainty) and allowing businesses to purchase permits both on the market or from the government at a specified trigger price. Other proposed systems have both long-term and short-term permits. The long-term permits allow a certain amount of emissions each year and can be traded. The short-term permits, which could be for one year, could be bought as needed from the government and act like a carbon tax with the price fixed for a period of time.

The price of emissions and the quantity of emissions reductions cannot both be controlled by the government. This is because control over one affects the other. Which to control is guided by the relative importance of having greater control over the emissions outcome or control over the cost imposed.

Both carbon trading and carbon taxing present some difficulty for trade-exposed industries in a country where they have to pay for emissions but their products compete against goods produced in other countries where there is no cost on emissions. There is a risk that the trade-exposed industry may relocate to the cheaper country and continue to produce the same emissions — sometimes known as 'carbon leakage'. This would lead to an economic loss in the country that imposes a price on emissions for no environmental benefit as the emissions would continue to be produced. In some cases, governments may be forced to compensate these trade-exposed industries to ensure they do not relocate.

How Are Emissions Targets Set and Permits Allocated?
Emissions targets usually refer to a target percentage reduction in greenhouse gas emissions from some base year. For example, a state's 2030 emissions target may be a 30% reduction from the level of emissions in 1990. If no base year is set, we probably tend to assume that

it means this year but this is often not the case and leads to ambiguity. Targets can be either aspirational targets or binding targets. Aspirational targets are really 'hoped for' targets which are important in setting intermediate targets and trading caps. Binding targets have to be met.

Typically a government or international body, such as the EU, will set emissions targets and trading caps and determine how permits are to be allocated. Long-term targets are usually aspirational, for example a 50% cut in 2000 emissions by 2050, and are usually based on the emissions reductions needed to meet a particular IPCC stabilisation level (see Chapter 13). A binding intermediate target for emissions can then be set for the next period of the scheme which acts as the cap for that period. The EU has recently set a binding target of 20% reduction from 1990 levels by 2020.

The government will then decide how many permits will be allocated to meet that target. Clearly if emissions are to be reduced, then the total number of permits issued must be less than the current actual emissions. Allocating permits across businesses needs care. It will reduce profitability for some businesses unable to pass on the full cost to their customers and provide benefits to others, particularly renewable energy generators who might be able to readily sell their permits. It will also increase costs for households.

How the permits are allocated can address some of these inequities between businesses. Some could be allocated for free to some disadvantaged businesses. They could be allocated for free depending on historical emissions (often called 'grandfathering'). They could be allocated for free based on industry benchmarking — how a business is doing against its peers or against best practice. Some permits could also be auctioned where a business can bid for a quantity of permits.

A regulator will allocate the permits to businesses based on the rules set by the government. It will also record permit ownership changes (through trading or auctioning) and register surrendered permits. Usually businesses report their own emissions to the regulator, who will monitor and verify those emissions. The regulator will collect permits (usually annually) to match the emissions and levy emissions penalties on businesses that do not hold sufficient permits.

What About International Regulation?

Because global warming and the need for emissions reduction are global in nature, there is a need for international regulation of emissions. This is performed by the United Nations (UN) through its international treaty the UN Framework Convention on Climate Change (UNFCCC) and the Kyoto Protocol, an international and legally binding agreement to reduce greenhouse gas emissions worldwide.

The Kyoto Protocol requires developed countries to reduce their emissions below levels specified for each country in the treaty. Review and enforcement of these commitments are carried out by the UN. The Protocol developed three market-based mechanisms to reduce emissions known as emissions trading, joint implementation (JI) and the clean development mechanism (CDM). We have already discussed the principles of emissions trading. JI and CDM are carbon offset arrangements that allow countries to invest in emissions reducing projects in other countries as an alternative to emissions reductions in their own countries. We will discuss the principles of carbon offsets in the next section of this chapter.

The Kyoto Protocol sets caps for country emissions and a framework and set of rules for carbon trading but does not set up an international emissions trading scheme for businesses. This has been left for individual countries to do. It does allow countries which cannot meet their targets to 'buy' offsets by investing in reduction projects in other countries under JI and CDM. It also allows government to government trading of emissions units.

There are several business to business emissions trading schemes and carbon markets in existence around the world with some part linkage between them. Given that global warming and greenhouse gas emissions are a global problem, it could be an advantage to have a truly global emissions trading scheme with a single regulator that all countries and businesses could trade in. Getting agreements between all countries to this will be quite a challenge, however.

What Are Carbon Offsets?

So far in this chapter we have generally focused on businesses reducing or avoiding their own emissions. Ideally, businesses will accurately assess all the emissions from their operations as well as their products and reduce those emissions where possible. Sometimes it will be too costly or impossible to reduce all the emissions so the businesses may have to pay a price to continue their operations, whether through a tax or to buy permits. Alternatively, it is possible to achieve the same environmental result by investing in projects which will remove an equivalent amount of emissions elsewhere. The damage caused by a unit of emissions is the same no matter where it comes from.

The process of purchasing emissions reductions from other projects is called carbon offsetting. The offsetting project needs to prevent or remove the amount of emissions to be offset or, at least, promise to do so in the future. It also needs to do it at less cost than can be achieved by the buyers doing it themselves. Carbon offsets can be generated from different kinds of projects but they usually involve either renewable energy (usually wind, solar or geothermal), energy efficiency (upgrading buildings, installing energy saving appliances, switching fuels, etc.), methane capture (from landfill, agriculture or mining) or planting trees to soak up carbon dioxide from the environment during photosynthesis.

For offsetting to help mitigate climate change, it must actually be decreasing the total quantity of emissions. In other words the offsetting projects must be new projects that are only happening because of offsetting, not projects that would have happened anyway because of regulation or economic good sense. Further, the projects must actually reduce the amount of emissions claimed so they need to be verified. A high quality carbon offsets project needs to meet the following criteria:

• The project would not have occurred without the carbon offsets.
• We accurately know the quantity of emissions that would have occurred without the project.
• We can quantify the emissions that will be reduced by the project.
• The reductions will be permanent and not reversed later.
• The offsets will not be sold more than once.

Offsets typically fall under two different schemes: mandatory schemes such as emissions trading discussed earlier and voluntary schemes. Under mandatory schemes businesses must comply with regulatory requirements, usually set by governments to reduce emissions either through carbon trading or carbon taxes. Carbon offsets can be recognised as a legitimate reduction in emissions under these schemes as long as there is no double counting — that is, both the emitting business and the offsetting project operator don't claim the same reduction.

Worldwide, businesses have been keen to be seen to be doing something about climate change even if they are not required to reduce emissions under a mandatory scheme. This has led to the emergence of several voluntary carbon markets. The best know voluntary market is the Chicago Climate Exchange (CCX) where CCX members commit to annual emissions reductions targets. Those members who reduce below the targets have surplus allowances to sell to other CCX members. Those who emit above the targets can buy Exchange Offsets from verified high quality projects run by registered offset providers.

Carbon markets have created opportunities for enterprising groups to offer carbon offset services to businesses and individuals. Carbon offsets can be bought from these service providers which might be for-profit or non-profit organisations. Some may only invest in certain kinds of projects, such as renewable energy projects or tree planting, and the price per tonne of CO_2-e offset can vary significantly between providers. Internationally available offset service providers include the CarbonNeutral Company in the UK[36] and the Carbonfund.org in the US.[37]

It is clearly very important to assure the quality of these schemes and service providers. Voluntary offset markets are relatively new and there are no universally accepted product quality standards. There are global standards for measuring and accounting for greenhouse gas emissions and there are standards to determine the credibility of reductions such as the Voluntary Carbon Standard (VCS).[38] International standards are still being developed to certify offset selling schemes and providers. Given the lack of regulations in the voluntary market there is a risk of 'rent seeking'[39] by some providers making money out of offsets but not actually reducing overall emissions.

---

[36] www.carbonneutral.com.
[37] www.carbonfund.org.
[38] The VCS was founded by the Climate Group, the International Emissions Trading Association (IETA) and the World Business Council for Sustainable Development.
[39] Rent seeking occurs when a person or business obtains an economic gain from others without creating any wealth for society.

Businesses such as airlines sometimes offer us the ability to offset the greenhouse gas emissions that we may produce from using their products or services. This is usually done by effectively selling us carbon offsets to become 'carbon neutral'. The business will usually buy these offsets from one or more of the many services providers. Given the variation in the quality of these providers, we might be wise to satisfy ourselves that the offsets we have bought will really make us carbon neutral.

Some critics object to carbon offsets because it allows businesses to continue to produce emissions and many have questioned the benefits of certain types of offsets, such as tree planting. Critics also argue that businesses are offsetting emissions released now against emissions reductions some time in the future — in the case of tree planting, a long time in the future.

Are all Offsetting Projects Equal?

As discussed in the previous section, there are not yet any universal standards that can be applied to offset projects. To be high quality, projects need to meet the criteria we discussed earlier. Some governments offer accreditation for projects in their own country. So if this is available we should ensure that any project we 'invest' in is accredited.

Renewable energy projects usually involve building new energy generation plants that use wind, solar, biomass or possibly geothermal and hydro energy sources. We can only consider them to be high quality projects if these plants would not have been built without the offset scheme. This is usually because the present cost differential between renewable and fossil-fuel energy sources in generating electricity (see Chapter 1) makes them uneconomic without some form of subsidy. Renewable energy projects are generally long-term replacements for fossil fuels. The resulting emissions reduction from replacing the fossil-fuel energy delivers the carbon offset. The offset value diminishes, however, if the projects would have been built anyway as renewables become more cost competitive.

Energy efficiency offset projects have the advantage over others in that they actually reduce the total amount of energy that we use. An offset project that upgrades an older building to be more energy efficient is a very productive way to spend our offset dollars providing that building would not have been upgraded otherwise. The resulting emissions reduction from the energy saved generates the carbon offset. The accuracy of the saving may be difficult to verify and the saving may change over time as energy use changes.

Methane capture projects generally burn methane collected from landfills, industrial processes and farm animals to produce electricity or heat. Methane is a very potent greenhouse gas, so burning it can significantly reduce greenhouse gas emissions (see Chapter 10). As with renewable energy projects, methane capture projects have to be new projects that would not have happened without the offset scheme.

Forestry projects differ from the others because they actually soak up the carbon dioxide rather than prevent it being released. Reforestation projects are controversial because fires and tree death can return the carbon dioxide back into the environment which may compromise the permanent nature of the emissions reductions. It can also be difficult to accurately measure the amount of carbon dioxide soaked up by forestry projects. For example, once trees mature they remove carbon dioxide more slowly so the emissions offset value declines with time. Clearly forests grown for firewood are not going to be high quality offset projects as they are likely to be short lived and, once burned, return all the carbon dioxide back into the atmosphere. Likewise the forests grown for producing paper pulp are going to be relatively short lived as the paper products will soon finish up in landfill where they can release the carbon dioxide. Against that, timber grown for making long-lived wooden products like flooring, furniture or building timber will lock away the carbon for decades.

One of the most interesting prospects for offsets is to reduce carbon dioxide emissions in developing countries that do not have an emissions trading system. We have already discussed renewable energy projects which could be built in developing countries, but even technologies like IGCC and CCS (see Chapter 14) installed at coal-fired power stations could be considered as valuable offset schemes if the technology would not have been used without the outside investment. This could be one of the largest investment opportunities over the next few decades.

How Else Could Governments Provide Other Inducements to Reduce Emissions?

Carbon trading and taxing schemes are both likely to produce additional revenue for governments. Given that the aim of these schemes is to mitigate climate change, it would be wise for governments to invest this money in areas that will assist this process. Some possible areas could include:

- increasing investment in research and development and pre-commercial demonstration of low-emissions technologies,
- encouraging the use of energy efficiency measures,
- funding cooperative action on climate change with developing countries, or
- reducing other taxes to assist any business or person financially burdened by the emissions scheme.

Much of the cost from reducing emissions will ultimately be borne by households. We will face higher prices for electricity, gas, petrol and other carbon-intensive products. For example, the EU scheme could increase household electricity bills by 10–15%.[67] The impact on low-income households, in particular, may lead government to consider ways in which households might be assisted. We can, of course, reduce the impact of these higher prices by reducing our total consumption or, in the case of electricity, switching usage to low tariff times of day both of which will directly reduce emissions.

Any inducements to reduce emissions need to be made with care. There is a place for governments to provide incentives to encourage low-carbon solutions, but these solutions are generally technological in nature and governments are not necessarily the best at picking winning technologies. Subsidies for particular solutions will likely go to those with the greatest lobbying power, not the best solutions, and subsidies don't tend to encourage reduction in energy demand.

Regulation can be used as a big-stick inducement. Mandatory emissions targets can be set for particular industries. Mandatory targets can be set for renewable energy sources. This seems particularly popular in some countries to ensure that a certain percentage of electricity comes from renewable sources. Such regulations, which can be appealing to particular lobby groups, are likely to be high cost rather than least cost approaches to addressing the climate change problem. On the other hand, regulations and consumer information concerning building energy efficiency or motor vehicle fuel consumption might be the best approach to addressing the energy demand issue.

Addressing climate change is a risk management issue on a global scale. While there are costs in acting now, the consequences of inaction (more severe climate change) are potentially large for many countries. To reduce greenhouse gas emissions we need to shift from high-carbon to low-carbon goods and services. Given the potential for significantly higher costs from climate change in the future, the best risk management approach is to take steps now to reduce emissions rather than do so later.

17 — The Price We Have to Pay

The changing climate for energy will impact energy prices. Both peak oil and global warming are likely to increase prices. The new technologies we discussed will not decrease prices but should minimise the increases. The politics could go either way as the quest for votes often overrides good economic management, but the best of management probably can't avoid some increase to prices.

In this chapter we will look at possible net cost increases for energy from a combination of peak oil, our desire to address climate change and the way industry and governments set about dealing with it all.

What Will Be the Cost of Peak Oil?
This question will be impacted by when the demand for oil outstrips the availability of supply. As we saw in Chapter 12, there is no consensus on this. The UK *Times* in January 2008 reported that in an email to staff, the Chief Executive Office of Shell, the second largest oil company, told staff that supplies of easy-to-access oil and gas will no longer keep up with demand after 2015.[68] (This is conventional oil and does not include unconventional sources such as oil sands.) As a result, society has no choice but to add other sources of energy such as renewables, more nuclear power and unconventional fossil fuels. Using more fossil-fuel energy inevitably means emitting more carbon dioxide at a time when climate change has become a critical global issue.

The Shell CEO also sets out two scenarios for the world's energy future.[69] The first scenario envisages a free-for-all for energy resources
around the world with a mad dash by nations to secure resources leaving both winners and losers. The alternative scenario envisages a world
of political cooperation between governments and industry on efficiency standards, taxes and the environment and a convergence of policies
on emissions trading.

These Shell scenarios are just two of many and probably express two
extremes. The first scenario will initially minimise the impact on those
countries that have adequate energy resources but could be devastating
for those that don't, with prices for imported fossil fuels, particularly
oil and gas, rising sharply. This is already happening. Supplies of oil
and gas will eventually run short for everyone unless consumption is
curtailed and the looming threat of climate change will still need to be
addressed.

The alternative scenario is more attractive, will spread the cost pain
around and deal with climate change early on. Shell's alternative scenario assumes that carbon dioxide is captured at 90 per cent of coal and
gas power plants (using CCS) in developed countries by 2050, plus at
least 50% of those in the developing world. Shell recognises that this
will be hard work and there is little time.

Rising oil prices from the shortage of conventional oil and the higher
cost of extracting unconventional oil (see Chapter 12) will push up
transport fuel prices. At some point this will drive us to buy electric or
hydrogen cars. Both these require significantly greater use of electricity (as much as 50% greater) to charge the batteries and produce the
hydrogen. Hydrogen can be made from natural gas but that too will
peak at some point and it may be more efficient to use the natural gas
to run the cars directly. In many countries, generating more electricity
to replace motor fuels means using more coal. If we are to reduce greenhouse gas emissions and use more coal then we need carbon capture
and storage (CCS) which could add 70% to the generating cost for
coal-fired power stations (see Chapter 14). Nuclear power and electricity generated from wind might be a bit cheaper in some countries but
increases in electricity prices are inevitable.

The impact of rising crude oil costs on petrol pump prices depends

on the refining and transport costs and, in particular, local fuel taxes. In Europe, fuel taxes range from 50% to 65% of the pump price.
In the US, fuel tax is only 13% of the pump price so the impact of
crude oil costs on the price is likely to be much higher in the US
than in Europe. According to the IEA, over the year 2007, crude
oil prices rose 44% while petrol prices in the US rose 33%, in the
UK 15% and in Germany 10%. The weighted average increase for
petrol prices across eight major developed countries on 2007 was
29%.[15] Other transport fuel prices such as diesel have risen by
similar amounts.

The cost impact isn't just in transport fuel prices — it would be across
the whole economy. Fuel costs impact the price we pay for many of our
goods, particularly food, that are transported by road, diesel rail, air
or ship. As we discussed briefly in Chapter 12, oil is widely used in
industrial processes. Products made in part from oil appear in many of
the goods and food products we buy. Oil prices have long been a key
determinant of global economic performance.

Over the last century, the development and lifestyle of most of the
developed world has been shaped by the availability of low cost energy,
oil in particular. Over the past 50 years, world economic performance
has been negatively impacted by periods of increased oil prices as in
the oil shocks of 1973 and 1980 (see Chapter 15). According to the
Hirsh Report into the impacts of peak oil in the US, each 50% sustained increase in the price of oil will lower US GDP by 0.5%.[70] A
sustained increase in crude oil prices could have a significant impact
on world GDP unless we can mitigate the impact by greater efficiency
in oil consumption and switching to alternative sources for transport
fuels and industrial usage.

What Will Be the Cost of Climate Change?
Climate change really has two distinct cost components. The first is
the cost of mitigation. This is the cost of minimising the long-term
impact of climate change by reducing greenhouse gas emissions. The
second component is the actual cost of the adaptation needed to help
human and natural systems to adjust to rising temperatures, sea levels
and extreme weather patterns (see Chapter 15). The cost of mitigation

is reasonably well understood and can be quantified. The cost of adaptation is less certain.

Saving the cost of mitigation, in other words ignoring climate change, is likely to do far more damage to economic growth in the long term than tackling the problem now. Both the IPCC and Stern tell us that climate change presents very serious global risks with potentially severe, and expensive, consequences in the future.

Stern in particular believes that our inaction over the next few decades could seriously disrupt economic and social activity later in this century and finish up costing us significantly more than if we had dealt with the problem sooner rather than later. For example, the risks of severe weather events (storms, hurricanes, typhoons, floods, droughts and heat waves) will increase rapidly at higher temperatures. Stern estimates that the cost of extreme weather alone could reach 0.5–1% of world GDP per year by the middle of this century.

Stern goes on further to estimate the total cost of climate change over the next two centuries from continuing business-as-usual greenhouse gas emissions is equivalent to an average reduction of at least 5% in global consumption per head, now and forever.[47] There are some economists such as William Nordhaus who question some of the modelling assumptions made by Stern and disagree with his estimates.[71]

To address climate change we need both mitigation and adaptation. Climate change is probably inevitable whatever we spend on mitigation, so we will be forced to invest, to some degree, in adaptation and we will have to pay for both. However, the more successful we are at reducing greenhouse gas emissions, the less we should need to spend on adaptation such as water resource management, coastal protection, building and infrastructure protection and crises and disaster management.

If we fail to do enough to reduce emissions, and temperatures start to rise much higher, then the cost of adaptation to buildings and infrastructure could rise sharply. Much of the risk of climate change can be reduced through a strong mitigation policy and the cost of mitigation is likely to be far lower than the cost of the impacts, so mitigation is actually highly productive. Some economists argue that the most cost effective way to slow climate change is to reduce emissions slowly in the near term while the low-carbon technologies are being developed, followed by sharp reductions in the medium to longer term when the technologies are proven.[71]

In Chapter 13 we discussed stabilising greenhouse gas levels at 550ppm CO_2-e as probably the most realistic target. Both the IPCC and Stern estimated that stabilising at this level will cost around 1% of annual global GDP by 2050 with a range that could be slightly negative (that is, a small net gain) to 4% depending on the assumptions made. A cost of around 1% of GDP is small relative to the costs and risks of climate change that will be avoided.

Both the IPCC and Stern also looked at the social cost of carbon (SCC), which is the marginal damage caused by an additional tonne of carbon dioxide emissions. This social cost is likely to increase over time because the environmental damage increases with the amount of greenhouse gas in the atmosphere which will increase with time.

Stern suggests that the social cost of carbon today is $85 per tonne of CO_2-e if no mitigation was made. However, if mitigation was made to sta-bilise concentrations at around 550ppm the social cost of carbon would start at $25-30 per tonne. The IPCC estimates the social cost of carbon at $12 per tonne of CO_2-e based on a range of estimates that went from -$3 to $95.[46] In Chapter 16 we discussed carbon trading and taxing where a price is set on emissions.[40] The optimal carbon price is the price that bal-ances the incremental costs of reducing emissions against the incremental benefits of reducing climate change. So ideally the price of an emissions permit or a carbon tax should be related to the SCC.

What Will We Need to Pay for all the New Technology to Help Reduce Emissions?

Table 7 in Chapter 14 identified the cost impact of some of the new technologies we discussed in that chapter. These technologies are all still in development phase and basically fall into three groups: low-car-bon electricity generation, grid electricity storage and alternative fuels for motor vehicles. All of these technologies are likely to be more ex-pensive than currently used technology.

---

[40] A quick word of caution here. Sometime SCC is quoted as cost per tonne of carbon not carbon diox-ide. To convert from a carbon cost to a carbon dioxide cost multiply by 12/44.

The low-carbon electricity generating technologies in order of likely generation cost are:

• Next generation nuclear power plants	$0.05/kWh–$0.09/kWh
• Carbon capture and storage (CCS)	$0.05/kWh–$0.10/kWh
• Concentrated solar power (CSP)	$0.08/kWh–$0.11/kWh
• Tidal and wave power	$0.45/kWh–$1.35/kWh

This compares with the cheapest, and most widely used, source of power which is coal-fired power without CCS at around $0.04/kWh–$0.06/kWh or the cheapest renewable source, wind power, at $0.05/kWh–$0.14/kWh. So we can expect an increase in our cost of electricity. For those countries which decide not to use nuclear power or CCS this could rise by 100% or a doubling of cost.

The developing grid storage technologies in order of likely storage cost are:

• Compressed air storage (CAES)	$0.02/kWh–$0.05/kWh
• Flow batteries	$0.05/kWh–$0.90/kWh
• Sodium-sulphur battery	$0.09/kWh–$0.30/kWh

Grid storage does not replace existing generation sources but improves the efficiency by storing low cost off-peak electricity so it can be used during peak periods (see Chapter 14). It is difficult to assess what the cost impact of storing electricity will have on the price we pay for our electricity. For example, wind power generation costs range from around $0.05/kWh to $0.14/kWh, depending the availability of wind. An electricity utility would only use these storage technologies where it would improve the capacity factor of the power station so storage may actually reduce the cost of low-carbon electricity from solar or wind.

The alternative fuels we discussed for motor vehicles were electricity and hydrogen. Hydrogen will require extensive refuelling infrastructure before it becomes widely commercially available. There are some hydrogen cars in use in California, where Honda is prepared to service and refuel them. It may be some time before we get a good understanding of their commercial viability and cost. The running cost for electric cars is likely to be cheaper than oil-based products. We will discuss this in Chapter 22 when we discuss the future of transport.

What Will a Price on Emissions Cost Us?
In Chapter 16 we looked at carbon trading and taxing and the need for a price on emissions which businesses will include in the prices of their goods and services. This price will eventually be paid by all of us. So how much can we expect to pay?

There are few emissions trading schemes in operation but they may give us an indication of what the carbon price might be. The Chicago Climate Exchange was trading at $4 per tonne of CO_2-e in February 2008. The European Energy Exchange started emissions trading in July 2005 at €20 ($24) per tonne of CO_2-e. By February 2006 it had risen to €30 ($36). It then fell over the next two years to €0.03 ($0.04). This substantial price drop in Europe was caused by over generous emissions caps in Phase I in some countries that minimised the need to reduce emissions and trade permits. A strong warning to future national trading schemes about getting the caps right. This was addressed in Europe in the second phase, started in January 2008. In August 2008 trading was back up at €23 ($34).

Another place to look for emissions prices is carbon offset schemes. These vary significantly from around $7 per tonne of CO_2-e to $36 with an average around $19.

The IPCC indicated that a carbon price in the range $20–50 by 2020–2030 would deliver deep emissions reductions by mid-century consistent with stabilising the concentration of greenhouse gases at around 550ppm CO_2-e, which was the target we discussed earlier in Chapter 13.[72]

When we looked at the cost of climate change we said that the emissions price should be related to the social cost of carbon. The IPCC estimated the SCC at $12 and Stern put it at $25–30, assuming a mitigation strategy was in place. So we can probably expect the price on emissions to be in the range $10–30 to stabilise at 550ppm. To stabilise at 450ppm would require the price to be much higher — possibly over $100 (see Chapter 18).

In Part One we identified the emissions intensity of various fuels, that is, kilograms of emissions per unit of energy generated or used. If we convert this to a dollar cost we can start to see the likely impact on our energy bills if the full emissions cost is passed to the customer.

Table 8 sets out the emissions intensities for major fuel sources and calculates the impact on average domestic fuel bills based on a $20 emissions cost per tonne of CO_2-e. The fuel costs vary significantly around the world and the numbers shown are simple averages, which may be very different from what we actually pay in our own country.

At $20 a tonne, the actual increases to our fuel bills will be relatively small except for electricity generated from coal and oil. This is to be expected as these fuels are the biggest producers of greenhouse gas emissions. In Chapter 14 we noted that the IPCC estimated the cost of carbon capture and storage (CCS) for a coal-fired power station without enhanced oil recovery at $30–70 per tonne of carbon dioxide avoided. If this estimate is correct, an emissions price of $20 per tonne is unlikely to encourage coal electricity generators to install CCS technology when it would be cheaper to buy permits. This may mean that the initial emissions price needs to be much higher than $20, which would make the fuel price increases proportionately greater.

Table 8

Impact of Emissions Price on Energy Costs

Fuel Source	Emissions Intensity	Emissions Cost at $20 per tonne of CO_2-e	Impact on Average Fuel Bill
Electricity:	kg CO_2-e/kWh	Per kWh	@$0.16/kWh
Coal-fired	1.1	$0.022	+14%
Oil-fired	0.8	$0.016	+10%
Natural gas	0.5	$0.010	+6%
Current world average	0.6	$0.012	+8%
Nuclear	< 0.1	<$0.002	+<1%
Wind	< 0.1	<$0.002	+<1%
Solar	0.2	$0.002	+1%
Hydro	< 0.2	<$0.002	+<1%
Heating and cooking:	kg CO_2-e/MJ	Per MJ	@$0.02/MJ
Natural gas	0.052	$0.0010	+5%
LPG	0.068	$0.0014	+7%
Transport fuel:	kg CO_2-e/litre	Per Litre	@$1.50/litre
Petrol (gasoline)	2.35	$0.047	+3%
Diesel	2.68	$0.054	+4%
LPG	1.53	$0.031	+2%
Jet fuel	2.53	$0.051	+3%

Part Three
The Future of Energy

So far in Part One and Part Two we have looked at energy and the impact of changes in the world. Our human history has gone from using only renewable energy resources to primarily using non-renewable resources (mainly fossil fuels) which must eventually run out. When they do run out, we will have to revert to renewables. We will go from renewables to renewables in 15 generations.

Making long range future predictions is always problematic but crude oil will probably go from being our principal primary energy source to probably being a relatively minor contributor to our energy mix by the end of the 21st century. Natural gas may last a little longer, but not much. Even coal and uranium will probably run out within a couple of centuries — a relatively short time in the history of man. Times they are a-changin'![41]

But it isn't just the demise of non-renewable energy resources that we need to worry about. Burning all those fossil fuels for over 250 years may well have done some serious damage to our atmosphere, causing it to trap too much heat near the Earth's surface and potentially causing serious climate change. We need to reduce the greenhouse gases emitted from energy usage if we are to minimise this damage. This means changing the way we generate and use electricity, how we fuel

[41] With apologies to Bob Dylan

our vehicles and how we heat and cool our buildings and power our factories.

We have to do all this in a world of ever growing population and the very reasonable desire by the poorer countries to enjoy the standard of living of the more wealthy. Historically there has been a strong relationship between gross domestic product (GDP) and energy use, so more people and a higher average standard of living has meant using more energy, not less.

The challenge ahead is to reduce greenhouse gas emissions to minimise harm to the environment, while at the same time not adversely affecting our standard of living or those of our neighbours. We need affordable energy for everyone. We also need energy security for everyone. This means a range of energy sources with minimal emissions.

So what is the roadmap to get us there? We will aim to answer this question in this final part of the book.

18 — What's Needed to Save the Planet?

We are fairly certain that we need to reduce greenhouse gas emissions if we are to minimise the harm from climate change. The questions we aim to answer in this chapter are: how much do we need to reduce them? ... by when? ... and what are the implications for our energy generation and usage?

This is a relatively complex chapter with many calculations. Some may be happy to just have a summary of the findings without ploughing through all the reasoning so here it is:

- To stabilise greenhouse gas emissions at the level of 550ppm discussed in Chapter 13 we will need to reduce worldwide energy emissions in 2030 by 20–25% below the forecast business-as-usual (BAU) level. This is a reduction of between 9 and 12 billion tonnes of emissions. The 2030 energy emissions will still be about 20–30% above the 2000 level but trending down. This should be possible at a carbon price somewhere between $20 and $50 per tonne. This will be the roadmap we will follow for the rest of this book.

- The roadmap does not demand a slowing of world population growth or GDP. The reductions in energy emissions will come from improved efficiency and switching to low-carbon energy sources not from significant social change.

- The burden of energy emissions reductions will fall on the OECD countries. We can expect that the developing world will actually *increase* emissions by 2030 so the cuts in the developed world will need to be deeper, to levels 30% below their 2000 level.

- If we want to stabilise at 450ppm we will need to cut the BAU level in 2030 by almost 60%. This will require a carbon price above $100 and substantially increase fuel prices which could be very damaging financially.

For those of you who would like to understand how we got to these conclusions — read on.

What Kind of Reduction Are We Actually Talking About?

In Chapter 13 we discussed the need to stabilise the concentration of greenhouse gases in the atmosphere to manage climate change. Stabilising means reducing the amount of new greenhouse gas emissions we are releasing into the atmosphere.

We suggested that we need to stabilise the concentration of greenhouse gases at 550ppm CO_2-e to manage climate change. This would still lift the average global temperature by around 3°C above pre-industrial levels and sea level will eventually rise more than 0.6 metres. Not ideal, and some would argue potentially catastrophic.

The cost of reducing greenhouse gas emissions is significant and the lower the level of concentration, the greater the reductions will need to be. The greater the reduction, the greater the cost. The quicker the reduction, the greater the cost because not all the technology we need is in place today but could be within the next few decades.

To stabilise at 550ppm, the IPCC estimated we would have to peak worldwide emissions between 2010 and 2030 and reduce emissions to up to 30% below the 2000 level by 2050.[46] The emissions levels would also need to be trending downward. This is in contrast to today, where they are still trending upwards (see Figure 4 in Chapter 13).

According to the World Resource Institute (WRI)[2], the level of total annual emissions in 2000 was about 44 billion tonnes of CO_2-e and energy contributed about 28 billion tonnes or 63% to the total (see Table 6 in Chapter 13). A 30% reduction below this level means reducing total emissions to 31 tonnes and energy emissions to 19.5 billion tonnes a year by 2050. Currently world energy emissions are growing at an average of 0.5 billion tonnes or about 2% a year.

So now we know what the 2050 target is for emissions — how do we get there? To answer that question we need to know how to reduce emissions while recognising the growing population and the demand for increasing GDP.

Where Will the Energy Emissions Reductions Come From?

There are basically two ways we can reduce energy emissions. The first way, and probably the cheapest and quickest to implement, is to improve energy efficiency so we actually use less primary energy to get the same or a similar result. Less energy used means fewer emissions produced. The greatest energy savings can be made in buildings, followed by transport. The second way to reduce emissions, and generally more expensive and slower to implement, is to get our energy from low-carbon sources. Low-carbon sources also mean fewer carbon emissions.

The most likely places to find energy emissions reductions over the next few decades are show in Box 14. Many of these have already been discussed in some detail in Part One and Part Two of this book.

Box 14

Sources of Energy Emissions Reductions

1. Improving energy efficiency in buildings through improved heating and cooling, better insulation, low-energy lighting, more efficient appliances and improved building control systems.
2. Increasing efficiency in vehicles through fuel economy measures such as reducing the weight of light-duty vehicles, improved aerodynamics, more efficient engines and transmissions, more use of diesel for light-duty vehicles, switching from road transport to rail and public transport, and improved road vehicle operating efficiency through driver education.
3. Reducing the use of high-carbon fuels in vehicles by switching to hybrid or plug-in vehicles (assuming low-carbon electricity generation) or using biofuels.
4. Reducing carbon emissions in electricity generation by using more low-carbon primary energy sources such as nuclear, wind, solar and geothermal, switching from coal-fired to gas-fired, improving power plant efficiency and using CCS[a] technology.

[a] Carbon Capture and Storage — see Chapter 14.

How Much Emissions Reduction Can We Get From Each Source?

To help us here we will actually look at the reduction needed in the short to medium term (by 2030) rather than the long term (2050). This is because we have a much better idea about what technology is likely to be available in the short to medium term and the IPCC and the IEA can offer some insights on energy emissions reductions to 2030. If we are to minimise the damage from climate change then the greatest changes in energy use are needed over the next few decades, so looking at what is needed to meet the 2030 target will set the roadmap for the rest of the century. As this book is about energy, from now on we will just focus on the energy related emissions.

The IEA in its Outlook 2007 report[62] forecasts that in a business-as-usual (BAU) scenario the global energy related emissions will jump 57% from 2005 to 2030. BAU means no significant change to the way things are done today — behaviourally, technically, economically and in policy terms. Based on 2005 energy emissions of about 28.5 billion tonnes of CO_2-e,[42] then the BAU energy emissions in 2030 would be about 45 billion tonnes of CO_2-e. Compare this with our target of 19.5 billion tonnes needed by 2050 and we can start to see that substantial reductions are needed in energy emissions if we are to manage climate change. Business as usual is just not an option.

IEA forecasts that to be on track to stabilise greenhouse gases at 550ppm we need to reduce the BAU emissions in 2030 by 19%. This means a reduction in worldwide energy emissions of around 9 billion tonnes per year by 2030.

The IPCC believes that to be on track to stabilise greenhouse gases at 550ppm we need to peak around 2010–2030 and return to 2000 levels by 2040.[73] The 2000 level for energy emissions was 28 billion tonnes. To achieve this by 2040, energy emissions would probably need to be about 33 billion tonnes by 2030, which would require a reduction in energy emissions below BAU of around 12 billion tonnes per year by 2030.

We are probably looking for a reduction in energy emissions somewhere between IEA's estimate of 9 billion tonnes and the IPCC's estimate of 12 billion tonnes. So where will these reductions come from?

[42] This is an estimate for 2005 based on IEA projections for 2030. Note that the IEA uses CO_2 not CO_2-e. All figures used in this book are CO_2-e.

The IPCC has looked at the economic potential for reducing emissions in various sectors by 2030. An estimate was made for different carbon prices using what is called a 'bottom-up' analysis.[43] A summary of the range of possible reduction for energy emissions at carbon prices below $20, $50 and $100 is shown in Table 9. Emissions reduction from end-use electricity savings are allocated to energy supply. These electricity savings come largely from buildings but also from industry.

Table 9

Energy Emissions Reduction Potential by Sector

Energy Emissions Reduction Potential by 2030	Reduction (billion tonnes of CO_2-e per year)		
Carbon price per tonne CO_2-e	<$20	<$50	<$100
Energy supply	4.4–6.4	5.6–8.4	6.3–9.3
Transport	1.3–2.1	1.5–2.3	1.6–2.5
Buildings	1.9–2.3	1.9–2.3	2.3–2.9
Total	7.6–10.8	9.0–13.0	10.2–14.7
Electricity savings included in above	3.2–4.0	3.4–4.2	3.9–4.6

Source: **IPCC.[72]**

As we can see in the table the ranges are fairly broad (as are most ranges in the IPCC reports) but they indicate that our 9–12 billion tonnes energy emissions reduction target is likely to be possible at a carbon price somewhere between $20 and $50 per tonne.

The table also shows that about a third of the reductions can come from electricity savings through greater efficiency in buildings and industry. Electricity savings reduce the demand for electricity generation. These savings can be made at relatively low cost and we can expect these savings will be made first.

The IPCC estimated the amount of emissions reduction from electricity savings using the average emissions intensity[44] for the

---

[43] See Chapter 17 for a discussion on carbon prices. Bottom-up analysis in this context means considering reduction opportunities to derive an overall reduction potential.

[44] Emissions intensity is the amount of kilograms of CO_2-e per kWh — see Table 3 in Chapter 1..

expected electricity supply in 2030 (about 0.3 kg/kWh) which includes low-carbon sources such as renewables and nuclear. In reality, because these savings can be made early, they are more likely to reduce emissions from fossil-fuel power stations (about 0.6 kg/kWh) than from low-carbon electricity sources so these emissions reduction estimates from electricity savings may be very conservative.

What Does the Roadmap Mean for the World and GDP Growth?
We have already discussed the strong relationship between population, GDP and energy use in Chapter 15. The IEA in its World Energy Outlook 2004 report predicted population and GDP growth for the period to 2030.[74] Based on these growth rates, world population will rise 24% from 6.7 billion in 2007 to 8.3 billion in 2030. Most of this growth will be in the less developed regions where the population will rise from 5.4 billion to 6.9 billion (83% of the world).

World GDP growth is expected to be 3.2% per year to 2030. This will more than double world GDP from $48 trillion in 2006 to $100 trillion in 2030. In the two key developing countries of China and India, which represent 37% of the world population, the annual GDP growth is expected to be 5.0% for China and 4.7% for India — well above the global average.

In terms of energy demand, IEA predicts that by 2030 demand will have risen to 17.7 billion TOE,[62] a rise of 53% from 2006, so for every 1% increase in global GDP there will be a 0.5% increase in primary energy consumption. China and India alone will account for 45% of this increase. These IEA energy demand and growth figures are for business-as-usual (BAU) and do not take into account the energy saving measures we discussed earlier in this chapter. If we can reduce energy consumption by say 25% through greater efficiency (not reduction in services) then the energy demand in 2030 would fall to around 13 billion TOE. This is in line with what the IPCC believes will deliver the reduction potential shown in Table 9.

The roadmap does not demand a slowing of world population growth or GDP. The reductions in energy emissions will come from improved efficiency and switching to low-carbon energy sources not from significant social change.

The changes in energy growth and reductions in energy emissions will not be uniform across the whole world. We can probably expect that much of the developing world will actually *increase* energy emissions by 2030. Population and GDP growth in developing countries will drive up energy usage faster than improved efficiency and fuel switching can reduce emissions. This means the developed world (largely the OECD countries), which generates roughly 45% of world emissions, will need to shoulder the burden of reducing energy emissions and they will have to set much more aggressive emissions targets than might be implied by our 9–12 billion tonnes reduction target.

A 10 billion tonne worldwide reduction in energy emissions in 2030 will reduce energy emissions to 35 billion tonnes in that year. This is still 25% *higher* than 2000 energy emissions levels but lower than the expected peak around 2020 so the trend will be in the right direction — downwards.

The developed world will set targets that will actually reduce emissions levels in 2030 to below 2000 levels. If the developing world energy emissions grow 75% by 2030 (as seems likely) then OECD emissions would need to be reduced by 35% of the 2000 level to reach the 35 billion tonne target by 2030. The European Union (EU) is already planning to reduce its total greenhouse gas emissions by 20% from 1990 levels by 2020. The EU had already reduced emissions between 1990 and 2000.

What if We Need to Stabilise the Temperature at 2°C Rather Than 3°C?

There are many conservationists and members of the European Union (EU) who believe that a 3°C increase in average global temperature will create too much damage to the environment, so let's look at what kind of energy emissions reductions would be needed by 2030 to be on track to lower the temperature growth to just 2°C.

The IPCC tells us that to stabilise at 2°C above pre-industrial levels we would need to stabilise greenhouse gas concentration at 450ppm. This means peaking emissions before 2015 and reducing emissions to less than 50% of the 2000 level by 2050.[46] Based on the 2000 level of energy emissions of 28 billion tonnes, this would mean reducing energy worldwide emissions to less than 14 billion tonnes by 2050.

Bringing this back to 2030 to consider the reduction potential, the 2030 energy emissions target would need to be reduced from 35 billion tonnes to no more than 25 billion tonnes to stabilise greenhouse gases at 450ppm rather than 550ppm. BAU energy emissions for 2030 are 45 billion tonnes so we are seeking a total reduction in energy emissions of at least 20 billion tonnes.

When we now consider the reduction potential identified by the IPCC in Table 9 we see that the IPCC does not consider that such a reduction is possible by 2030 below a carbon price of $100 a tonne. A very high carbon price above $100 would significantly drive up the cost of energy — at least in the short term. At $100 a tonne our electricity bills will increase by over 60% for electricity largely coming from coal-fired power stations (see Table 8 in Chapter 17). We cannot just turn off our coal-fired power stations in the next few decades in most parts of the world without substantially impacting the reliability of our electricity grid, particularly in Australia where 80% of electricity comes from coal. Most of us will need to continue to use electricity largely generated from coal and we will pay a significant premium for it. This indicates the potentially severe economic implications of setting very aggressive short term targets for emissions reduction. A 60% increase in electricity doesn't just impact our energy bills. It impacts the cost of most of what we buy, from food to motor vehicles.

We are going to have to trade off some of the benefits from reducing climate change early against the costs associated with greater mitigation, particularly from early emissions reductions. It may still be possible to reduce 2050 emissions to less than 50% of the 2000 level if we make much more severe cuts in emissions after 2030, once we have the technology to do so and it is commercially available at the right price.

As we saw in Table 7 in Chapter 14, much of the technology we need to make deep cuts in emissions, without significantly disrupting the electricity supply, is yet to be proven commercially. Attempting to quickly stabilise at 450ppm is probably ambitious at best. To attempt to do this before the technology is available will be very expensive and potentially very damaging financially.

What Will Be the Impact on Energy Generation and Usage?

From what we have seen so far in this chapter, it should be possible to reduce our energy emissions by 9–12 billion tonnes by 2030 while still maintaining similar world population and GDP growth and without requiring massive changes in lifestyle or substantial increases in costs. Most importantly, this reduction will deliver the level of energy emissions we need to be on track to manage climate change although maybe not at the level possible below 450ppm stabilisation requested by many conservationists.

The emissions reductions will come from improved energy efficiency and low-carbon primary energy sources. Reducing the demand for electricity and reducing the demand for oil and gas for heating and transport fuel will improve energy efficiency. Low-carbon primary energy sources will come from energy substitution in electricity generation and energy switching in transport.

The IPCC suggests that, by 2030, 4.3 billion tonnes of emissions reductions can come from electricity savings and a further 4.7 billion tonnes from energy substitution in electricity generation.[72] If these IPCC estimates are correct, two-thirds of our 12 billion tonnes target can come from the electricity sector alone, depending on the carbon price. Further savings from transport and heating in buildings will make up the difference. We will discuss how this can be done over the next few chapters.

19 — Getting More From Less

Energy efficiency is about getting more from less. Using less energy to get the same outcome. Energy efficiency does not necessarily mean less total demand for energy but it helps slow down the growth in energy demand.

The cost of energy savings is the difference between what we have to invest in a new energy-efficient product such as new lighting or appliances and the savings we can make on our energy bills over the life of the investment. Sometimes this will be a negative cost — in other words a true financial saving.

How Do We Calculate the Cost of Reducing Energy Emissions?
For any emissions reduction opportunity it is possible to work out the cost of that opportunity and how much greenhouse gas emissions can be saved. From this we can work out the cost (or savings) per tonne of emissions to make the reductions. In Box 15 we look at a worked example for the compact fluorescent lamp we discussed in Chapter 1.

Similar analysis has been performed by Enkvist, Naucler and Rosander from McKinsey in Stockholm[75] for emissions reduction opportunities by 2030. McKinsey's assessment of the total worldwide emissions reduction potential is generally higher than the IPCC estimates that we showed in Table 9 in Chapter 18 but it offers an insight into the cost effectiveness of each opportunity. McKinsey believes

Box 15

Worked Example of Energy Emissions Reduction Savings

1. A 25W compact fluorescent lamp (CFL) might cost $5 more than a 100W incandescent lamp that it replaces. At an electricity cost of 16 cents a kWh we can save 1.2 cents in electricity every hour we use the CFL (75W at 16¢/kWh).

2. Once we have used the CFL for 420 hours it has paid for itself and starts to save us money. If the CFL lasts 6000 hours then it would save us $67 ($72 in electricity less $5 lamp cost) over its lifetime.

3. It also reduces electricity usage by 450 kWh over its lifetime (75W for 6,000 hours), which in turn reduces energy emissions by about 0.27 tonnes at an average emissions intensity of 0.6kg/kWh.

4. In this example the real cost of reducing emissions from electricity generation by using more efficient lighting is minus $248 per tonne ($67 saving divided by 0.27 tonnes emissions avoided) over the life of the lamp.

5. If the lamp is used for six hours a day and lasts for 6,000 hours it will last for 2.7 years (1,000 days). The annual saving from reducing emissions is therefore $91 per tonne ($248 over 2.7 years).

almost three-quarters of the potential to reduce emissions comes from measures that are either independent of technology or rely on mature rather than new technologies. We will only consider the energy related opportunities here.

Where Are the Opportunities to Get More From Less?
Throughout this book we have discussed many ways to reduce energy use in our homes, workplaces and when we are on the road. The big savings — more than half — can be made in improved building insulation and using more energy-efficient lighting and appliances. Improved motor vehicle design can improve fuel economy, as can driver education.

McKinsey estimates that nearly one-quarter of the total emissions reduction potential can come from using less energy through improving energy efficiency. Table 10 shows the major measures that can be taken to save energy in order of potential financial savings. This means the ones highest on the list deliver the best financial return and logically should be done first. The potential energy emissions reduction by 2030 from using less energy is over 5 billion tonnes. This gets us well on our way to our target for reducing energy emissions by 9–12 tonnes by 2030.

Table 10

Opportunities to Reduce Emissions With Potential Savings

Opportunity to Reduce Emissions From Saving Energy	Potential Emissions Reduction (billion tonnes of CO_2-e per year)	Potential Savings From Reduction (US$/tonne [a])
Building insulation	1.3	$210–$150
Fuel economy in commercial vehicles	0.5	$120
Building lighting and appliances	1.1	$115–$100
Building air-conditioning	0.4	$100
Water heating	0.6	$75–$65
Fuel economy in light vehicles	0.6	$40
Standby power	0.3	$15
Industrial energy efficiency	0.6	$0
Total potential reduction	**5.4**	

[a] Converted from Euro @ 1 Euro = 1.3 US$ December 2006.   *Source:* McKinsey[75]

If These Energy Savings Come at Negative Cost, Then Why Aren't We Doing Them Already?

Many of these savings are related to buildings and transport. These financial savings can be made with or without climate change or a price on carbon as they all yield a net positive saving in the same way our compact fluorescent lamp example did in Box 15. Most of these savings can be made with current technology. The key question is why aren't these savings being made already? What are the barriers that are preventing what would seem to be a rational decision to reduce energy use and save money?

One of the barriers is that often the person who pays the cost for the savings investment doesn't receive the benefit from the resulting energy savings. For example, the house builder has little incentive to provide all the best energy saving fittings and appliances if they are going to make the building more costly and the builder isn't going to be paying the future energy bills. Another barrier is that some of these savings accrue over a significant period — say 10 to 15 years for solar PV panels. The home owner may not intend to stay in the home long enough to get the return.

The same problem arises with motor vehicle efficiency. Until fuel economy becomes an important customer purchasing decision, the vehicle manufacturers have little incentive to improve vehicle designs as they don't pay the fuel bills. Most manufacturers do provide some energy-efficient vehicles in their fleet to meet market demand, but until the price of oil rises substantially customer preference will not be sufficient to realise all the potential savings unless we introduce efficiency regulations.

How Do We Maximise Energy Efficiency in the Future?

Many countries already recognise these barriers to maximising efficiency and regulate energy efficiency for new buildings and new motor vehicles. This means that the house builder and vehicle manufacturer have no choice but to build in the efficiency upfront. This only addresses the new housing or vehicle market. Vehicles have a 12–20 year life and buildings a 50 year life, so much of the potential savings will be in existing buildings and motor vehicles. It will take time to realise the benefits in existing buildings and vehicles unless the governments legislate to have the efficiency measures retrofitted or the energy prices increase sufficiently that the payback period for the user becomes much shorter.

Peak oil and carbon pricing are expected to drive up the price of transport fuels and the cost of electricity. Higher fuel prices reduce payback periods and provide greater incentive for energy efficiency. If the carbon price rises to $50 then electricity cost could rise 30%, which would reduce the payback period by 30%.

By 2030, most of the fleet of existing motor vehicles will have been replaced. The sooner we legislate for better transport fuel economy the more confident we can be about getting the full emissions reduction potential from this source. We discussed in Chapter 15 that the European Union was planning to set an emissions target of less than 130g of CO_2 per km for manufacturers' car fleets. Given that many cars on the road today emit almost twice this amount we can see why there is significant emissions reduction potential in the transport sector at a real financial saving.

20 — Energy Without Carbon

Reducing the emissions from energy is largely about switching to low-carbon energy sources. In some cases this will be a switch in primary energy source, such as from coal to nuclear power. It can also come from improving technology such as using carbon capture and storage (CCS) with coal or gas.

How Do We Calculate the Cost of Reducing the Emissions by Decarbonising?

All the opportunities to reduce energy emissions by decarbonising require some capital investment. In most cases it requires a considerable investment in new plant and equipment, such as building a new wind farm. The cost to reduce emissions is the additional cost of producing the energy with this zero or low-emissions technology instead of the cheaper fossil-fuel-based power production it would replace. Typically, low-carbon technologies will only be introduced when new capacity is required or to replace retiring plants. A worked example of building new wind farms rather than a coal-fired power station is shown in Box 16.

Table 11 shows a number of opportunities from McKinsey[75] for reducing energy emissions by 2030 at a cost of $50 per tonne or less. Most of these (6 billion tonnes) are in electricity power generation of which half involve using CCS which will probably not be commercially

Box 16

Worked Example of the Cost of Reducing Emissions by Decarbonising

1. To reduce the emissions from electricity generation it is necessary to build a new zero or low emissions plant rather than a traditional high emissions plant. The cost to reduce emissions is the additional cost of the low-emissions technology over the cheaper high-emissions technology. Let's take the example of building new wind farms instead of a new modern generation coal-fired power station.

2. A 2005 IEA study on the cost of generating electricity determined that a typical levelised[a] cost of electricity from a new coal plant at a discount rate of 10% is around $50/MWh.[8]

3. The comparable cost from a new wind farm is $70/MWh or $20/MWh more than for the coal plant.

4. From Table 3 in Chapter 1, the new generation coal plant without CCS will produce 0.8 kg/kWh or 0.8 tonnes/MWh of emissions and we will assume the wind farm produces no emissions.

5. The real cost of reducing emissions by using wind farms in this example is therefore $25 per tonne ($20 per MWh additional cost divided by 0.8 tonnes/MWh reduction).

[a] Levelised cost is the present value of the total cost of building and operating a generating plant over its economic life, converted to a cost per MWh generated during that life.

Table 11

Opportunities to Reduce Emissions From Decarbonising Energy

	Potential Emissions Reduction (billion tonnes of CO_2-e per year)	Potential Reduction Cost (US$/tonne[a]; figures in brackets are negative costs)
Ethanol	0.3	($15)
Nuclear power	1.1	$0–$5
CCS with enhanced oil recovery, new coal	0.6	$20
Renewables for power	1.4	$25
Industrial biofuel switching	0.6	$25
CCS, new coal	1.6	$35
Industrial motor systems	1.3	$45
CCS, coal refit	0.9	$50
Others for power (eg coal-to-gas shift)	0.4	$50
Biodiesel	0.3	$50
Total potential reduction	**8.5**	

[a] Converted from Euro @ 1 Euro = 1.3 US$ December 2006.

Source: McKinsey[75]

available until 2015. McKinsey has assumed that 17% of the world's electricity generation will use CCS by 2030 from zero today. This compares with the IPCC which assumes that only 8% will come from CCS by 2030. We discuss electricity generation in more detail in the next chapter.

Where Are the Opportunities to Generate Low-Carbon Energy?
McKinsey expects that most of the opportunities (70%) are in the electricity generation sector. A further 23% can be found in industrial processes and a relatively small 7% in switching transport fuels from petroleum-based products to ethanol and biodiesel.

McKinsey found that some 70% of the total potential reductions (not just energy) would not depend on any major technology developments, suggesting that low-tech solutions will be the main source of reductions up to 2030.

21 — What Next for the Watt?

With global warming and peak oil the 'watt's' future is looking pretty bright! Changes in electricity usage and supply can make a substantial contribution to addressing global warming. As oil runs out, we will be forced to find other ways to power our vehicles and electricity will pay a big part. What will change for electricity is the fuel technology that drives the generators, and that's what we will discuss in this chapter.

What Have We Learned so far About the Future for Electricity?

Most of the easy reductions in greenhouse gas emissions can be made from improving the ways we use electricity. We saw in Chapter 19 that we can save over 3 billion tonnes of emissions by using less electricity with better building insulation, more efficient lighting and appliances, improved building cooling and water heating and using less standby power. All these changes will have little or no impact on our way of life and can be done using available technology. What's more, we can do it with a real cost saving.

More challenging, but with greater potential to reduce emissions, we can change the way we generate some of our electricity. We saw in Chapter 20 that we can save up to 6 billion tonnes of emissions by using different primary energy sources such as nuclear power and renewables and decarbonising fossil fuels using CCS. Some of these can be done with existing technology but require significant additional investment in new plant.

How Will the Electricity Generation Energy Mix Change by 2030?
Today electricity is mostly generated from fossil fuels (about two-thirds of it). This makes electricity generation the biggest single contributor to total greenhouse gas emissions. Large-scale power stations have a long life, between 30 and 100 years, so many of the existing fossil-fuel plants will still be operating in 2030. As these plants reach the end of their useful life they will need replacing. If the world moves towards setting a price on carbon then the electricity generating industry will look towards switching to newer low emissions technologies. At the same time, there could be a switch to more distributed or decentralised generation (DG) using smaller scale distributed energy plants with local energy resources (such as wind, solar or biomass) and cogeneration for both electricity and heat (CHP).

In Table 12 we look at how the energy mix might change by 2030. We consider two scenarios from the IPCC and the one from McKinsey used in the previous chapters. We also compare them with the actual primary energy mix in 2004.

Table 12
Electricity Generation Primary Energy Mix to 2030

Electricity Mix From	2004	2030		
Primary Energy Source	Actual[4]	BAU[72]	IPCC[72]	McKinsey[75]
Coal	41%	39%	21%	11%[a]
Gas and oil	25%	33%	19%	19%[a]
Nuclear	16%	9%	18%	21%
Renewables (hydro, wind, solar, bio)	18%	19%	34%	32%
Coal with CCS	0%	0%	8%	17%
Electricity generation (billion kWh)	16,424	31,656	23,295	23,000[a]
Emissions (billion tonnes CO_2-e)	9.7	15.8	6.8	7.2
Emissions intensity (kg/ kWh)	0.6	0.5	0.3	0.3

[a] Author's estimates.   *Sources:* US DOE/EIA, IPCC and McKinsey.

The first scenario is the business-as-usual (BAU) case from the IPCC where we continue to use and expand our electricity generation capacity in much the way we do today. This means we get none of the savings we discussed in Chapter 19 and we make minimal switch away from carbon intensive energy sources other than using more efficient gas turbines and more gas. In the BAU scenario total electricity generation almost doubles from 2004 to 2030 and energy emissions from electricity generation increase by 6.1 billion tonnes.

The second IPCC scenario takes the BAU case and applies a 26% reduction in electricity demand from improved energy efficiency. Getting more from less by using many of the opportunities identified in Table 10 in Chapter 19. It also reduces the emissions intensity of electricity generation by half by using more nuclear, more renewables and applying CCS to a portion of the coal generation. This scenario assumes that total electricity generation will increase by 42% from 2004 but, at the same time, eliminates 9 billion tonnes of emissions below the BAU level. That is almost enough from electricity alone to meet our target of reducing energy emissions by 9–12 billion tonnes to stabilise greenhouse gases at 550ppm.

The table also shows the McKinsey estimates for 2030 as a comparison with the IPCC second scenario. The most obvious difference is the proportion of energy that will come from coal using CCS. McKinsey believes that twice as much electricity will be generated in power stations using CCS than does the IPCC. McKinsey started with a higher BAU emissions level for the power sector of 16.8 billion tonnes rather than the IPCC's value of 15.8 billion tonnes so the potential reduction in the McKinsey case is actually 9.6 billion tonnes, 0.6 billion higher than the IPCC.

Table 13

Electricity Generation 2004 to 2030

Electricity Generation (billion kWh)	2004 Actual[4]	2030 IPCC[72]	Change
Coal	6,734	4,918	-27%
Gas	3,231	3,813	18%
Oil	781	698	-11%
Nuclear	2,619	4,111	57%
Hydro	2,722	3,899	43%
Biomass and waste	141	1,578	1,019%
Other renewables (wind, solar, geothermal)	196	2,316	1,082%
Coal with CCS	0	1,962	
Total Generation	**16,424**	**23,295**	**42%**

Source: US DOE/EIA and IPCC plus author's calculations.

In Table 13 we look at the amount of electricity that the IPCC expects to be generated from each energy source in its second scenario. The table also includes a comparison to 2004 so we can see how the electricity generation industry might change by 2030. What we can clearly see from this table is that the key electricity generation technologies we can expect to be used to reduce energy emissions are nuclear power (57% growth), renewable energy like hydro (43% growth), biomass, waste, wind and solar (over 1,000% growth or 10 times) and CCS. IPCC believes the greatest single source of low-emissions electricity in 2030 will be nuclear power. We will spend the rest of this chapter looking at each of these and the possible implications for our electricity supply.

What Will Happen to Fossil-Fuel Plants by 2030?

We need a significant swing to lower carbon emitting technologies to reduce greenhouse gas emissions from global electricity generation by 2030. This will be done with a combination of substituting fossil fuels with nuclear, hydro and other renewable resources and by lowering the emissions intensity by switching from coal to gas and using CCS.

Existing fossil-fuel plants will be replaced as they reach the end of their useful life. This will depend on when they were built and the cost of keeping them producing emissions. Depending on the carbon price, some plants may well be retired or modified long before the end of their normal life. New generation plants will be built to replace the old ones as well as provide new capacity to meet the increasing power demand, particularly in developing countries. These new plants will be shared by fossil fuels, renewables, nuclear and, after 2015, coal and gas with CCS.

From Table 13 we can see that about one-quarter of the existing tradition coal-fired plant capacity may be closed or modified and replaced by low-carbon plants by 2030. This replacement rate would be in line with the anticipated natural rate of replacement. The actual carbon price might influence the actual share for each replacement technology. Local geographical and political issues will also influence the primary energy choice for new plants. For example, some countries will not have suitable sites for hydro power and other countries will refuse to build nuclear plants for political reasons.

Where a country elects to build a new fossil-fuel plant (either coal or gas), it should give serious consideration to designing and locating the plant so it can be readily converted to CCS when the technology is available. This means reserving space in the design for CCS capture as well as siting the plant to allow access to a carbon dioxide storage site.

Even by 2030, we can still expect that nearly half our electricity will be generated from fossil fuels although at a much lower emissions intensity than today.

What Part Will Nuclear Play?

In some countries we can expect some retiring or planned fossil-fuel plants to be replaced by nuclear power plants. This is already happening in many countries, with 34 reactors under construction as at January 2008, mainly in developing countries, and a further 93 on order or planned.[25] These new plants will generate some 900 billion kWh or about 60% of the planned nuclear growth to 2030. Of the new plants, 40% will be in China and India. The design of the planned reactors is a mixture of Generation II, III and III+.

The IPCC sees nuclear power increasing its share of electricity generation slightly from 16% to 18%. Nuclear power is probably the most effective way to reduce greenhouse gas emissions from electricity generation at the lowest cost per kWh with minimal changes to the distribution networks as nuclear can supply high availability baseload power. This will be one of the primary reasons that the IPCC sees nuclear power as the greatest source of low-emissions electricity in 2030. Nevertheless, community concern about the safety of nuclear power and the storage of the waste continues to hold back its development in many countries.

What Will it Mean to Have More Renewable Energy?

Supplies of our major existing primary energy resources for electricity — coal, gas and uranium — are still abundant and will remain that way through to 2030. These resources will not last forever, so the long-term switch to renewable resources — wind, sun, hydro, ocean, geothermal, biomass — is inevitable. It's just a matter of when.

The major renewable resource used today for electricity is hydro, which contributes 16% of total generation. Electricity generated from hydro plants with adequate, year-round water supply and located close to demand is economical and reliable, with generally low (but not zero) emissions. Hydro uses proven, mature technology. For those countries with suitable sites for new hydro plants, this will be an attractive option for replacing aging fossil-fuel plants and providing additional baseload or peaking capacity as well as energy storage. A full hydro storage facility can replace a conventional power station for several hours if needed. Suitable sites are an issue for many countries either because of insufficient year-round water flows, unacceptable environment impacts or distance from where the electricity is needed. Many of the best sites have been used already. Total hydro generation is expected to grow by over 40% by 2030, in line with total generation. The 'sleeper' with hydro is the effect of climate change on running-water supply which could be significant in some parts of the world.

Using biomass and waste combustion to generate electricity also involves mature technology but contributes less than 1% of total generation today. This is expected to grow by more than tenfold by 2030, particularly in the developing world where biomass could produce 10% of the total electricity. Biomass and waste are particularly useful for smaller scale distributed generation (DG) plants using CHP. We will discuss DG later in this chapter.

Both wind and solar PV are growing rapidly, although they remain a very small contributor to total electricity demand (< 2%). They both suffer from being intermittent and variable sources of supply, which provides challenges when trying to match supply for electricity with demand. Today's grid systems can cope with a certain amount of variable supply, perhaps 15–20%. Above this figure, we will need to improve weather forecasting significantly and upgrade the networks with advanced control systems to incorporate more solar and wind energy plus storage and/or capacity reserves. Despite this, some industry observers (not completely unbiased) have predicted that close to 30% of world electricity could come from wind by 2030.[76] The IPCC assumes a more modest 7% for on- and off-shore wind by 2030, mainly in OECD countries.[49]

Even at 7%, this means that some 1,600 billion kWh will be generated by wind turbines. A typical 2MW turbine will generate around 5 million kWh/yr so it will take 320,000 2MW turbines to generate 7% of world electricity demand. That is 3,200 wind farms with an average of 100 turbines each.

Solar PV installations are also growing significantly — by over 30% a year. About half these may be connected to the grid but they will still make a very small contribution to meeting total electricity demand by 2030. The relatively high cost of some renewable plants compared to coal, gas and nuclear, the variability issues and environmental impact issues will constrain the use of wind, solar PV and solar CSP plants in the period to 2030. We can probably expect a greater switch to renewables after 2030 as costs fall and technology better addresses the variability.

What Would it Mean to Have all the Increase in Demand Met by Renewables?

Some conservationists would like to see all new electricity power from now on to come from renewable resources. Table 13 tells us that electricity demand is expected to increase by over 6,000 billion kWh/yr by 2030. This is after we have made significant savings in electricity usage. If we were to use renewables for all the increase in demand then about 43% of supply would come from renewable resources and this would require major upgrades to the grid networks at additional cost (see 'How Much Will Electricity Cost in 2030?' below).

To provide all new supply to 2030 with wind or solar power alone (and ignoring any existing plant replacement) would mean over 1 million new 2MW wind turbines or 6,000 500MWe solar CSP plants. It would mean installing 50,000 wind turbines or 300 CSP plants *every year* for the next 20 years. Fifty thousand wind turbines is over five times the number of new wind turbines installed in 2007. So far no 500MWe CSP plants have been built and even the solar industry is expecting less than 100 billion kWh of CSP by 2025[77] or 15% of the expected increase in demand for electricity.

Will There Still Be a Role for Coal in Electricity Production?

Coal is a dirty, non-renewable source of energy but it is cheap and plentiful in some countries. In some regions there are several hundred years of supply and some countries will want to continue to use local coal to generate electricity for energy security reasons. In the medium term, coal gasification and using the resulting gas rather than burning the raw coal can reduce greenhouse gas emissions (see Chapter 14). This process (IGCC) also helps separate out the carbon dioxide for carbon capture and storage (CCS) when the technology is commercially available. It is possible that most new coal-fired plants will use coal gasification.

For those countries that choose to continue to use coal, CCS will be essential if they are to achieve their longer term greenhouse gas emissions targets without replacing their coal-fuelled power stations. In these cases, coal plants using CCS may become a medium to long-term solution. This will not be possible for the world as a whole. Worldwide coal supplies might run out within this century so CCS is necessarily a stopgap solution for some countries. In these countries, CCS will be seen as a transitional technology only while coal-powered stations are being phased out and replaced with nuclear or other low carbon energy sources.

An alternative to CCS is biological removal of carbon dioxide from fossil-fuel-powered plant flues. Algal systems could remove the carbon dioxide from the flue gases and the algae can be used to produce biodiesel. This sounds like a wonderful win-win — reduce greenhouse gas emissions and produce transport fuel. This is very much in the experimental stage although there have been some successful trials.[78]

Coal use in electricity generation is likely to be with us for many decades yet. Applying the right technologies can get the emissions intensity of coal down to that of renewable resources so global warming isn't a reason for abandoning coal. That will happen when the competing comparable technologies become less expensive than coal with CCS.

How Will Electricity Distribution Change?

Electricity transmission networks have successfully supplied us with the vital link between the generators and our homes and workplaces for decades (see Chapter 1). These networks were designed to meet the need to generate electricity in large (generally polluting) fossil-fuel-based generators located some distance from the towns and cities to avoid the pollution or to be close to coal mines. It can cost $1–2 million per km for high voltage transmission lines. Over half the capital assets of electricity generation and distribution are tied up in these transmission networks covering hundreds of kilometres.

These networks have needed regular upgrades to meet the growing demand for more electricity and more base, intermediate and peak-load generators (see Chapter 1). They also need to handle a certain degree of supply variability to cope with a generator unexpectedly going off-line. Over the next few decades they will be faced with maintaining system performance and reliability while handling many more generators that are generally smaller, more distributed and produce more variable and sometimes unpredictable supply. This may require using more fossil-fuel intermediate and peak-load generators to provide reserve capacity during wind calms or cloudy periods. It will also require upgraded network control systems to handle the dispatching of more reserve systems and possibly more voltage and frequency fluctuations.

The grid electricity storage technologies — pumped storage, CAES, flow batteries, CSP storage — we discussed in Chapter 14 can help address some of the issues with variability on the grid. Both pumped storage and CAES are proven technologies but require suitable sites that will not be available everywhere. CAES needs to use gas turbines so will have a limited place in an all-renewable future. Flow batteries and CSP storage are still in the development stage and may not make a significant contribution to supply before 2030, so upgrading the transmission networks and building more fossil-fuel reserve capacity to cope with wind and solar is probably inevitable even using only 30% renewable resources.

It is more likely that the wind will be blowing or the sun shining somewhere in a country than just relying on one or two locations with large-scale renewable resource plants. Having many geographically dispersed wind farms or solar systems spread throughout a country's network will smooth variations in output but not completely eliminate it. Long periods of widespread still or cloudy weather could have a high impact on total electricity supply in a future relying heavily on wind and solar.

Distributed generation (DG) systems are geographically located close to the electricity demand and typically use small to medium generation facilities. DG systems may become much more popular with the move away from large fossil-fuel plants and the increased use of wind, solar PV and biomass. They can provide both local supply as well as some grid supply in both urban and rural areas. They can also increase energy efficiency by providing local heating and cooling as well as electricity from medium-scale combined heat and power (CHP) systems using gas, biomass or waste. DG systems can be built more quickly than large, centralised plants but they do have power limitations and reliability issues as well as added cost. DG's share of the total world power capacity has been estimated at some 8–9%.[79]

In rural areas, where the grid connection cost may be high, DG systems can be used along with distributed or mini-grids that service a community. The generation sources could be a mix of renewables plus gas or diesel back-up generators, depending on the need for reliability of supply. DG can reduce the need for costly, long distance, very high voltage transmission systems and reduce the associated power losses (see Chapter 1). It may also defer the cost of upgrading transmission lines to cope with growing rural demand. DG systems and mini-grids could also be used in urban areas when they are cost effective and they may become popular in developing countries for supplying electricity to rural areas.

If these DG networks are to be monitored and controlled locally but also integrated into a wider grid they will need to exchange information to ensure smooth operation of the total system.

How Much Will Electricity Cost in 2030?

We can expect the generation cost from renewable resources to reduce over the next few decades from technology development and economies of scale. The IPCC assessed the future cost from various resources as shown in Table 14. We can expect that cost per kWh will significantly influence which substitution energy resources are selected to replace fossil fuels as new plants are built. The table also shows that there are many different primary energy sources that could be cost competitive in 2030 with today's generation costs.

We can see a distinct shift in the generation costs from now to 2030 for some renewables, particularly solar. This will bring the cost per kWh much closer to that of fossil fuels with CCS. These costs only include the cost of generation and do not cover any additional network costs or electricity storage or reserve capacity costs needed to handle any variability. The IEA estimates that these additional system costs for a 20% renewable share of total supply at between 10% and 30% of the generation costs.[80]

Table 14

Electricity Generation Costs 2005 to 2030

Electricity Generation Cost	US $/kWh	
	2005	2030
Coal	~0.020	0.040–0.055
Coal with CCS		0.060–0.085
Natural gas	~0.037	0.040–0.060
Natural gas with CCS		0.060–0.090
Oil	~0.048	0.050–0.100
Nuclear	0.010–0.120	0.025–0.075
Hydro	0.020–0.100	0.030–0.070
Solar PV	0.250–1.600	0.060–0.250
Solar CSP	0.120–0.450	0.050–0.180
Wind	0.040–0.090	0.030–0.080
Geothermal	0.040–0.100	0.030–0.080
Ocean	0.080–0.400	0.070–0.200
Biomass	0.030–0.120	0.030–0.100

Source: IPCC[49]

What Low-Carbon Technology Solutions Are We Unlikely to See Before 2030?
From the customer side we are likely to be paying a different electricity tariff through the day, depending on the real-time cost of generation. This will help match demand with supply, reduce wastage and reduce the overall cost for both the utilities and the customers.

Three things will restrict the widespread implementation of some low-carbon technologies over the next couple of decades. The first is technology maturity — has it been commercially proven? The second is relative cost — relative to other commercially available solutions. The third is unacceptable environmental impact. The first two can be related and are commercial decisions made by the infrastructure investors. The third is largely a political decision.

Some technologies may have been demonstrated and look attractive but are yet to be proven commercially. Examples include ocean power, CSP storage, flow batteries and EGS geothermal. It can often take decades for promising technologies to become high capital cost commercial realities.

Some technologies may be commercially viable and environmentally acceptable in some locations and not others. The reasons can be geographic and geological such as with hydro, pumped storage, solar CSP, geothermal, CCS and ocean power. Some such as hydro, nuclear and CCS will be ruled out in some countries for political reasons.

Technologies that may be held back by commercial acceptance and/ or cost before 2030 are:

- Ocean power (technology, cost),
- Solar CSP with heat storage (technology, cost),
- EGS geothermal (technology),
- Flow batteries (technology, cost), and
- Generation IV nuclear plants (technology).

Where the technology issues have been addressed before 2030, some of these may be introduced even though they may be commercially unattractive.

Technologies that may be held back by environmental concerns before 2030 are:

- Nuclear power in some countries (safety, long lived waste, proliferation),
- CCS in some countries (safety, long-term impact), and
- EGS geothermal (earthquakes, water usage).

As technology improves with more research and development and political climates change, some of these may be implement after 2030 and may well be needed before 2050 to address climate change.

What Are We Likely to See After 2030?

Time to get out the crystal ball.

Some technologies are well down the development track and are very likely to be seen post-2030. These include concentrated solar power (CSP) with heat storage and geothermal energy from hot dry rocks (EGS). Barring major unforeseen technical barriers, both these technologies could be making a significant level of contribution to electricity supply post-2030 and possibly earlier.

We can expect improved transmission networks to reduce transmission losses and to manage many more smaller and widely distributed variable generators and storage devices such as flow batteries and CAES. Transmission technologies that reduce losses include superconducting cables and high voltage DC lines.

By 2030, the nuclear high-level waste storage problems will have been solved and this will start to look like a non-issue. Despite today's community resistance in many developed countries, we will see much more baseload generation coming from very safe and clean next generation nuclear power plants (see Chapter 24).

Improvement in solar PV cell production will significantly reduce the cost and flexibility of solar cells, as can be seen in Table 14. Nanotechnology may play a part to revolutionise the PV cell industry and remove the high cost disadvantage that solar PV has today.

If CCS proves to be successful we can expect future technology improvements to reduce the cost of capture. Bioengineering may produce an answer to carbon dioxide storage by getting organisms such as algae to convert it to biofuels.

22 — Where to for Transport?

Transport is a big energy user and it has played a key role in the development of the human race. It is the area most affected by peak oil, with 95% of transport energy coming from crude oil. It is also responsible for over 20% of energy greenhouse gas emissions. We can expect big changes in how we build, use and power our transport over the next few decades.

If we are to build a transport system that doesn't rely on oil and produces near zero emissions then we only have three practical fuel choices — low-emissions biofuels, electricity and hydrogen. We will discuss all three of these in this chapter.

Where Are We at Today With Motorised Transport?
Motorised transport really started to develop rapidly about 100 years ago following the invention of the internal combustion engine (ICE) and the production of fuels from crude oil. Vast industries grew up to service our transport needs and to produce and distribute fuels. These industries are still based on the same basic ICE technology and petroleum fuels we used 100 years ago. We know that crude oil will not always be available so these technologies may now be potential barriers to our future.

We have become an urban society. Three-quarters of the population in the developed world and 40% in the developing world live in towns and cities. Cities have grown larger and spread into lower density sub-urban areas and edge cities. This urbanisation spread has increased the demand for travel but reduced the effectiveness of public transport. We have seen a rapid growth in personal vehicles needed to travel from home to work. Intercity and international travel are also growing rapid-ly and cities can no longer exist without being able to transport people and goods effectively and cheaply.

Urbanisation is also on the rise in the developing world. But much of the world still has low incomes and is yet to become motorised. Most people in the world don't have personal vehicles and many don't have access to affordable public transport. As the non-OECD countries be-come more developed, we can expect the world demand for both per-sonal and public transport to increase significantly.

In terms of energy use, the transport sector can be split into several groups. Light-duty vehicles (LDV) plus motorbikes form the largest group at around 46%, freight trucks at 25%, public transport (buses and trains) at 8%, air transport at 12% and shipping at 9%. The big growth sectors are LDVs, freight trucks and air travel.[81]

Economic development increases the demand for freight transport. Urban freight is largely done by trucks of varying sizes. Intercity and regional freight mainly involve large trucks with some rail. Internation-al freight is dominated by ocean shipping with some air freight. Freight carriers are under pressure to cut costs so fuel economy in trucks and other freight transporters already receives high priority.

We can expect that all sectors of motorised transport will continue to grow rapidly throughout the world. Transport already contributes over 6 billion tonnes of greenhouse gas emissions every year and around three-quarters of this comes from road transport.

Energy efficiency of personal LDV technology has improved over time but much of this benefit has been offset by increasing vehicle size, weight and power. Features such as increased safety systems, improved driving characteristics, reduced noise and emissions and increased comfort have all added to vehicle weight.[82] On average, LDV weight in Europe has increased about 30% over the last 30 years. This increase in weight has increased fuel consumption (litres per 100 km) for cars and sports utility vehicles.

Fuel consumption is important because the twin transport challenges ahead are: how do we reduce our vulnerability to peak oil and how do we reduce transport greenhouse gas emissions when demand for transport fuel continues to grow?

Where Will Transport Be in 2030 if We Do Nothing Different?
Probably whatever we do, short of banning private motor vehicles, there will be many more vehicles in 2030 than now. The IEA projects that there will be another 600 million vehicles by 2030 of which 400 million will be in developing countries.[74] China is the world's fastest growing new car market. Currently China has only 17 cars for every 1000 people compared with 626 in North America and 417 in Europe[83] so there is plenty of scope for fleet expansion!

Table 15

Vehicle Stock by 2030

Region	Vehicles (millions)		
	2002	2030	Growth
OECD (developed world)	500	700	40%
Non-OECD (developing world)	150	550	267%
Total	650	1250	92%

Source: IEA[74]

IEA's business-as-usual (BAU) growth scenario assumes that world oil supplies will be sufficient to meet demand to 2030. In other words, no major impact from peak oil. Total transport energy demand is projected to rise by over 80% with a small shift away from petroleum products.

Even allowing for some improvement in fuel consumption and more use of biofuels in the BAU scenario, transport greenhouse gas emissions will increase 66% from 6.4 billion tonnes in 2004 to 10.6 billion tonnes in 2030.[72] From Table 14 in Chapter 18 we saw that the IPCC estimated the emissions reduction potential from this BAU scenario in 2030 at between 1.5 and 2.3 billion tonnes at a carbon price less than $50. Let's look at where these reductions could come from.

Where Can We Get 'More From Less' From Our Vehicles?
There is plenty of scope to improve worldwide transport fuel economy. The fuel economy of new vehicles already varies significantly between countries. For LDVs in the US the average fuel consumption is close to 10 litres/100 km whereas in Europe it is below 7 litres/100 km.[74] There are several ways that vehicle fuel economy can be improved.

Reducing vehicle weight can make a significant contribution to fuel economy. The weight of LDVs could be reduced by 20–30% which could mean a fuel economy improvement of 8–24%.[81] There are two main ways to reduce the weight of new vehicles. One is to redesign the size and shape of the vehicle. The other is to use lighter materials. Existing mild-steel designs can be replaced with lighter materials like aluminium, high-strength steel, magnesium and plastics. Generally such material changes will be more expensive, so the improvement in fuel economy may be offset by increased vehicle cost but the vehicle will use less fuel and produce fewer greenhouse gas emissions.

Improving what is called the drive train (engine and transmission) in new vehicles can also improve fuel economy. Using direct injection (DI) turbocharged diesel engines in LDVs instead of conventional petrol engines can improve fuel economy by 35%. Newer engines like DI petrol engines will also improve fuel economy.

Reducing vehicle air resistance can reduce fuel consumption — particularly at higher speeds over 80 km/h. Air resistance depends on the vehicle size and shape. Significant improvements in LDV air resistance have already been made over the last few years, but incremental improvements are still possible. Significant improvements are still possible for trucks and buses. Reducing our driving speed can significantly reduce air resistance and improve our fuel economy. Driving at 80 km/h rather than 110 km/h can improve our fuel economy by 27%.[81]

Rolling resistance is also a factor in fuel consumption. Rolling resistance is the force required to push a vehicle along the road. The higher the rolling resistance the more energy (from fuel) is needed to move the vehicle. Unlike air resistance, rolling resistance is significant at any speed. Tyre rolling resistance is impacted by the tyre design and materials but also by the amount of air in the tyre (the tyre pressure). We can reduce our fuel consumption by just ensuring our tyres are inflated properly.

Our car air-conditioning systems can consume 7–8% of total vehicle energy consumption. More efficient climate control systems that require less heating in winter and less cooling in summer can reduce the energy used in vehicle heating and cooling.

Fuel economy can also be improved by using a hybrid electric vehicle (HEV) — see Chapter 3. A smaller engine can be used which uses less fuel. The engine can be turned off completely when the vehicle is stopped and the vehicle can switch to electric mode at low speed when the engine efficiency is low. Even more energy savings can come from using battery electric vehicles (BEV).

Many of these efficiency improvements are being built into new vehicles now. The average life of a vehicle is 12–20 years so it will take some time for these various improvements to be standard in all the vehicles on the road.

We can also improve fuel economy by switching vehicles. In Table 4 in Chapter 3 we looked at the greenhouse gas emissions of various modes of transport. We generate nearly four times as many emissions travelling in a two-person car than we do in a 40-person bus. This means we also use about four times as much fuel in a car per passenger kilometre than we do in a bus. Switching our mode of transport from private to public will reduce fuel consumption and transport emissions. Some governments have introduced congestion charges in cities to encourage this transport mode shift. Possibly the best known was in London in 2005. The challenge for governments is to improve public transport systems to encourage us to use them more. After all, it is often cheaper to expand public transport capacity than to build new roads and bridges.

Freight mode switching from road trucks to rail or ships can also reduce fuel consumption and greenhouse gas emissions. Freight fuel savings can also come from improved logistics to combine shipments and making sure that trucks use the most efficient routes. IEA believes that freight fuel consumption and therefore greenhouse gas emissions can be cut by 25–30% over the next 15–20 years.[84]

What Are the Transport Fuel Options by 2030?
We can only go so far with reducing petrol and diesel consumption

with better vehicle design and usage. The big reductions in use of these fuels and their associated greenhouse gas emissions will come from fuel switching. Before we can discuss switching we need to understand what our options are.

Petrol and diesel are likely to remain the major road transport fuels for the internal combustion engine (ICE) to 2030. Significant investment has been made for these liquid fuels in production processes (refineries) and supply infrastructure (pipelines, tanks and filling stations). Some new fuels will mean new and different infrastructure. Expanding the existing infrastructure to meet the growing demand is much cheaper than developing new infrastructure. What we are likely to see over the next few years is a switch from petrol to diesel for LDVs and this trend is already happening in Europe. Diesel engines use about 18% less fuel than current petrol engines.

In the short to medium term it is likely that petrol and diesel will increasingly contain blended components derived from sources other than crude oil. These components will be selected to reduce emissions, offer greater energy security (see Chapter 15) and/or reduce dependency on expensive oil. These blended fuels can largely use the existing supply infrastructure. These are some of the alternative liquid fuels or components that can be used in this way:

- Ethanol and biodiesel are generated from biomass as we discussed in Chapter 10. Ethanol can be blended with petrol and biodiesel with diesel and both are used today in relatively small quantities. The scope to expand biofuels depends on the extent to which they compete for cropland with food and other commercial crops plus the availability of water resources.

- Advanced biofuels are being developed that do not use food crops but use grasses and woody material known as cellulosic sources. These materials can come from crop residues such as wheat and rice straw, and corn stalks and leaves. Cellulosic crops have a much higher yield per hectare than sugar and starch crops and may be grown in areas unsuitable for food crops. These cellulosic biofuels are yet to be produced commercially.

- Synthetic petrol and diesel can be made from natural gas and coal as well as biomass. Gas-to-liquid (GTL) and coal-to-liquid (CTL) processes we discussed in Chapter 12 can be used to produce FT[45] diesel and FT gasoline. Synthetic fuels can be blended like biofuels with petrol or diesel for use in ICEs but are expensive to make. As the oil price increases or crude oil becomes scarce, these synthetic fuels may become attractive alternatives.

We do have alternative gas-like fuels that can be used in ICEs but they cannot utilise the existing liquid fuel supply infrastructure which means they are unavailable in some countries. These gas fuels include liquid petroleum gas (LPG) and compressed natural gas (CNG) we discussed in Chapter 2. They also include hydrogen which we discussed in Chapter 11. The easiest to store and distribute is LPG, which requires a low pressure tank, can be distributed by road or rail and is already widely available in some countries. CNG and hydrogen require more sophisticated high pressure storage and safe distribution.

There are other ways to propel a transport vehicle that don't require using an ICE. Electric motors have been used for years in buses, trams and trains using electricity delivered through conductive contact such as overhead wires or trains using a third rail. Electric motors can also be used with on-board batteries but are usually restricted to a short driving range and have a relatively short battery life. Historically they have been limited to forklift trucks, golf carts or local delivery vans. As battery technology improves, work is progressing to deliver passenger battery electric vehicles (BEVs) that can be used in urban areas — see Chapter 3.

Electric motors used in combination with an ICE are starting to become more popular in LDVs, particularly in the US and Japan, to improve fuel economy. Hybrid electric vehicles in use today use batteries to store electricity generated by the ICE and by the electric motors when decelerating and braking. Fuel cells allow the vehicle to generate the electricity from an on-board fuel source — with or without batteries. The most promising fuel cell technology uses hydrogen as the fuel source — see Chapter 11.

Fuel cell vehicles (FCV) offer a higher overall efficiency than ICE vehicles and produce fewer greenhouse gas emissions. FCV's can offer energy security as they do not require fossil fuels if the hydrogen is

---

[45] FT stands for Fischer-Tropsch — the process used to produce the fuel.

produced from fossil-fuel-free electricity (for example, solar or wind).
There are many FCV demonstration projects underway using both
cars and buses but there are still many barriers to be overcome (see
Chapter 11) and FCV drive trains are substantially more expensive
than ICE drive trains. It is not clear how big a part FCVs and hydrogen
will play in transport fuels in 2030.

How Can We Decarbonise Our Transport by 2030?
Decarbonising transport involve improving vehicle efficiency to use less
fuel plus fuel switching to lower carbon fuels. Figure 5 shows the well-
to-wheel greenhouse gas emissions we might expect by 2030 from various vehicle fuel/drive train combinations as calculated by WBCSD.[46]
This is both the emissions from using the fuel in the vehicle plus the
emissions produced during the fuel production and distribution process. The drive train as well as the fuel can have a significant effect on
fuel consumption.

Figure 5

Well-to-Wheel Emissions (g/km) for Various Fuel-Drive by 2030

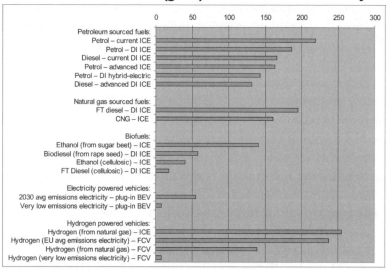

ICE = internal combustion engine, DI = direct injection, HEV = hybrid electric vehicle, FCV =
fuel cell vehicle, BEV = battery electric vehicle.
Note: Electricity powered vehicles from author's assessment.
Source: WBCSD — Mobility 2030[82]

[46] World Business Council for Sustainable Development

It is essential that the full well-to-wheel cycle is used. For example, for fuels produced from biomass, such as ethanol and biodiesel, emissions are actually saved during the production process because the plants absorb more carbon dioxide from the atmosphere during growth than the emissions generated in producing the fuel. These savings can significantly offset the emissions produced in the vehicle. Similarly, hydrogen used in a fuel cell vehicle (FCV) produces no greenhouse gas emissions in the vehicle, but if the hydrogen is made from fossil-fuels then there are significant emissions generated in the production process.

There are difficulties in accounting accurately for emissions but Figure 5 gives a comparison of the various options available to decarbonise our transport. We can expect some improvement in efficiency in both petrol and diesel ICE vehicles by 2030 from advanced drive train technology. Clearly some of the biofuels options like biodiesel from rapeseed (sometimes called RME diesel) and cellulosic ethanol and FT diesel look attractive with emissions levels one-quarter those of current petrol and diesel.

Plug-in electric vehicles using electricity with the anticipated emissions intensity in 2030 (See Table 12 in Chapter 21) produce one-quarter of the emissions of conventional petrol ICE vehicles today. Even using electricity with the average emissions intensity we have today produces about half the emissions. Plug-in battery electric vehicles may be an immediate option to decarbonise transport fuel in vehicles that only make short trips away from a recharging point like a home or workplace (if we are prepared to pay the extra vehicle cost).

Today nearly all hydrogen is made from natural gas (without CCS) and, as we can see from Figure 5, doesn't do much to decarbonise transport fuels even when used in an FCV. Hydrogen is really only going to be an attractive way of decarbonising fuel when the hydrogen is produced using very low emissions electricity such as wind, solar, nuclear power or using CCS. Until then, hydrogen might be used for energy security reasons to protect against dwindling supplies of crude oil or to reduce total transport energy use. FCVs have a well-to-wheel efficiency that is significantly higher than a current petrol ICE vehicle. So FCVs will require less fuel to provide the same transport services.

The production and distribution cost of these various fuel options vary but generally low-carbon fuels are more expensive to produce than existing petrol or diesel with the exception of electricity. For hydrogen and CNG to be used widely, they will need new distribution and storage infrastructure. Vehicle modification costs also vary significantly. More advanced drive trains could add 10% to vehicle cost. Some of these advanced engines are already on the market, like DI petrol engines. Fuel cells are very expensive today but may become cheaper with more technical development. Even so, FCVs could cost over 50% more than standard petrol ICE vehicles.[82]

WBCSD is of the view that the current cost of cellulosic biofuels, hydrogen and fuel cells is much too high for them to compete with today's vehicles and fuels. Our governments will continue to provide us with incentives (through subsidies and taxes) and regulations (to reduce fuel consumption and emissions) to encourage us to switch to some of the low-carbon fuels options discussed so far. The incentives required for some of the more expensive solution such as fuel cells are probably beyond governments' ability. The possible increase in the cost for petrol and diesel fuel may make many of us see these alternatives as attractive by 2030 even without government incentives and regulations.

How Much Can We Reduce Transport Greenhouse Gas Emissions by 2030?
As we said earlier, greenhouse gas emissions from transport are expected to rise to 10.6 billion tonnes by 2030 unless we do something about it. This business-as-usual (BAU) case does assume that substantial amounts of biofuels will be used in some parts of the world such as Brazil and significant improvements will be made in fuel economy in the developing world. But as we have seen so far in this chapter, we can do much better than that with improved vehicle design and fuel switching to lower carbon fuels.

Table 16 shows the IPCC's estimate of the additional reductions that can be made from the BAU case by 2030 at various carbon prices. As we can see, most of the savings can be made at less than $20 per tonne in both light duty vehicle fuel economy and greater use of biofuels. The IPCC did not include heavy duty vehicles but LDVs represent two-thirds of road transport.

Table 16
Transport Emissions Reduction Potential by Sector

Transport Emissions Reduction Potential by 2030	Reduction (billion tonnes of CO_2-e/yr)			
Carbon Price per tonne CO_2-e	<$0	<$20	<$50	<$100
LDVs — petrol, diesel	0.4–0.7	0.7	0.7	0.7–0.8
Biofuels		0.6–1.5	0.6–1.5	0.6–1.5
Aircraft			0.2	0.3
Total	0.4–0.7	1.3–2.2	1.5–2.4	1.6–2.6

Source: IPCC[81]

If we take the average potential emissions reduction at less than $50 a tonne from the IPCC we get a saving of just under 2 billion tonnes of emissions from transport. We can compare this figure with IEA's estimate of 1.0 billion tonnes[74] and McKinsey's estimate of 2.9 billion tonnes.[75]

Given the potential for savings in transport emissions we have discussed so far, and the opportunity for significant 'low cost' savings, we can probably be confident of stripping between 1.0 and 2.0 tonnes of emissions per year from transport by 2030 at less than $20 per tonne.

Is There a Long-Term Future for the ICE?

Our current transport industry has been built on the back of the internal combustion engine. These are the engines that burn up half our crude oil and produce about a fifth of our energy emissions. Without cheap oil their future looks bleak.

We can use hydrogen and natural gas in them but that doesn't greatly help greenhouse gas emissions. We can use biofuels and synthetic fuels in them and that will prolong their life after petroleum products becomes too expensive to burn (except for the vintage car enthusiasts). Today biofuels compete with food and gas- and coal-to-liquid rely on other depleting fossil fuels — natural gas and coal.

The ICE's best long-term hope is biofuels that do not compete with food (cellulosic) and hydrogen made from low-emissions electricity. Both these technologies are still being developed but we can expect to see some progress and early adoption by 2030.

The efficiency of the ICE can be enhanced through the use of hybrid electric propulsion systems. Today's hybrids use about 30% less fuel than a pure petrol ICE vehicle. We are probably likely to see more diesel ICEs rather than petrol for light vehicles. A diesel ICE uses about18% less fuel than a petrol ICE.

In the shorter term, as petrol and diesel become more expensive, we will see more use of conventional and advanced biofuels in ICEs to reduce greenhouse gas emissions and, eventually, to improve their fuel cost economy.

The ICE is not dead but we can feel that its days are numbered.

What Part Will Electric Vehicles Play?

If we don't use an ICE to drive our vehicles' wheels what could we use? Electric motors.

Electric motors have been used for powering vehicles since the middle of the 19th century — almost as long ago as the first ICEs. They have many technical advantages over ICEs, they are much more fuel efficient, they don't need gear boxes, they are very quiet and release almost no air pollution. If they are that good, why haven't we used them much more in the past?

Electric motors need a continuous supply of electricity to drive the wheels. This either has to be supplied to the vehicle as it travels along or produced or stored somehow on the vehicle. Where the electricity can be supplied externally, such as with electric trains, tramcars and trolley buses with the electricity supplied through overhead wires or the rails, this is an attractive option that is widely used in some countries and cities. There is additional costly infrastructure to be built and maintained to supply the electricity but this is offset by cheaper fuel and less noise and air pollution.

For trains or other large vehicles without access to external electricity, the electricity can be generated on board the vehicle using a diesel ICE powered generator — known as a diesel-electric locomotion. The same principle can be applied to ships and buses. For smaller road vehicles the electricity needs to be generated on board using a small ICE or a fuel cell. Modern hybrid-electric vehicles (HEVs), like the Toyota Prius, use both an ICE and an electric motor to drive the wheels and store electricity in batteries (see Chapter 3). Hydrogen fuel cells are being developed to generate electricity on board an electric motor driven vehicle (see Chapter 11).

Electric motors can also be used in vehicles without externally supplied or internally generated electricity. They require a storage system such as batteries that can be charged externally. These vehicles are called battery electric vehicles (BEVs) or popularly called plug-ins. The problem with batteries is that they have low energy density — in other words the energy stored per kilogram of battery is very low compared to say petrol or diesel in a fuel tank. This means the batteries take up much more space and weigh more than a fuel tank and need recharging much more frequently than the tank needs refilling. Typical plug-ins can only travel 100–200 km between charges and take a few hours to recharge which limits their use to urban runabouts. However, they are very cheap to run. Tesla Motors claim they can recharge the batteries using 11 kWh per 100 km.[85] If we assume our average electricity cost at $0.16/kWh then the cost per 100 km is $1.76 compared to an ICE at 10 litres of petrol per 100 km at a cost of $15 (at $1.50 per litre).

There are vehicles planned that share the characteristics of both the HEV and BEV called plug-in hybrid electric vehicles (PHEV) using larger batteries for electric only use and an ICE to extend the travel range between recharging the batteries. They can share the benefits of all electric usage with low petroleum fuel usage if the ICE is needed.

In Chapter 14 we discussed battery technology with improved energy density over traditional lead-acid batteries. We can expect improvements in battery performance by 2030 but it may be some time before we see a plug-in BEV that can travel 500–600 km between charges.

How About Air Transport?

Air travel is becoming more and more popular as cheap tickets become the norm. Air travel has the highest growth rate of all transport modes at around 5% per year and uses about 12% of all transport fuel. We can expect that aircraft manufacturers will make planes more efficient over the next few decades as fuel represents about 20% of total aircraft operating costs. However, increases in air traffic growth are likely to exceed improvements in fuel economy so fuel use and total aircraft greenhouse gas emissions will increase.

Aviation has a larger impact on global warming than just the carbon dioxide emissions. Aircraft also produce nitrous oxides, water vapour and soot particles which all increase global warming. In addition, jet aircraft at high altitude produce long plumes of exhaust that can be seen behind the plane called condensation trails or contrails which mainly consist of water droplets and ice. These contrails can last several hours and spread a couple of kilometres wide. Contrails contribute to global warming by trapping heat from the Earth that would otherwise escape. The net effect of these additional contributors to global warming can double the impact of the carbon dioxide alone.

Aircraft fuel consumption can be impacted by aviation operational systems controlled by air traffic management. Taxi-times on the runway, cruising altitude, flight path between destinations, flight speeds and holding and stacking at airports can all impact fuel economy.

Aviation is likely to depend on fossil fuels for the foreseeable future. There have been successful trials with biofuels in commercial jet aircraft but cost will be a big factor. Research into biodiesel made from algae and suitable for aircraft has shown some promise and could be a long-term solution (next 50 years?). Ideally, any synthetic aviation fuel to be used in the shorter term should be able to work in the existing aircraft engines and fuel tanks without significant modification.

It is possible to use hydrogen as an aircraft fuel with some modification to accommodate larger tanks needed for hydrogen, and this will increase aircraft weight and energy consumption. Although hydrogen from low emissions electricity will produce low well-to-wheel carbon dioxide emissions, hydrogen used in an aircraft will produce much more water vapour than jet fuel and water vapour is a greenhouse gas.

What Will Transport Be Like in 2030?

Transition to new technologies takes time — particularly in transport. Once some new technology, like fuel cells, has been successfully demonstrated commercially it can take 10 to 20 years to become 'standard equipment' in all new vehicles. It will then take a further 12 to 20 years to replace all the existing vehicles that were built before the introduction of the new technology. So if a major technology isn't under development today it is unlikely to have much impact before 2030.

With that in mind, it's time to get out that crystal ball again.

New internal combustion engine (ICE) vehicles will still be sold in 2030 but about half of these will use diesel rather than petrol. Half of all the new ICE LDVs and medium trucks being manufactured will be hybrid electric vehicles.

Most of the petrol and diesel used in 2030 will be blended with conventional and advanced biofuels. Biofuels will cost less, probably below the petroleum-based fuels depending on whether oil has peaked. Conventional ethanol is likely to be made from sugarcane grown in warm climates rather than from corn or sugar beet. Production of biofuels is likely to be in developing countries closer to the equator with lower costs of production and plenty of rainfall. Competition with food crops will continue to be an issue for biofuels and although using cellulosic biofuels reduces this competition (assuming they are commercially available by 2030) they still need arable land to grow the feedstock which may compete with other crops.

We will see electricity becoming much more widely used in road transport by 2030, particularly in hybrids. Pure electric plug-in vehicles, including cars, bikes and scooters, will get some use in urban areas for short journeys and may even become more widely used as battery technology improves. Public recharging stations in urban areas like shopping centre car parks will expand the use of plug-in vehicles. Plug-in hire cars for use around cities may replace some taxis and personal vehicles. We are unlikely to see electric or hybrid heavy duty vehicles without significant battery development.

However, there is no such thing as a free lunch. Switching to electric cars from petrol or diesel will require a significant increase in domestic electricity demand. Based on the values quoted earlier for Tesla of 11 kWh per 100 km, for a family with two cars travelling a total of 30,000 km per year, they will increase their annual electricity usage by 3,300 kWh. If we assume the average home in 2030 uses 7,000 kWh without electric cars then switching fuels will increase the electricity usage by almost 50%. There could also be a problem if we all decided to recharge our cars in the early evening after coming home from work. The extra demand on the grid at that time could be unmanageable. We will probably need some kind of network management system that ensures that car recharging is spread over the night.

Some hydrogen fuel cells may be used in buses and selected urban commercial vehicles with depot refuelling by 2030. High volume production of fuel-cell passenger cars seems unlikely although some will probably be available by then. The availability of hydrogen refuelling stations is likely to be very limited.

More electric rail systems will replace diesel rail and reduce personal vehicle use by expanding urban and intercity public transport systems. This will reduce transport energy consumption as well as greenhouse gas emissions.

We will start to see more intelligent transport infrastructure to reduce congestion and assist drivers to find the shortest and quickest routes using real-time in-vehicle information and navigation systems that can be installed in new and existing vehicles.

What Might Be the Future for Transport After 2030?

There is a real possibility of near zero transport emissions by the second half of the century. With greater use of hybrids, electricity and fuel cells, vehicle energy use per kilometre could be halved. The complete stock of vehicles will have turned over two or three times by then so we will not have a legacy of old vehicle technology (read ICEs using fossil fuels).

We can be reasonably confident that should crude oil be no longer economic for transport use then we will have three possible options: pure electric vehicles, hydrogen FCVs and advanced biofuels that don't compete with food crops. The crystal ball thinks that a combination of all three is the most likely outcome.

Technology improvements are needed for widespread use of pure electric or fuel cell vehicles. Substantially improved battery technology is needed for pure electric road vehicles and possibly for fuel cell vehicles. Battery technology has improved significantly over the last few years and improvements will continue over the next decades. Further development on other storage systems such as supercapacitors[47] or flywheels could augment batteries. The crystal ball might even be able to see a future that uses on-road battery recharging using inductive charging.[48]

If hydrogen FCVs become operationally and financially attractive we will need hydrogen distribution infrastructure with high pressure pipelines and road transport in cryogenic liquid form. Hydrogen production can be from biomass gasification or electrolysis using low carbon electricity. Alternatively, the electrolysis could be at the fuelling station or at home which would avoid the need for pipelines and cryogenic transport. If all vehicles were fuelled by hydrogen, IEA estimates it would take 2 terawatts (2 billion kW) of additional generation capacity.[84] This is a 50% increase over the 2030 electricity usage we saw in Table 13 in Chapter 21. [49]

Biofuels will play a part either for producing hydrogen for use in FCVs or for ethanol and biodiesel for use in ICE hybrids. Biodiesel from algae that capture carbon dioxide produced in fossil-fuel power stations is an attractive possibility. Technically it will be possible for biofuels to provide all our transport fuel needs post 2030 but this is not the most likely outcome. Probably 20% will be more likely.

At some stage non-hybrid ICE vehicles will cease production. All vehicles being made will either be pure electric, fuel cell or advanced biofuel ICE hybrids.

We may even see some real innovation in shipping. In Germany they are testing using wind power for large cargo ships. The ship uses a large kite to reduce bunker fuel use. Solar panels could also be used on large ships to power electric motors. High fuel prices will stimulate all kinds of interesting ideas for the future.

---

[47] A capacitor is an electrical device that can store energy. A supercapacitor has very high energy density.
[48] Inductive charging uses electromagnetic induction to charge the batteries on the vehicle from an electromagnetic field in the road as the vehicle drives along.
[49] Assuming an average capacity factor of 70%, 2 billion kW = 2 x 0.7 x 365 x 24 = 12,264 billion kWh.

23 — Building Better Buildings

Most building energy today comes from fossil-fuel-sourced electricity along with gas, oil, coal and wood for heating and cooking. This means buildings offer big opportunities to reduce greenhouse gas emissions. We can make our biggest impact on saving energy by using our buildings more energy wisely.

Where Are Buildings at Today?
Residential and commercial buildings consume over a third of all the energy we use. Building emissions have increased steadily over the last 30 years but that growth is starting to slow, particularly in residential buildings. The growth in the commercial sector is much higher than in the residential sector. The IPPC believes there is a global potential to cost effectively reduce 29% of the projected emissions from residential and commercial buildings by 2020.[86]

In 2004, we generated 10.6 billion tonnes of CO_2-e emissions in residential and commercial buildings of which more than half was from electricity. The remaining 5 billion tonnes CO_2-e were the direct energy related emissions largely from heating and cooking in those buildings using fossil fuels (gas, oil and coal) and wood plus 1.5 billion tonnes of halocarbons (HFCs, CFCs and HCFCs) from refrigerators and air-conditioning systems.[86]

What Potential Energy Savings Can We Make in Buildings?
Much of the possible energy savings in buildings can be made with current technology and can generate a positive cost saving over a relatively short timeframe. We have discussed many of these already throughout the book, including more efficient lighting, reducing standby power, solar hot water heating, better insulation, passive and active solar heating and heat pumps. These are all covered in some detail in Chapter 14.

One of the big energy users in buildings is electric lighting. About one-third of building electricity emissions derive from lighting. The IPCC believes lighting energy use can be reduced by 75–90% with better use of daylight, better positioning of lighting and using more efficient light fittings. Appliances such as household appliances (refrigerators, washing machines, dishwashers, etc.), office equipment and consumer electronics are other big energy users. This equipment uses 40% of total residential primary energy use in the larger developed countries.[86] Equipment efficiency varies significantly, so choosing energy-efficient appliances can reduce our building energy use substantially. Standby power used by this equipment can also be significant (see Chapter 14).

Building control systems can use computers and electronic sensors to improve the energy use in a building. Smart meters plus temperature, occupancy and lighting sensors can be attached to the control systems to minimise energy use by automatically shutting down appliances and lighting when they are not needed or when they are more expensive to run. These systems can be used in both commercial and residential buildings.

Better building design allows many of these improvements to be built in right from the start. Key design decisions, often made by the architect, can significantly influence how effective the building will be at saving energy. There is a place for government regulations to ensure this happens as we discussed in Chapter 19.

Of course buildings can have a 50 year life, so many of the savings by 2030 will require retrofitting into existing buildings at greater cost, but they can still generate real savings. Some improvements like better use of daylight and passive solar heating may be very difficult or costly to retrofit. There may be a place for governments to provide incentives for building owners to make these improvements, although this may no longer be needed when the cost of greenhouse gas emissions is factored into the fuel price.

Savings in one area can create increases in other areas. In Chapter 22 we discussed the option of switching transport fuels from oil to electricity to reduce oil usage and reduce transport greenhouse gas emissions. In that chapter we discussed that some families might increase their electricity usage in the home by 50% by switching to plug-in battery electric vehicles. This would probably more than negate any home electricity savings we have discussed so far.

How Much Can We Reduce Building Greenhouse Gas Emissions by 2030?
Table 17 shows the IPCC's estimate of the building emissions reductions that can be made from the BAU case by 2030 at various carbon prices. As we can see, most of the savings can be made at less than $20 per tonne. Some additional savings are possible above $50 but these are of the order of only 10%.

Table 17

Building Emissions Reduction Potential by Sector

Building Emissions Reduction Potential by 2030	Reduction (billion tonnes of CO_2-e per year)		
Carbon price per tonne CO_2-e	<$20	<$50	<$100
Electricity savings	3.0–3.8	3.0–3.8	3.1–3.8
Fuel savings	1.9–2.3	1.9–2.3	2.3–2.9
Total	**4.9–6.1**	**4.9–6.1**	**5.4–6.7**

Source: IPCC[72]

The electricity savings in buildings are already included in the end-use electricity savings shown in Table 9 in the chapter on emissions reduction — Chapter 18. We can see that electricity emissions savings in buildings shown above make up around 90% of the total end-use savings from electricity shown in Table 9.

If we take the average potential building emissions reduction at less than $50 a tonne from the IPCC we get a saving of 5.5 billion tonnes of emissions. We can compare this figure with McKinsey's estimate of

3.7 billion tonnes.[75] We can reasonably expect that a reduction in building emissions of 2 billion tonnes over and above the electricity savings will be possible by 2030 at less than $20 a tonne.

What Changes in Building Energy Can We Expect by 2030?

Long before 2030, we will no longer be able to buy incandescent lamps for general lighting. Some may still be available for special purposes but most will be replaced by low-energy substitutes such as compact fluorescent lamps or light-emitting diodes.

We will see continued improvements in appliance efficiency. Average appliance standby power will be limited to one watt (see Chapter 14). Solar heated hot water will be standard in most countries, with water-saving devices to minimise hot water wastage. Solar heating will be used more widely for space heating as well as hot water. Improved building control systems will further help reduce the energy we use in buildings.

Building integrated PV cells consisting of PV modules that function as part of the building such as roof tiles, skylights or shading devices are available today but expensive. New thin film technology (perhaps using nanotechnology) will significantly reduce the cost of these integrated cells by 2030, making solar power in new buildings much more financially attractive and much more common.

We can expect more awareness by builders and renovators of better use of daylight, insulation and passive solar heating to reduce building energy use. Governments will introduce building standards and codes to ensure that higher efficiency appliances and designs are used.

24 — The Nuclear Explosion

So far in Part Three we have looked at how much we need to reduce energy greenhouse gas emissions in the future. A key part of this reduction involves decarbonising the primary energy source used in electricity generation. We have several options for this and different technologies will be used in different parts of the world depending on the circumstances. One of those technologies is nuclear power. This is a highly charged political issue but the potential of nuclear power as a cost effective way to reduce greenhouse gas emissions cannot be dismissed lightly.

Where Is Nuclear Power at Today?
Producing electricity from nuclear power has been around for over 50 years, so it is a mature and well understood technology. We have 440 operating nuclear plants spread throughout the world. Nuclear power produces 16% of the total world's electricity, about the same as hydro-power.

There is a great deal of misinformation about the cost effectiveness of nuclear power for reducing greenhouse gas emissions. By 2030, it is expected to be the most cost effective technology for low-carbon electricity generation based on the full life cycle cost per kWh (see Table 14 in Chapter 21). According to the IPCC, the full life cycle emissions from nuclear power stations are below 0.04 kg/kWh, which is similar to renewables such as wind and solar.[49] Nuclear power already makes a significant contribution to emissions reduction by avoiding between 1.5 and 2.5 billion tonnes per year compared to using fossil fuels. This is around 15–20% of the total emissions from electricity generation.

The capacity factors for nuclear power plants (the annual energy output divided by the theoretical maximum) are some of the best of any power plants at 80–90%. Compare this with solar PV at 25%, wind at 30%, hydro at 30–80% and coal at 75%.

Contrary to popular belief, we have sufficient supply of identified uranium reserves to last 80 years using current nuclear power technology. If we include probable reserves, we have over 200 years.[25] Any new nuclear power plant built in the next few decades will not run out of fuel and the next generation of nuclear plants will use even less fuel than the current generation.

Why Does Nuclear Power Have Such Bad Press?

Unfortunately, in the minds of many people, nuclear power is infamous for Chernobyl, plant safety, radiation dangers, nuclear waste storage, and the risk of nuclear proliferation and of terrorist attacks. We discussed most of these in detail in Chapter 5 and Chapter 15. The nuclear industry is only too aware of the bad press that nuclear power receives. Since the Three Mile Island accident in 1979 and Chernobyl in 1986 the orders for new nuclear plants fell substantially and many proposed plants were cancelled.

Back in the 1980s only a few scientists and knowledgeable conservationists really understood the impact of greenhouse gas emissions on the environment. For politicians in the last two decades of the 20th century it was easier to approve new fossil-fuel power stations than risk electorate wrath by approving new nuclear ones in the supercharged emotional backlash against nuclear power. In much of the world there was still plenty of coal. Natural gas discoveries in the North Sea made gas-fired plants a much safer political option in Europe.

In the last decade, understanding about greenhouse gas emissions has reached the public consciousness and a more balanced debate is starting to take place about nuclear power and its place in electricity generation.

What is the Future for Nuclear Power?

In Chapter 15 we discussed the politics of energy. In particular, we discussed whether we really needed nuclear power given all its 'baggage'. Nuclear power will need to climb a few hurdles before it becomes widely accepted by everyone as a significant part of the solution. Next generation nuclear plants are being designed and built to address waste directly and to improve safety, and further reduce the risks of proliferation and terrorism. The main safety objective of the nuclear industry is that human health and the environment are protected now and into the future without undue burden on future generations.

The nuclear waste problem is still not solved however, and won't be for another few years. Long-term, safe and secure nuclear waste storage will need to be in place before some will accept new nuclear power stations. Others will always worry about burying today's sins for future generations to stumble over. The same argument is levelled at CCS where today's carbon dioxide is buried for future generations to worry about — or use as a future energy source once the technology is in place to convert it economically into usable fuel.

In the meantime the world needs practical and affordable solutions to global warming. It takes a number of years to build and commission new power generation plants and many countries are not waiting for long-term nuclear waste storage before planning and building new nuclear power plants.

Where Will Nuclear Power Be by 2030?

Nuclear power is just part of the solution for generating our electricity needs by 2030, as we saw in Table 13 in Chapter 21. The IPCC sees the generation capacity from nuclear power increasing 57% by 2030 which will probably mean another 200–250 nuclear power stations. This means commissioning an average of 10 new nuclear plants each year from now to 2030.

Planning and building a new nuclear power plant can take several years. With 35 reactors currently being built, 91 on order or planned and 228 proposed, the target looks achievable. The location of these new plants will be widespread with 121 in China, 35 in Russia, 32 in the US and 25 in India and South Africa.[25] Not all the proposed plants may get built by 2030 but we can expect that many of them will.

Even with this significant increase in nuclear power it will still only represent 18% of the electricity generation capacity. By 2030, according to the IPCC, there will actually be more electricity coming from all renewable sources than from nuclear power. There will still be plenty of coal and gas used for electricity generation as well.

What About Nuclear After 2030?

With Generation IV reactors, the nuclear industry is aiming to build on current technology and answer many of the criticisms targeted at nuclear power. Generation IV plants should be available after 2030. Key design features aim to get the maximum return from the uranium fuel used and to reduce the amount of high-level waste produced to assist the long-term storage problem. Additional features of Generation IV reactors are minimising the risk of proliferation and reducing the risk of theft of weapons-usable material. These reactors will operate at higher temperatures than today's reactors and some are designed for low-emissions hydrogen production which can be used in transport. See Box 11 in Chapter 14 for more technical details about next generation nuclear reactors.

As we discussed in Chapter 6, the sun is a giant nuclear reactor that produces energy through nuclear fusion rather than nuclear fission used in current nuclear power reactors. For over 50 years researchers have been working at developing nuclear power reactors that would use fusion rather than fission. Fusion has two major benefits over fission. Firstly the reactor fuel (deuterium) is readily available from the ocean and provides a virtually unlimited source of fuel. Secondly there are no long-lived radioactive waste products. The scientific feasibility of fusion energy has been proven but the technical feasibility is yet to be demonstrated. The concept is taken very seriously however, with a $10 billion pilot plant planned for construction in France (the ITER[50] project). There are still many technical challenges to be overcome, so nuclear fusion for power generation is probably another 50 years away.

---

[50] International Thermonuclear Experimental Reactor.

Diminishing supplies of fossil fuels will probably guarantee a long future for nuclear power. When the coal, gas and oil have all run out and we still need reliable baseload capacity then all that will be left in some parts of the world will be nuclear power. Nuclear power will not be for everyone. A few countries will continue to ban it for political reasons. Others will just not need it because they have ample supplies of coal, hydro or geothermal power. But in some countries, nuclear power may be the only way they can meet their greenhouse gas emissions targets and reliably supply their population with adequate 24 by 7 low-carbon energy.

25 — The Sun Will Always Shine and the Wind Will Always Blow (at Least Some of the Time)

Eventually all non-renewable resources will run out — by definition. The debate about using renewable sources for energy is not about if, it's about when. Some will say now and the sooner the better! Others are more cautious on how quickly we can switch from non-renewable to renewable energy. Everyone agrees it will have to happen eventually. In this chapter we look at what it will take to move to all-renewable energy in a way that won't disrupt society as we know it.

Where Are Renewables at Today?

Renewable resources from solar, wind, hydro, geothermal and biomass supply about 13% of our primary energy. The largest renewable energy resource is still biomass — mainly used in developing countries for heating and cooking. Renewables supply 18% of our electricity, almost all of it hydropower.

In the first three-quarters of the 20th century, renewable resources in developed countries were largely limited to hydro-electric and geothermal heat and power plants where the resources were available. In the last quarter of the century we saw the growth in solar heating and cooling, wind power, solar PV and biofuels.

Over the last 30 years, the growth in renewable energy has been only slightly higher than the growth in total energy used. The 'new' renewables — solar, wind and geothermal — have grown at nearly four times the rate of total energy use with the fastest growth in wind power. These new renewables represent only 0.5% of our total primary energy today but are expected to become significant contributors to energy over the coming decades.[1]

What has held back the growth in renewables in developed countries has largely been cost. In a world of cheap fossil fuels, it has been hard for renewables to compete except for large-scale hydro and geothermal plants (not including EGS). This is starting to change. Once the cost of carbon is factored into energy prices, plus further investment made in renewable technology development, then renewable sources will start to look much more financially attractive.

In terms of electricity generation, renewables play a significant part but different challenges are present by different sources. Hydro can provide large-scale baseload and peak-load supply depending on water availability. Geothermal can provide baseload but is only available in limited areas. Biomass and waste plants are generally small in scale and probably better suited to distributed generation (DG). Wind can be intermediate scale but is intermittent and variable. Solar PV is both small-scale and intermittent.

What Renewable Resources Will We Use in the Future?
Hydro and geothermal sources will always be limited to locations with suitable resources but where they are available they can provide a ready replacement for fossil fuel. Not all countries have such resources so these options will not be open to everyone. These sources also need to meet environmental and social acceptability (see Chapter 8 and Chapter 9).

Solar heating and cooling, biofuels, wind power and solar PV are commercially available today, albeit with government subsidies and incentives in many countries. Demand for wind and solar PV electricity generation is increasing significantly. As the number of installations increase, technology will improve the products and costs will come down. 5MW wind turbines are already available but they are over 180 metres tall (the hight of a 50-storey office tower) and over 120 metres in diameter. Proposals have been made for 10MW wind turbines which will need to be much larger.

Newer renewable technologies like advanced biofuels, concentrated solar power with heat storage (CSP), enhanced geothermal systems (EGS) and ocean energy are not yet fully commercialised and some are not yet demonstrated. These technologies need much more research and development before we can be certain about their future contribution to energy supply.

In Chapter 21 we looked at the future of electricity and in Table 13 we analysed electricity generation. By 2030, about a third of electricity will come from renewables compared to 18% today. The big growth will be in the new renewables plus biomass, but hydro will still dominate renewable electricity generation in 2030 producing about half of it.

What Would be Needed for an All-Renewables Future?

The most challenging area for renewable energy is electricity generation. Over the last 100 years, electricity generation has been built around large coal-fired power stations that run 24 hours a day usually located away from population centres. This means that electricity generation is largely centralised with extensive networks of power lines to distribute the electricity to where it is used. This structure is fine for large fossil fuel and nuclear power stations. It can also readily incorporate large renewable hydro and geothermal plants that can run continuously.

In those countries that can generate sufficient hydro and geothermal power, the existing networks may work fine in an all-renewables future. Most countries are not in this position. They will need to rely on solar, wind, biomass and possibly ocean power for the renewable sources. The proven technologies we have today for these sources are either intermittent, variable or small scale and more suited to distributed generation (DG) systems (see Chapter 21).

Solar, wind and biomass can make a valuable medium-scale contribution (<20%) to a centralised grid system today but they cannot readily provide the large-scale 24 by 7 coverage that consumers in the developed world have grown up to expect without adequate electricity storage facilities or reserve fossil-fuel capacity to cope with the variability. Lead acid battery storage can work fine for small-scale domestic supply but it will not cope with the high energy demands of large industry or commercial complexes. Wind advocates have proposed interconnected, geographically distributed wind farms as a solution but they will not provide adequate power during wide-area calm weather. Solar advocates believe that CSP with thermal storage will provide the answer but current storage systems will not survive a long-lasting cloud event of several days. For most of us in the developed world, our lifestyle relies on large industry and continuous access to plenty of cheap, reliable electricity. Without it we would need a massive change to the way we run our economies and live our lives.

Pumped hydro storage is a mature renewable technology for storing large amounts of electricity but it requires suitable sites (see Chapter 8). For those countries that cannot use pumped storage, we still need substantial technology development in renewable energy storage systems before an all-renewable future is a reality. The most promising renewable storage technologies are CSP with thermal storage and large flow batteries that can store electricity from wind turbines and solar PV cells. These technologies are still in the development phase and may be some years before they are commercially available in the scale needed. In the meantime we will need to rely on fossil-fuel-powered reserve supply to cover for those times when mother nature fails to deliver sufficient sun or wind to run our solar and wind-powered systems. Even when available, CSP will probably be limited to countries in lower latitudes closer to the equator where there is sufficient solar availability and plenty of flat available land.

With these technology developments, it seems likely that our electricity networks will need to cope with many, smaller, renewable energy powered generators and storage systems. Upgrading those networks will not happen overnight and will cost billions of dollars.

For most of us, unless we are prepared to restructure our lifestyle and live in decentralised, self-sufficient communities without the fruits of mass-production like motor vehicles, we will need to wait for large-scale storage and upgraded electricity networks before we can embrace an all-renewables energy supply and turn off all those centralised fossil-fuel and nuclear power plants.

We still need extensive research and development in renewable technologies to deliver the dream of an all-renewable future. As I said in the Preface, we need our governments to actively encourage the development of new technologies because private industry won't do it on its own.

What Is a More Likely Future for Renewables?

Modern industry in both the developed and developing world needs plenty of reliable, 24 hour a day baseload electricity (see Chapter 1). In many countries about two-thirds of the total power consumption is baseload. Until renewable energy can reliably provide this level of baseload service then countries will continue to use some fossil fuels or nuclear energy. In some countries, some of this renewable baseload can come from hydro or geothermal plants. Others could use geographically distributed large interconnected wind farms to provide some of this baseload demand because while one farm may have calm conditions another may have gusty winds. But they will often need some intermediate level non-renewable backup supply as well to cover for widespread calm days.

The future 'white knights' of renewable baseload supply are CSP with thermal storage and geothermal power from hot dry rocks (EGS). Both these technologies are under development with demonstration plants built or under construction. It can take many decades to move from demonstration phase to full commercial availability and there is always a risk that some technology problems may not be overcome. This is probably more of a risk for EGS than CSP, which is a more mature technology.

Both these white knights will need suitable locations that are likely to be away from existing high voltage grids. EGS needs the right geological rock structure and CSP will probably need large flat desert areas (low rainfall, high sunshine) in low latitudes. This will mean the costly building of new grid interconnections, possibly over several hundred kilometres using HVDC.[51] It can cost $2 million per kilometre for a high voltage transmission link. If the EGS or CSP station has to be located 500 km from the grid the transmission link might double the cost of a 500MW power plant and double the cost of the electricity generated.

[51] High voltage DC — see **Chapter 1.**

In many countries, the speed of adoption of renewables for baseload power will depend on how successful we turn out to be at cleaning up the fossil-fuel plants. Most new coal plants under construction today produce much less greenhouse gas than their old thermal predecessors by using technologies like IGCC (see Chapter 14). If carbon capture and storage (CCS) is successfully delivered by 2020 then this may be a more attractive solution financially to greenhouse gas emissions than either CSP or EGS, particularly in those countries with large reserves of coal like Brazil, Russia, India and Australia. If CCS proves to be unsuccessful then new nuclear plants may also look more attractive financially.

Over the next few decades, the likely future for renewables in electricity supply is in DG systems (particularly solar PV in buildings) and as contributors to intermittent-load and peak-load grid supply (particularly wind farms and CSP) where they augment existing gas turbines. This will probably limit renewables contribution to about one-third of the total generation capacity until cost competitive energy storage systems are available.

Solar technology will improve over the next 30 to 50 years with better sunlight conversion efficiency and large-scale effective thermal or chemical storage systems that can last several days. We have plenty of solar energy hitting the Earth to satisfy our energy needs. We just need to be able to harness and store it for that string of cloudy days.

26 — Is There Still Hope?

We have now looked at all our energy options for the foreseeable future and considered what needs to be done to the energy mix to cope with the changing climate. We need to reduce greenhouse gases to an acceptable level. It will not be an easy journey but we have tried not to rely on false hope. So can we make it unscathed?

Can We Meet Our Emissions Reduction Targets and Keep the Lights On?
The answer to this question depends on how fast we try to reduce our emissions. Some very aggressive emissions targets set by some conservationists may well cause severe energy reliability issues in some countries and substantially decrease GDP and possible damage the social fabric.

In Part Three of the book, we have looked at what is possible to be on track to stabilise greenhouse gases at 550ppm by 2030. The estimate we made in Chapter 18 was that we need a reduction in energy emissions of 9–12 billon tonnes below the business-as-usual level to stabilise at 550ppm. In Chapter 21 we identified 9 billion tonnes that could be saved in electricity generation, in Chapter 22 we identified 1–2 billion tonnes from transport and in Chapter 23, 2 billion tonnes from buildings over and above the electricity savings which are included in electricity generation. This gives us a total of between 12 and 13 billion tonnes of identified energy emissions reductions by 2030. From this we can say that a reduction of 9–12 billion tonnes of emissions is achievable at a carbon price between $20 and $50 a tonne.

We can achieve this by making energy savings, mostly at negative cost so they should be done anyway, plus technology changes to our electricity generation, transport and buildings that do not require a significant change to our lifestyle. To increase the reduction above 12 billion tonnes will require a much higher carbon price with an associated increase in energy prices.

Energy will be more expensive at a carbon price of $20 (see Table 8 in Chapter 17) but not so expensive that we will all have to stop turning on the lights or driving our cars. We are likely to have to pay no more that 10% extra on our fuel bills. We may be turning on lights that work differently and driving cars that are powered differently but we can read at night without using candles and travel comfortably from place to place without resorting to pedal power.

What Can't We Change?

We are stuck with running out of oil eventually. Whatever can be done about peak oil will be done by using fewer oil products and finding unconventional oil replacement as we discussed in Chapter 12. We need to plan for a future with much higher oil prices and higher petrol and diesel costs. We have finite supplies of coal, natural gas and uranium. There are many arguments about how long the supplies will last but they will all run out eventually.

The potential consequences of global warming could be catastrophic. We need to reduce greenhouse gas emissions in case it really is causing global warming. If it is, we need to address the problem as soon as realistically possible because the longer we leave it the greater the risk that we may pass the point of no return. If it turns out that that the Earth's warming isn't caused by human produced carbon dioxide then we will have mitigated against a possible risk by buying ourselves a relatively inexpensive insurance policy that we are more than happy not to claim on.

What Do We Need to Do?

Probably very few of the changes to energy we have discussed in this book will take place without some action from us and our governments.

We need to support our governments to introduce market-based systems such as emissions trading schemes or carbon taxes so that the cost of climate change is paid by the producer of the emissions. This will provide real financial incentives for emitters to reduce carbon emissions and consumers to not waste energy.

We need government sponsored financial incentives such as research and development grants or tax benefits to encourage investment in low-carbon technologies. We want the kind of investments that will ultimately bring down the price of clean energy to the price of dirty coal today. This would be the most effective way to encourage developing countries like China and India, as well as the developed world, to switch from dirty coal to clean energy.

We need our governments to mandate energy efficiency levels for new vehicles, appliances and buildings. This can ensure that the most efficient technology is used by the manufacturers and builders right from the start rather than just building the products or homes for the lowest cost.

We need to support our governments to review and reform energy subsidies. Some of these subsidies can be productive such as encouraging efficiency but others are counterproductive such as subsidies for fossil fuels like diesel. Those that are counterproductive should be phased out. We need to co-opt those who retain a strong (vested) interest in maintaining the status quo such as coal miners, the oil and gas industry, and motor vehicle manufacturers. They can be powerful lobby groups that can divert government policy away from the direction we want.

We need to prepare for the impacts of inevitable climate change. We discussed adaptation in Chapter 15. We therefore need to encourage our governments to have an adaptation strategy as well as the mitigation reforms above.

What Is Already Happening?

Energy systems in some countries are already evolving from fossil-fuel dependence in response to climate change and need for energy security. Oil seems to be the resource that most worries countries that don't have their own supply. Some countries, such as Sweden, are being proactive at replacing oil with renewable energy and reducing oil demand through energy conservation.

The European Union (EU) has now entered the second phase of its Emissions Trading Scheme (EU ETS) which runs from 2008 to 2012. Valuable lessons were learnt from Phase I which have led to changes in Phase II. Australia is also now preparing its own ETS that will commence in 2010. We can expect other countries to follow with their own market-based systems to reduce emissions.

Regulations are being implemented to improve energy efficiency and reduce emissions from appliances, buildings and vehicles. The EU proposes an average vehicle emissions target for new cars. Many countries use a mandated energy rating system for appliances so that consumers can compare energy efficiency between competing brands when buying a new appliance. Similar rating systems are used for buildings so that a purchaser can gauge the energy efficiency of a home. The US has the HERS index (Home Energy Rater) where a reference home is rated at 100 and a rating of zero means the building uses no net purchased energy.

Subsidies are being provided in many countries to encourage renewable energy sources such as wind and solar. We discussed some of the pitfalls with subsidies in Chapter 15 but they can be a way of getting a new industry off the ground when it would otherwise be unable to compete financially with existing alternatives. The common example is the installation of solar PV cells on domestic buildings. The upfront cost is significant and the payback period may be longer than the home owner expects to remain in the property, so the domestic solar PV industry would struggle without government subsidies. Once an effective market-based system like an ETS or carbon tax is in place there should be less need for such subsidies as fuel prices will rise and payback periods will reduce.

What Do We Need to Recognise?

Simplistic solutions to energy emissions reduction are unlikely to be successful. Making hard and fast demands — no nuclear power, no more coal, no carbon capture and storage, use 100% solar power — are not the answer. Nor is expecting everyone in the world to use much less energy. We need a realistic balance between reducing energy emissions and not wrecking the world economy. This may mean that some 'sacred cows' like banning nuclear power need to be set aside.

Fossil fuels will not last forever. Peak oil may happen much later than even the oil industry thinks but it will happen eventually. But we cannot get rid of fossil fuels quickly. We should see renewable energy resources as augmenting our existing fossil-fuel energy sources and then progressively replacing them. If we head down the path of improving energy efficiency — getting more from less — and reducing our reliance on fossil fuels we will have helped ourselves and the planet even if global warming turns out not to be caused by human emissions or not to be occurring at all!

Developing countries are key contributors to addressing our future energy and greenhouse gas levels but we cannot expect them to make substantial sacrifices in growth just because the rest of us did our developing when no one cared about carbon emissions. An argument often raised by developing countries — that the developed world created the problem so they can fix it — has a ring of fairness about it. The developed world will need to carry the lion's share of reducing emissions in the next few years and decades but it cannot do it alone.

There is no one solution for every country. We need regional solutions that recognise local growth rates, local availability of natural resources and local existing infrastructure. This will almost certainly mean that some countries cannot rely solely on renewable energy resources for some time to come. They will all have to get there eventually but it may be well into the 22nd century, and who knows what technology will be available by then?

Whatever happens, we will not run out of primary energy. There is enough sunlight falling on the Earth to allow us to use 7000 times the energy we use today. The world population is likely to be limited by food supply and water long before it runs out energy.

What Can We Look Forward To?

We can look forward to a future were we no longer remove non-renewal resources from the Earth to power our lifestyle. This is an easy prediction to make. We don't even need a crystal ball for this one. What is less clear is when. Some would like to see it this century but I doubt that will happen.

Out of all this effort to reduce greenhouse gas emissions and maintain energy security, we will make wonderful new inventions that will make life (for some of us) even more comfortable and (I trust) the environment cleaner and greener. We will need to spend up big on renewable energy technology research to reduce costs and improve output and we need to do it before all the non-renewables are gone.

Some of the most exciting technologies may be biological solutions. After all, that's all Mother Earth had in the past. Technologies like algae that can convert carbon dioxide to biodiesel would be a wonderful win for the energy industry as well as the planet. In the shorter term, it could address the thorny issue of storing carbon dioxide from fossil fuels and longer term could remove past carbon dioxide emissions from the atmosphere. It would also allow us to keep using internal combustion engines where they are still needed.

We can expect nanotechnology to play a part (see Chapter 14). Super thin, super cheap solar PV cells that can cover the outer skin of all our buildings could make a substantial contribution to a renewable energy supply. Along with this will come much more distributed energy generation where the electricity is generated at the place it is used rather than centrally.

Looking again at the crystal ball, we seem to be heading for a future where electricity is our major energy carrier along with (possibly) hydrogen. We can expect substantial improvements in hydrogen fuel cells which may prove a better solution than batteries for transport vehicles. But this seems unclear at this stage. Either way, electricity-powered vehicles seem to be the future for transport unless burning hydrogen proves to be a better solution.

And above all else, we can look forward to reducing greenhouse gas emissions and limiting global warming to a level that we and the planet can tolerate. This will prove the doomsayers wrong about the planet's future and give comfort to all those IPCC scientists who will be able to say, 'we told you so.'

References

Reference numbers are in square brackets in the text.

1 International Energy Agency — Renewables in Global Energy Supply January 2007 http://www.iea.org/textbase/papers/2006/renewable_factsheet.pdf
2 World Resources Institute — Climate Analysis Indicators Tool (CAIT), http://cait.wri.org
3 US DOE Energy Information Administration — France, http://www.eia.doe.gov/emeu/cabs/France/Background.html
4 US DOE Energy Information Administration — International Energy Outlook 2007 Chapter 6 http://www.eia.doe.gov/oiaf/ieo/pdf/electricity.pdf
5 US DOE Energy Information Administration — End-Use Consumption of Electricity 2001 http://www.eia.doe.gov/emeu/recs/recs2001/enduse2001/enduse2001.html
6 Alan Meier and Benoit Lebot — One Watt Initiative a Global Effort to Reduce Electricity 1999 http://www.osti.gov/bridge/servlets/purl/795944-XFu5mJ/native/795944.pdf
7 US DOE Energy Information Administration — Direct Use and Retail Sales of Electricity 2005 http://www.eia.doe.gov/cneaf/electricity/epa/epat7p2.html
8 OECD/International Energy Agency — Projected Costs of Generating Electricity-2005 Update, http://www.iea.org/textbase/nppdf/free/2005/ElecCost.pdf
9 US DOE Energy Information Administration — International Electricity Prices for Households Feb 2007 http://www.eia.doe.gov/emeu/international/elecprih.html
10 US DOE Energy Information Administration — Average Retail Price of Electricity Feb 2007 http://www.eia.doe.gov/cneaf/electricity/epm/table5_6_a.html
11 International Atomic Energy Agency — Nuclear Power and Climate Change http://www.iaea.org/OurWork/ST/NE/Pess/assets/03-01708_Rognerspeech.pdf
12 US DOE Energy Information Administration — International Natural Gas Prices for Households Feb 2007 http://www.eia.doe.gov/emeu/international/ngasprih.html
13 US DOE Energy Information Administration — International Energy Outlook 2007 Chapter 3 http://www.eia.doe.gov/oiaf/ieo/pdf/oil.pdf
14 US DOE Energy Information Administration — International Energy Annual 2005 World Petroleum Data http://www.eia.doe.gov/iea/pet.html

15 International Energy Agency — End-User Petroleum Product Prices, http://www.iea. org/Textbase/stats/surveys/mps.pdf

16 US DOE and US EPA Energy Efficiency and Renewable Energy http://www. fueleconomy.gov/feg/driveHabits.shtml

17 US DOE and US EPA Energy Efficiency and Renewable Energy http://www. fueleconomy.gov/feg/findacar.htm

18 Boeing Commercial Airplanes — Products — 787 Dreamliner, http://www.boeing. com/commercial/787family/background.html

19 US DOE Energy Information Administration — Fuel and Emissions Coefficients http://www.eia.doe.gov/oiaf/1605/factors.html

20 US DOE Energy Information Administration — Steam Coal Prices 2007 http://www. eia.doe.gov/emeu/international/stmforelec.html

21 The Australian Coal Association — Coal in a Sustainable Society 2000 http://www.australiancoal.com.au/Pubs/CISS%20Summary.pdf

22 International Iron and Steel Institution — A Policy to Reduce Steel-related Greenhouse Gas Emissions http://www.jernkontoret.se/jernkontoret/pressmeddelanden/2007/climate_change_policy_final.pdf

23 World Coal Institute — Coal Facts 2006, http://www.worldcoal.org/pages/content/index.asp?PageID=188

24 US DOE Energy Information Administration — World Net Electricity Generation by Type 2005 http://www.eia.doe.gov/emeu/international/RecentElectricityGenerationBy Type.xls

25 World Nuclear Association — Information Papers , http://www.world-nuclear.org/info

26 World Business Council for Sustainable Development , http://www.wbcsd.org

27 Solarbuzz LLC — Photovoltaic Industry Statistics August 2008, http://www.solarbuzz. com/StatsCosts.htm

28 Solarbuzz LLC — Solar Electricity Prices August 2008, http://www.solarbuzz.com/SolarPrices.htm

29 Windustry — Wind Energy Today and Tomorrow 2007, http://www.windustry.com/basics/01-windenergytodayandtomorrow.htm

30 American Wind Energy Association — Wind Energy Costs accessed August 2007, http://www.awea.org/faq/wwt_costs.html

31 World Wind Energy Association, http://www.wwindea.org/home/index.php

32 US DOE Energy Information Administration — World Net Electricity Generation by Type 2005 http://www.eia.doe.gov/emeu/international/RecentElectricityGenerationBy Type.xls

33 US DOE Energy Efficiency and Renewable Energy — Geothermal Technology Program 2006 http://www1.eere.energy.gov/geothermal/faqs.html

34 US DOE Energy Efficiency and Renewable Energy — Biomass Program Environmental Benefits http://www1.eere.energy.gov/biomass/environmental.html

35 Air Products and Chemicals, Inc — Hydrogen Energy Frequently Asked Questions http://www.airproducts.com/Products/LiquidBulkGases/HydrogenEnergyFuelCells/FrequentlyAskedQuestions.htm

36 Australian Govt Greenhouse Office — Advanced Electricity Storage Technology Programme Dec 2005, http://www.greenhouse.gov.au/renewable/aest/pubs/aest-review.pdf

37 BP statistical review of world energy 2007 http://www.bp.com/productlanding.do?categoryId=6848&contentId=7033471

38 US DOE Energy Information Administration — World Oil Production Projections 2007 http://www.eia.doe.gov/oiaf/forecasting.html

39 Energy Watch Group — Crude Oil Supply Outlook Oct 2007 http://www.

energywatchgroup.org/fileadmin/global/pdf/EWG_Oilreport_10-2007.pdf
40 The Association for the Study of Peak Oil and Gas — Newsletter No. 80 August 2007
    http://www.aspo-ireland.org/contentFiles/newsletterPDFs/Newsletter80_200708.pdf
41 Cambridge Energy Research Associates Inc. — Press Release November 2006
    http://www.cera.com/aspx/cda/public1/news/pressReleases/pressReleaseDetails.
    aspx?CID=8444
42 The World Bank Data & Statistics — Population Dynamics 2007, http://www.
    worldbank.org/data
43 Jean Laherrere — Future of Natural Gas Supply ASPO Berlin May 2004 http://www.
    peakoil.net/JL/BerlinMay20.pdf
44 Intergovernmental Panel on Climate Change — Working Group 1 AR4 Report' http://
    www.ipcc.ch/ipccreports/ar4-wg1.htm
45 NASA Goddard Institute for Space Studies, http://data.giss.nasa.gov/gistemp/graphs/
46 Intergovernmental Panel on Climate Change — The AR4 Synthesis Report November
    2007 http://www.ipcc.ch/pdf/assessment-report/ar4/syr/ar4_syr_spm.pdf
47 The Stern Review on the Economics of Climate Change October 2006, http://www.
    hm-treasury.gov.uk/independent_reviews/stern_review_economics_climate_change/
    stern_review_report.cfm
48 Intergovernmental Panel on Climate Change — Carbon Dioxide Capture and Storage
    Special Report 2005 http://www.ipcc.ch/ipccreports/special-reports.htm
49 Intergovernmental Panel on Climate Change — Working Group 3 AR4 Report Chapter
    4 http://www.ipcc.ch/pdf/assessment-report/ar4/wg3/ar4-wg3-chapter4.pdf
50 NREL Parabolic Trough Power Plant Market, Economic Assessment and Deployment
    April 2007 http://www.nrel.gov/csp/troughnet/market_economic_assess.html#cost
51 Nanosolar Inc, http://www.nanosolar.com
52 CSIRO Australia — Smart approaches to electricity use ECOS 135 Feb-Mar 2007
    http://www.publish.csiro.au/?act=view_file&file_id=EC135p12.pdf
53 International Energy Agency — Standby Power Use and the IEA '1 Watt Plan' April
    2007 http://www.iea.org/textbase/papers/2007/standby_fact.pdf
54 International Energy Agency — IEA Standby Power Policy Summary July 2007 http://
    www.iea.org/textbase/papers/2007/Standby_Summary.pdf
55 Electricity Storage Association — Technology Comparisons Per Cycle Cost http://
    electricitystorage.org/tech/technologies_comparisons_percyclecost.htm
56 The New Scientist Environment — Climate change: A guide for the perplexed May
    2007 http://environment.newscientist.com/channel/earth/climate-change/dn11462-
    climate-change-a-guide-for-the-perplexed.html
57 MSNBC — staff and news service reports January 2007, http://www.msnbc.msn.com/
    id/16593606/
58 The US Senate — EPW Press Blog December 2007 http://epw.senate.gov/public/
    index.cfm?FuseAction=Minority.SenateReport#report
59 UxC Consulting Company, LLC — World Uranium Production 2006 http://www.uxc.
    com/fuelcycle/uranium/production-uranium.html
60 United Nations — Population Newsletter June 2007 http://www.un.org/esa/
    population/publications/popnews/Newsltr_83.pdf
61 Greenpeace International — Energy [R]evolution Report January 2007 http://www.
    greenpeace.org/raw/content/international/press/reports/energyrevolutionreport.pdf
62 International Energy Agency — World Energy Outlook 2007, http://www.iea.org/
    Textbase/npsum/WEO2007SUM.pdf
63 European Commission — Externe, *External Costs: Research results on socio-environmental
    damages due to electricity and transport.* 2003, http://www.externe.info
64 Caithness Windfarm Information Forum. Summary of wind turbine accident data to

Nov 2007 http://www.caithnesswindfarms.co.uk

65 World Nuclear Association — Waste Management in the Nuclear Fuel Cycle http://www.world-nuclear.org/info/inf04.htm

66 The New York Times — Nukes are Green by Nicholas Kristof April 2005 http://www.nytimes.com/2005/04/09/opinion/09kristof.html?_r=1&hp&oref=slogin

67 ueobserver.com — New EU emissions trading system to increase electricity prices January 2008 http://euobserver.com/9/25500?rss_rk=1

68 Timesonline — Shell chief fears oil shortage in seven years January 25, 2008 http://business.timesonline.co.uk/tol/business/economics/wef/article3248484.ece

69 Shell Group — Two Energy Futures by Jeroen van der Veer Chief Executive of Royal Dutch Shell plc http://www.shell.com/home/content/aboutshell-en/our_strategy/shell_global_scenarios/two_energy_futures/two_energy_futures_25012008.html

70 Robert Hirsh et al — Peaking of World Oil Production: Impacts, Mitigation & Risk Management 2005 http://www.netl.doe.gov/publications/others/pdf/Oil_Peaking_NETL.pdf

71 William Nordhaus — The Stern Review on the Economics of Climate Change — May 2007, http://nordhaus.econ.yale.edu/stern_050307.pdf

72 Intergovernmental Panel on Climate Change — Working Group 3 AR4 Report Chapter 11 http://www.ipcc.ch/pdf/assessment-report/ar4/wg3/ar4-wg3-chapter11.pdf

73 Intergovernmental Panel on Climate Change — Working Group 3 AR4 Report Chapter 3 http://www.ipcc.ch/pdf/assessment-report/ar4/wg3/ar4-wg3-chapter3.pdf

74 International Energy Agency — World Energy Outlook 2004 http://www.iea.org/textbase/nppdf/free/2004/weo2004.pdf

75 McKinsey Quarterly — A Cost Curve for Greenhouse Gas Reduction January 2007 http://www.mckinseyquarterly.com/PDFDownload.aspx?L2=3&L3=41&ar=1911

76 Global Wind Energy Council — Outlook 2006 http://www.gwec.net/fileadmin/documents/Publications/GWEC_A4_0609_English.pdf

77 2008 14th biennial CSP Solarpaces Symposium Las Vegas, Nevada March 2008 http://www.solarpaces.org/

78 Greenfuel Technologies Corporation — MIT Cogeneration Plant Trial October 2004 http://www.greenfuelonline.com/gf_files/CK_Test_Report.pdf

79 World Alliance for Decentralized Energy — World Survey 2006 http://www.localpower.org/documents/report_worldsurvey06.pdf

80 International Energy Agency — Variability of Wind Power and Other Renewables 2005 http://www.iea.org/textbase/papers/2005/variability.pdf

81 Intergovernmental Panel on Climate Change — Working Group 3 AR4 Report Chapter 5 http://www.ipcc.ch/pdf/assessment-report/ar4/wg3/ar4-wg3-chapter5.pdf

82 World Business Council for Sustainable Development — Mobility 2030 http://www.wbcsd.ch/plugins/DocSearch/details.asp?type=DocDet&ObjectId=NjA5NA

83 World Business Council for Sustainable Development — IEA/SMP Model Documentation and Reference Project July 2004, http://www.wbcsd.org/web/publications/mobility/smp-model-document.pdf

84 International Energy Agency — Energy Technologies for a Sustainable Future in Transport 2004 http://www.iea.org/textbase/papers/2004/transport.pdf

85 Tesla Motors, Inc. San Carlos California, http://www.teslamotors.com

86 Intergovernmental Panel on Climate Change — Working Group 3 AR4 Report Chapter 6 http://www.ipcc.ch/pdf/assessment-report/ar4/wg3/ar4-wg3-chapter6.pdf

Bibliography

Books About Climate Change

Broecker, Wallace S., and Robert Kunzig, *Fixing Climate: What Past Climate Changes Reveal About the Current Threat—and How to Counter It*. Hill & Wang, 2008.

Emanuel, Kerry, Judith A. Layzer and William R. Moomaw, *What We Know About Climate Change*. The MIT Press, 2007.

Fagan, Brian, *The Great Warming: Climate Change and the Rise and Fall of Civilizations*. Bloomsbury Press, 2008.

Gautier, Catherine, and Jean-Louis Fellous, *Facing Climate Change Together*. Cambridge University Press, 2008.

Hansjürgens, Bernd, and Ralf Antes, *Economics and Management of Climate Change: Risks, Mitigation and Adaptation*. Springer, 2008.

Hillman, Mayer, Tina Fawcett and Sudhir Chella Rajan, *The Suicidal Planet: How to Prevent Global Climate Catastrophe*. Thomas Dunne Books, 2007.

Ibbotson, John, *Planning Ahead for Future Generations by Highlighting Climate Change Myths*. Australian Lighthouse Traders, 2007.

Johansen, Bruce E., *Global Warming 101*. Greenwood Press, 2008.

Lawson, Nigel, *An Appeal to Reason: A Cool Look at Global Warming*. Overlook, 2008.

Leichenko, Robin, and Karen O'Brien, *Environmental Change and Globalization: Double Exposures*. Oxford University Press, USA, 2008.

Lovelock, James, *The Revenge of Gaia: Earth's Climate Crisis and the Fate of Humanity*. Basic Books, 2007.

Monbiot, George, *Heat: How to Stop the Planet From Burning*. South End Press, 2007.

Morhardt, Emil J., *Global Climate Change and Natural Resources: Summaries of the 2007–2008 Scientific Literature*. Roberts Environmental Center Press, 2008.

Pearce, Fred, *With Speed and Violence: Why Scientists Fear Tipping Points in Climate Change*. Beacon Press, 2008.

Ruddiman, William F., *Plows, Plagues, and Petroleum: How Humans Took Control of Climate*. Princeton University Press, 2007.

Schott, Robin, *The Global Carbon Pricing Policy Solution to Climate Change*. VDM Verlag, 2008.

Shellenberger, Michael, and Ted Nordhaus, *Break Through: From the Death of Environmentalism to the Politics of Possibility*. Houghton Mifflin Co, 2007.

Singer, Fred, and Dennis T. Avery, *Unstoppable Global Warming: Every 1,500 Years, Updated and Expanded Edition*. Rowman & Littlefield Publishers, 2008

Solomon, Lawrence, *The Deniers: The World Renowned Scientists Who Stood Up Against Global Warming Hysteria, Political Persecution, and Fraud**And those who are too fearful to do so*. Richard Vigilante Books, 2008.

Spencer, Roy, *Climate Confusion: How Global Warming Hysteria Leads to Bad Science, Pandering Politicians and Misguided Policies that Hurt the Poor*. Encounter Books, 2008.

Speth, James Gustave, *The Bridge at the Edge of the World: Capitalism, the Environment, and Crossing From Crisis to Sustainability*. Yale University Press, 2008.

Spratt, David, and Philip Sutton, *Climate Code Red: The Case for Emergency Action*. Scribe Publications, 2008.

Books on Energy

Avato, Patrick, and Jonathan Coony, *Accelerating Clean Energy Technology Research, Development, and Deployment: Lessons from Non-Energy Sectors*. World Bank Working Papers. World Bank Publications, 2008.

Barbir, Frano, and Sergio Ulgiati, *Sustainable Energy Production and Consumption: Benefits, Strategies and Environmental Costing*. NATO Science for Peace and Security Series C: Environmental Security. Springer, 2008.

Bodansky, David, *Nuclear Energy: Principles, Practices, and Prospects*. Springer, 2008.

Coley, David, *Energy and Climate Change: Creating a Sustainable Future*. Wiley, 2008.

Cravens, Gwyneth, and Richard Rhodes, *Power to Save the World: The Truth About Nuclear Energy*. Vintage, 2007.

Freris, Leon, and David Infield, *Renewable Energy in Power Systems*. Wiley, 2008.

Grubb, Michael, Tooraj Jamasb and Michael G. Pollitt, *Delivering a Low Carbon Electricity System: Technologies, Economics and Policy*. Department of Applied Economics Occasional Papers. Cambridge University Press, 2008.

Hoffman, Jane, and Michael J. Hoffman, *Green: Your Place in the New Energy Revolution*. Palgrave Macmillan, 2008.

Hopkins, Rob, and Richard Heinberg, *The Transition Handbook: From Oil Dependency to Local Resilience*. Green Books, 2008.

Krupp, Fred, Miriam Horn and Dick Hill, *Earth: The Sequel: The Race to Reinvent Energy and Stop Global Warming*. W. W. Norton, 2008.

Lerch, Daniel, *Post Carbon Cities: Planning for Energy and Climate Uncertainty*. Post Carbon Press, 2008.

Pimentel, David, *Biofuels, Solar and Wind as Renewable Energy Systems: Benefits and Risks*. Springer, 2008.

Scott, David Sanborn, *Smelling Land: The Hydrogen Defense Against Climate Catastrophe — Enhanced Edition*. Queen's Printer, 2008.

Sen, Zekai, *Solar Energy Fundamentals and Modeling Techniques: Atmosphere, Environment, Climate Change and Renewable Energy*. Springer, 2008.

Tertzakian, Peter, *A Thousand Barrels a Second: The Coming Oil Break Point and the Challenges Facing an Energy Dependent World*. McGraw-Hill, 2007.

Vanek, Francis, and Louis D. Albright, *Energy Systems Engineering: Evaluation and Implementation.* McGraw-Hill Professional, 2008.

Wengenmayr, Roland, and Thomas Bührke, *Renewable Energy: Sustainable Energy Concepts for the Future.* Wiley-VCH, 2008.

Reference Material

European Commission — Externe, *External Costs: Research Results on Socio-Environmental Damages Due to Electricity and Transport.* 2003.

Greenpeace International, Arthouros Zervos et al., *Energy [R]evolution — A sustainable World Energy Outlook (Report Global Energy Scenario).* Greenpeace and EREC, 2007.

Hirsh, Robert L., et al., *Peaking of World Oil Production: Impacts, Mitigation and Risk Management.* Nova Science Publishers, 2005.

Intergovernmental Panel on Climate Change, *Carbon Dioxide Capture and Storage Special Report.* Cambridge University Press, 2005.

Intergovernmental Panel on Climate Change, *Fourth Assessment Report: Climate Change.* Cambridge University Press, 2007.

The AR4 Synthesis Report
Working Group I Report: 'The Physical Science Basis'
Working Group II Report: 'Impacts, Adaptation and Vulnerability'
Working Group III Report: 'Mitigation of Climate Change'

International Atomic Energy Agency, Hans Holger Rogner, *Nuclear Power and Climate Change.* 2003.

International Energy Agency, *Energy Technologies for a Sustainable Future — Transport.* IEA Publications, 2004.

International Energy Agency, *World Energy Outlook,* IEA Publications, 2004.

International Energy Agency, *Projected Costs of Generating Electricity.* IEA Publications, 2005.

International Energy Agency, *Variability of Wind Power and Other Renewables.* IEA Publications, 2005.

International Energy Agency, *Renewables in Global Energy Supply — Fact Sheet.* IEA Publications, 2007.

International Energy Agency, *Standby Power Use and the IEA '1 Watt Plan' — Fact Sheet.* IEA Publications, 2007.

International Energy Agency, *World Energy Outlook.* IEA Publications, 2007.

McKinsey Quarterly, Per-Anders Enkvist et al., *A Cost Curve for Greenhouse Gas Reduction.* January 2007.

Nordhaus, William, *The Stern Review on the Economics of Climate Change.* 2007.

Stern, Nicholas, *The Economics of Climate Change: The Stern Review.* Cambridge University Press, 2006.

US Department of Energy, Energy Information Administration, *International Energy Outlook,* 2007.

World Business Council for Sustainable Development, *Mobility 2030: Meeting the Challenges to Sustainability.* World Business Council, 2004.

World Resources Institute, *Climate Analysis Indicators Tool (CAIT)* http://cait.wri.org/

Index

adaptation, 121, 122, 148–149
alternating current (AC), 21, 56
ASPO, 82, 83, 84, 86
Association for the Study of Peak Oil and Gas.
  See ASPO
aviation, 41, 114

barrels of oil, 37, 85
base-load electricity, 28–29, 215
batteries, 27, 107–110
lead-acid, 107, 109
  lithium-ion, 110
  nickel-cadmium, 109–110
battery electric vehicle (BEV), 39, 191, 197
BAU. See business-as-usual
BEV. See battery electric vehicle
biodiesel, 39, 72, 113, 170, 179, 201
bioengineering, 113, 179, 184, 201
biofuels, 72–73, 113, 190–191, 201
biodiesel. See biodiesel
  cellulosic. See cellulosic ethanol
  ethanol. See ethanol
  FT diesel, 191
  methanol, 40
  RME diesel, 191
biogas. See landfill gas
biomass, 71–72, 177, 182
bitumen. See oil sands
BP, 53, 82, 83, 85
building control systems, 203
buildings, 110–113, 202–205
business-as-usual (BAU), 156, 157, 159, 161, 173,
  174, 187, 194

CAES. See compressed air storage
Caldicott, Helen, 50, 131
Cambridge Energy Research Associates. See
  CERA
cap and trade emissions scheme 133–135
capacity factor, 60, 207
carbon capture and storage. See CCS
carbon dioxide, 44, 73, 79, 90, 98–99, 120–121,
  140
carbon leakage, 137

carbon offsets, 139–143
carbon price, 100, 150, 152, 156, 157, 159–160,
  163
carbon taxing, 134–136
carbon trading, 133–134, 136, 139
CCGT, 22, 98
CCS, 98–100, 147, 153, 175, 208, 216
cellulosic ethanol, 72, 73, 113, 190
CERA, 82, 83, 84, 85, 86
CFL. See compact fluorescent lamp
Chernobyl, 51, 207
Chicago Climate Exchange, 141, 152
China and India, 13, 48, 85, 94, 124–125, 128,
  161, 176, 219
CHP, 21, 99, 173, 177, 181
Clean Development Mechanism, 139
climate change, 89–92, 118
climate change cost, 148–153
climate change sceptics, 120–121
CNG, 32, 33, 39, 85, 113, 191, 194
coal, 42–45
coal-to-liquid (CTL), 87, 190, 195
combined heat and power. See CHP
compact fluorescent lamp (CFL), 30–31, 111, 166
compressed air storage (CAES), 107, 115, 151,
  180, 184
compressed natural gas. See CNG
concentrated solar power. See CSP
conventional oil. See oil - conventional
crude oil, 36–37
CSP, 57–58, 104–106, 115, 178, 182, 183,
  214–216
CTL. See coal-to-liquid

decarbonising energy, 170–171, 192–195
decentralised generation. See distributed generation
developing world, 126–127, 156, 161–162,
  185–186
DG. See distributed generation
diesel, 36–41, 72, 87, 113, 158, 189–192, 196,
  199, 219
direct current (DC), 23, 56
distributed generation (DG), 173, 177, 180–181,
  212, 213, 216

DOE, 25, 36, 83

EGS, 68–70, 127, 183, 213, 215–216
electric vehicles, 39, 191, 193, 196–197
electricity cost, 26–27, 181–182
electricity generation, 20–23, 172–179
electricity grid, 23–24, 28, 50, 61, 103, 177, 179–181, 214
electricity load curve, 28
electricity storage, 27, 64, 65, 66, 106–110, 115, 150, 180, 200, 213–214
electricity transmission, 23–24, 179–181
emissions intensity, 29, 30, 44, 94, 152, 160, 173, 174
emissions reduction, 92–96, 157–161, 165–167, 169–171, 194–195, 204–205, 220
emissions targets, 137–138, 144, 217
emissions trading, 132–135, 139
energy carrier, 18, 75, 222
energy costs, 26–27, 30–31, 34, 49, 56–58, 61–62, 64, 69, 72, 153
energy efficiency, 14, 78, 121–122, 140, 142, 158, 165–168, 186, 219
energy mix, 154, 173, 217
energy security, 123–125, 155, 219, 222
Energy Watch Group, 82–84, 86
enhance oil and gas recovery, 99
ethanol, 72–74, 190, 199, 201
EU Emissions Trading Scheme, 134, 138, 144, 162, 220
EWG. See Energy Watch Group
Exxon Mobil, 119

fast neutron reactors, 101
FCV. See fuel cell vehicle
Fischer-Tropsch (FT), 191, 193
flow batteries, 108
    sodium-sulphur, 108, 115
    zinc-bromide, 108, 115
fossil fuel, 32, 36, 42
fuel cells, 23, 76–78, 191, 194, 222
fuel cell vehicle (FCV), 191–194, 200

gas
    compressed natural gas. See CNG
    liquified natural gas. See LNG
    liquified petroleum gas. See LPG
    natural gas. See natural gas
gas-to-liquid (GTL), 87, 190
GDP, 96, 148–150, 155, 161, 164, 217
General Motors Volt, 39
Geodynamics, 70
geothermal energy, 67–70, 182, 183, 215–216
global warming, 11, 89–92, 118
government action, 31, 115, 121–123, 125–126, 144–145, 218–219
government inducements, 144, 189, 194

government regulations, 111, 132, 139, 144, 168, 194, 205
greenhouse effect, 89–90, 116–118, 120
greenhouse gas emissions, 29, 34, 40, 44, 49, 73, 77–78, 89–91, 94–95
Greenpeace, 15, 127–128, 131
grid. See electricity grid
gross domestic Product. See GDP
GTL. See gas-to-liquid
Gulf of Mexico, 80, 123

heat pumps, 30, 68, 112, 203
HERS index (Home Energy Rater), 220
HEV. See hybrid-electric vehicle
Hirsh, Robert, 148
hot dry rocks, 68, 183, 215
household power usage, 23, 25, 26
HVDC, 24, 215
hybrid-electric vehicle (HEV), 39, 189, 196
hydro storage. See pumped storage
hydro-electric generator, 65
hydrogen, 75–78, 99, 101, 113–114, 151, 193–194, 198, 200–201, 222
hydropower, 63–66, 106–107, 130, 177, 182, 211–214

IAEA, 30, 129–130
IEA, 15, 17, 27, 102, 111, 124, 128, 148, 159–161, 182, 187, 189, 195, 201
IGCC, 98, 143, 179, 216
Industrial Revolution, 90, 116
Intergovernmental Panel on Climate Change. See IPCC
International Atomic Energy Agency. See IAEA
International Energy Agency. See IEA
International Thermonuclear Experimental Reactor. See ITER
inverter, 56
IPCC, 12, 90–96, 97, 98, 99, 110, 118, 119–120, 131, 150, 152–153, 157, 159–160, 162–163, 164, 173–175, 177, 181–182, 195, 203, 204, 206
ITER, 209

jet aircraft, 40–41, 195, 197–198
Joint Implementation, 139

Kyoto Protocol, 118, 119, 139

Laherrere, Jean, 86
landfill gas, 72–73, 74, 91, 143
LDV. See light-duty vehicles
LED. See light-emitting diode
light-duty vehicles, 158, 186, 188, 190, 191, 195, 199
light-emitting diode (LED), 111, 205
LNG, 32–34, 39

Lovelock, James, 131
LPG, 32-34, 37, 39, 41, 153, 191

McKinsey, 15, 165, 166, 170–171, 173–174
methane, 72, 73, 74, 90–91, 121, 140, 143
Middle East, 36, 117, 123
mitigation, 96, 121, 132, 148–150

nanotechnology, 106, 184, 205, 222
NASA, 76, 91, 118
natural gas, 13, 32–34, 40, 45, 72, 73, 75, 81,
    85–86, 87, 88, 107, 113, 190
Nordhaus, William, 149
North Sea, 123, 207
nuclear fission, 46, 47, 209
nuclear fusion, 46, 54, 209
nuclear power, 22, 46–51, 99–101, 128–131, 175,
    176, 184, 206–210
nuclear proliferation, 51, 129–130, 207
nuclear reactors, 47–48, 101
    ABWR, 48
    BWR, 48, 101
    EPR, 48
    GFR, 101
    HTGR, 101
    LFR, 101
    LWR, 48
    MHR, 101
    MSR, 101
    PBMR, 101
    PWR, 48, 101
nuclear safety, 50, 100–101, 130, 176, 207, 208
nuclear waste, 49–50, 100, 130–131, 176, 207, 208

ocean power, 63–64, 101–103, 182–183, 213
oil — conventional, 81, 82, 85
oil — unconventional, 81, 82, 83, 85, 87
oil prices, 37–38, 84, 118, 147–148
oil reserves, 81–83, 124
oil sands, 36, 81, 82, 85, 87, 146
oil shale, 87
oil shocks, 117, 148
OPEC, 83, 117, 123
oxy-fuel combustion, 98

peak oil, 80–85, 117, 146, 218, 221
plug-in vehicles, 39, 109, 110, 158, 193, 197, 199,
    204
public transport, 39, 41, 158, 186, 189, 200
pumped storage, 64–66, 106–107, 180, 214
PV. See solar PV

renewable energy, 11, 14, 52–78, 124, 142,
    176–178, 211–216, 220–222

renewables 'new', 212–213
rent seeking, 141
reserve capacity, 180, 182

Shell, 53, 146–147
smart meters, 31, 110, 122, 203
social cost of carbon (SCC), 150, 152 See also
    carbon price
solar power, 54–58, 103–106, 182
solar PV, 22, 56–57, 103–104, 106, 109, 167,
    178, 182, 184, 205, 222
solar water heating. See water heating
Solarbuzz LLC, 57
solar-thermal, 20, 55, 57, 104–106
solar-thermal storage. See thermal storage
standby power, 25, 31, 111, 203
steam turbines, 20
steel, 43, 44
Stern Review, 94–96, 149, 150, 152
supercapacitor, 201
syngas, 43, 75, 87, 98
technologies - new, 97–115

Tesla Motors, 197, 199
thermal storage, 104–106, 115, 213, 214, 215
Three Mile Island, 50, 51, 117, 207
tidal power, 64, 102, 115
Toyota Prius, 39, 110, 196
trade-exposed industries, 137
transport efficiency, 188–189
transport emissions, 41, 189, 192–195, 200
transport fuel, 33, 40, 73, 84, 88, 113–114, 171,
    189–192, 197, 201

unconventional oil. See oil - unconventional
UNFCCC, 139
uranium, 46–48 49, 50, 101, 124, 130, 207

vehicle emissions, 40, 192–195, 220
Voluntary Carbon Standard, 141

waste-to-energy, 71, 73
water heating, 57, 112, 205
watt, 19
Watt, James, 19, 116
wave power, 64, 103, 151
WBCSD, 15, 53, 192, 194
well-to-wheel emissions, 73, 77–78, 192, 193, 198
wind farms, 60–62, 130, 170, 178, 180, 214, 215,
    216
wind power, 59–62, 124, 201, 212
wind turbines, 59–62, 124, 178, 212
World Bank, 84
World Resource Institute (WRI), 95, 157